Resources for Preaching and Worship—Year A

Also by Hannah Ward and Jennifer Wild
from Westminster John Knox Press

The Westminster Collection of Christian Meditations

Resources for Preaching and Worship—Year B

Resources for Preaching and Worship—Year C

Resources for Preaching and Worship—Year A

QUOTATIONS, MEDITATIONS, POETRY, AND PRAYERS

Compiled by
Hannah Ward and Jennifer Wild

Westminster John Knox Press
LOUISVILLE • LONDON

Book design by PerfecType, Nashville, Tennessee
Cover design by Lisa Buckley

First edition
Published by Westminster John Knox Press
Louisville, Kentucky

This book is printed on acid-free paper that meets the American National Standards Institute Z39.48 standard. ∞

PRINTED IN THE UNITED STATES OF AMERICA

04 05 06 07 08 09 10 11 12 13 — 10 9 8 7 6 5 4 3 2 1

Library of Congress Cataloging-in-Publication Data is on file at the Library of Congress, Washington, D.C.

ISBN 0-664-22507-1

CONTENTS

PREFACE

In the three volumes of *Resources for Preaching and Worship,* we are offering, for each Sunday or special day in the Christian year, a "hamper" containing various kinds of written material. Anyone who is concerned with preaching on Sunday—or leading study groups or prayer groups during the course of the week—can find here something to feed personal reflection, to stimulate ideas for sermon themes, and to provide stories and poems as well as prayers that in some way relate to the biblical readings for the day concerned. On the great days of the annual cycle, especially between Advent and Pentecost, the Bible readings clearly reflect the season. During large parts of the year, however—the "Proper" Sundays—there is little or no thematic matching of the Bible readings with each other; our choice of companion passages for these dates is at once more arbitrary and, we hope, perhaps even more useful. The passages we have chosen offer possible themes that the preacher might choose to fasten on, or that the person reading the Bible, alone or with others, might find leading to lines of thought not otherwise obvious. If we in any way can enlarge or sustain the range of themes and forms of expression open to the preacher or worship leader, we will feel that our aim has been accomplished. Although the writers from whom we have quoted are almost all from the Judeo-Christian traditions, we have tried, overall, to bear in mind that the great themes of Christian faith and practice are embedded in the basic experiences of human life, and the range of human experience is (perhaps) nearer to infinity than we might sometimes suspect.

Christians of many denominations now use the Revised Common Lectionary in one form or another. If you do not find exactly what your own church's lectionary prescribes for any given Sunday or special day, the biblical index at the end of this volume, or the theme index, may point to helpful ideas in another part of this book. One way or another, everyone can find something in here for them—even, sometimes, a point of view with which to disagree. As people who appreciate good sermons, we hope our "hampers" will stir the senses and memory of others who preach the Word of God.

Hannah Ward
Jennifer Wild

First Sunday of Advent

Isaiah 2:1–5   Romans 13:11–14

Psalm 122   Matthew 24:36–44

The Peace

Leader: Brothers and sisters, before we offer ourselves and our gifts to God, let us turn to those near us, and with respect and affection, make our peace with them.

As Christ has accepted us into his peace,

People: **Let us all live in peace with one another.**

(The PEACE is expressed both by the gesture of Namaskara, and by hand-clasp)

Leader: Leaving all enmity behind,
we make our offering to the God of peace
As a sign that we will wage peace in the world,
We pick up a flower near the offering place.
It is with love for neighbour, compassion for the needy,
faith in the truth, and trust in God-weak weapons—
that we are called to do battle for peace.

(As music is played, expressing our peace-warfare, and as all bring their offerings, and take a flower, the following prophetic word is read loud and clear)

Leader: Come, let us go up to the mountain of the Lord,
to the house of the God of Jacob.
He will teach us his ways that we may walk in his path.
He will judge (and make peace) between the nations,
and will settle disputes for many peoples.
They will beat their swords into ploughshares
and their spears into pruning hooks.
Nation will not take up sword against nation,

nor will they train for war any more.
Come, let us walk in the light of the Lord.

From "Liturgy: Praying for Peace, Celebrating Peace," in *Worship in
an Indian Context: Eight Inter-Cultural Liturgies,* ed. Eric J. Lott
(Bangalore: United Theological College, 1986), pp. 96–97.
Used by permission.

Where people are praying for peace the cause of peace is being strengthened by
their very act of prayer, for they are themselves becoming immersed in the spirit
of peace.

George MacLeod

Pregnant with hope

Now is a time of watching and waiting
a time pregnant with hope
a time to watch and pray.

Christ our advent hope,
bare brown trees,
etched dark across a winter sky,
leaves fallen, rustling,
ground hard and cold,
remind us to prepare for your coming;
remind us to prepare for the time
when the soles of your feet will touch the ground,
when you will become one of us
to be at one with us.

May we watch for the signs,
listen for the messenger,
wait for the good news to slip
into our world, our lives.
Christ our advent hope,
help us to clear the way for you;
to clear the clutter from our minds,

to sift the silt from our hearts,
to move the boulders that prevent us meeting you.

Help us to make straight the highways,
to unravel the deception that leads to war,
to release those in captivity.
May sorrow take flight,
and your people sing a song of peace
and hope be born again.

Kate McIlhagga, from *Encompassing Presence: Prayer Handbook 1993*
(London: United Reformed Church, 1993), Week 48, Advent 1. ©
Donald McIlhagga. Used by permission.

A new vision

What the world needs now is a new vision, a renewed story to give it meaning and purpose. We do not need to look too far: it is already here for the finding. The universe is currently revealing itself to us in its admirable diversity and wonderful uniqueness. The universe is proceeding in its evolutionary growth according to certain definite laws which reveal a vision of communion and interdependence stunning to behold. One can only stand in awe at the comprehensiveness of it all. The human is the one created being in whom this conscious reflection and celebration can take place. The transition in the evolutionary process from inanimate and animate life to the human form of consciousness appears to be so designed: that humanity, aware of itself and its interrelation with the rest of created life, may be able to give voice to this communion and interdependence on behalf of all. And not just to give voice, but also to act with reverence, care and cooperation.

Within the context of this vision the whole of creation finds its place. The heavens, the earth, stars, meteors, mountains and oceans, the very air we breathe; insects, animals and human beings: all of these will be transformed by the love of God and share communion with him forever.

Peter Hooper, from a sermon for the Third Sunday of Advent in
Advent and Ecology: Resources for Worship, Reflection and Action, ed.
Martin Palmer and Anne Nash (Godalming: World Wide Fund for
Nature, in association with the BBC, 1988), pp. 56–57.

Strange wisdom

O come, O come, thou wisdom strange
from deep within God's womb to range
the earth at midnight's hour of fears
to make us wise beyond our years.
Rejoice! Rejoice! Our God shall leap
with light that rouses us from sleep.

> Jim Cotter, from *Expectant: Verses for Advent* (Harlech: Cairns
> Publications, 2002), No. 2 (for the second day of December).
> Used by permission.

Grow up!

A sign of maturity in the human species is the ability to be open and resilient, to be willing to listen to many viewpoints, to celebrate many cultures and ideas, not to tighten up and shut down in the face of adversity. When you are mature (whole) you realize that what is "you" is not threatened by what is "not-you"; rather the not-you can be recognized, respected, tested, and learned from. Too often religion's task has been one of defense, defining doctrine and reciting creed, rather than listening and dialoguing. All membership had to do was believe the truth presented and it could be sure of being right and saved. In this history there was no acceptance of doubt, no healthy dialogue, no ragged edges. The New Story calls us all to grow up and welcome other viewpoints, including all the ragged edges of human experience, not as competitors, not as suspect or threatening, but as partners and friends in the full circle of creation. This kind of partnership would promote an atmosphere of mutual critique as well as mutual respect and responsibility for working on the problems of the world community.

> Cynthia Serjak, *Music and the Cosmic Dance* (Washington, D.C.: The
> Pastoral Press, 1987), pp. 14–15.

The present tense

Thank you, O God, for the time that is now,
for all the newness your minutes allow,
make us alert with your presence of mind
to fears and longings that move humankind.

Thank you, O God, for the time that is past,
for all the values and thoughts that will last.
May we all stagnant tradition ignore,
leaving behind things that matter no more.

Thank you for hopes of the day that will come,
for all the change that will happen in time;
God, for the future our spirits prepare,
hallow our doubts and redeem us from fear.

Make us afraid of the thoughts that delay,
faithful in all the affairs of today;
keep us, Creator, from playing it safe,
thank you that now is the time of our life!

Fred Kaan, *The Only Earth We Know* (Carol Stream, Ill.: Hope
Publishing Company; London: Stainer & Bell, 1999), no. 53, p. 68. ©
1968, Hope Publishing Company, Carol Stream, IL 60188 for USA
and Canada; © 1968, 1998 Stainer & Bell Ltd. for all other territories.
All rights reserved. Used by permission.

The doctrines of the Lord are three: the hope of life is the beginning and the end
of our faith; righteousness is the beginning and end of judgment; and glad and
joyful love is the evidence of the works of righteousness.

Barnabas (early second century)

Second Sunday of Advent

Isaiah 11:1–10
Psalm 72:1–7, 18–19

Romans 15:4–13
Matthew 3:1–12

A prayer of praise and longing

Merciful God of all creation, Holy Parent of all peoples,
through our Lord Jesus Christ,
who united all things in his fulness,
we join your whole creation
in exultant praise of your bountiful goodness.
You have now touched us with new life,
and filled us with new hope that your kingdom will come,
and the hungry will be fed,
and the oppressed will be set free from evil,
and your reconciling work will be done,
and the earth filled with your glory.
For the kingdom, sovereign power and supreme glory
are yours alone, great Saviour of the world.

From "An Indian Liturgy for Celebrating the Eucharist," in *Worship in
an Indian Context: Eight Inter-Cultural Liturgies,* ed. Eric J. Lott
(Bangalore: United Theological College, 1986), p. 77.
Used by permission.

God's reign is already present on our earth in mystery. When the Lord comes, it
will be brought to perfection.

Oscar Romero

Viper's venom

In the gospel reading we hear John the Baptist's harsh words of reproach to the
Jewish leaders. He calls them "a brood of vipers." The graphic image portrayed is
one of snakes fleeing from a ravaging harvest or forest fire. The viper is a symbol

of the venom of deceitful, uncharitable and destructive speech and conduct. But John is not speaking about a viperous individual but of a community or, at least, a group, especially a group with power.... There are not a few governments today who behave like vipers vis-à-vis the poorer people.

Intercessions

> *For those in authority that they may never degrade themselves with falsehood:*
> *For reverence for our mother earth.*

J. Massyngbaerde Ford, Days of the Spirit, vol. 1, Advent to Lent
(Collegeville: The Liturgical Press, 1994), pp. 20–21.

Were John the Baptist to return and denounce the sin of the world, once more they'd cut off his head.

Jacopone da Todi (c. 1230–1306)

Gaining distance and coming closer

To counteract myth-laden readings of biblical texts and to avoid the risk of repeating the interpretations of other readers, I believe in the importance of gaining distance from the text, mainly from those parts that have been frequently read and therefore have become overly familiar to our ears. When I say "gaining distance" I mean picking up the book and ignoring the interpretations that almost automatically come to mind even before reading the actual text. To distance oneself means to be new to the text (to be a stranger, a first-time visitor to the text), to be amazed by everything.... It is necessary to take up the Bible as a new book, a book that has never been heard or read before.

This way of reading is going to be conditioned by or embedded in the life experience of the Latin American reader. Her or his experiences must be very consciously taken into account at the time of the reading. It is this experience, in the end, that will facilitate the distancing of oneself from the all-too-familiar interpretation of the common suppositions in the text, and will help to uncover keys to a liberation-orientated reading. This is the process of coming closer to daily life, which implies the experiences of pain, joy, hope, hunger, celebration, and struggle. It is clear from this process of gaining distance and coming closer that in Latin America the Bible is not read as an intellectual or academic exercise; it is read with the goal of giving meaning to our lives today. In the confusing situation we find ourselves, we want to discern God's will and how it is present in our history. We think that the written word offers us criteria for discerning.

Elsa Tamez, from "Women's Rereading of the Bible," in *Feminist Theology from the Third World: A Reader,* ed. Ursula King (London: SPCK; Maryknoll, N.Y.: Orbis Books, 1994), pp. 196–97.

Plight of the asylum seeker

He stood before the court in nondescript clothes,
no papers, no fixed address.
The judge cleared his throat,
"Have you anything to say
before I pass sentence?"
What might have been his answer
had the prisoner the gift of speech
and the court the gift of hearing?

"I am condemned because your law
allows no place for me.
My crimes I freely admit:
I am homeless, seeking shelter
where I may rear my family in modest decency.
I am stateless, seeking a country
where I may belong by right in God's good earth.
I am destitute, claiming a share of the wealth
that is our common heritage.
I am a sinner, needing aid from fellow sinners.

"You will dispose of me according to your law,
but you will not so easily dispose of him
who owns me citizen in his kingdom.
He frowns on crimes your law condones;
pride, selfishness and greed,
self-righteousness,
the worship of all things material
and the refusal to acknowledge me as brother.

"By your law I stand condemned;
but one day you must answer
to the master of us all
for the havoc caused by your law
in his realm."

Edmund Banyard, *Turn But a Stone* (Birmingham: National
Christian Education Council, 1992). © 1992 Revd. Edmund Banyard.
Used by permission.

Judgment

In his Advent sermon, Guerric of Igny understands that it is not easy to desire with fervor [the] second coming [of Christ]. There, he says that if we cannot prepare ourselves for the day of judgment by desire, let us at least prepare ourselves by fear. Now I see better how part of Christian maturation is the slow but persistent deepening of fear to the point where it becomes desire. The fear of God is not in contrast with his mercy. Therefore, words such as fear and desire, justice and mercy have to be relearned and reunderstood when we use them in our intimate relationship with the Lord.

Henri J. M. Nouwen, *The Genesee Diary: Report from a Trappist Monastery,*
2d Image ed. (New York: Doubleday, 1989), pp. 199–200.

Hymn of the Word*

Your word is like a guiding lamp
which lights the path ahead,
it shows us where our feet may go
and makes it safe to tread.

Your word is like a living fire
that burns within our bones,
to share the message you have given
with clear courageous tones.

Your word is like a hammer blow,
that breaks our hearts of stone,

*Suggested tune: YOUR WORD

and makes our minds and wills anew
so serving God alone.

Your word is like the smallest seed
that falls into the ground,
which, fed and watered every day,
makes fruitfulness abound.

Your word is like a two-edged sword,
which, taken in the hand,
will help us fight your kingdom's cause
in this and every land.

Your word is like the purest milk,
which nourishes the soul
then weans us onto solid food,
until we are made whole.

Richard Firth, in *Worship Live* no. 23 (London: Stainer & Bell,
Summer 2002), p. 20. © 2002 Richard Firth. Used by permission.

Third Sunday of Advent

Isaiah 35:1–10   James 5:7–10

Psalm 146:5–10   Matthew 11:2–11

Who are the prophets?

Who are the prophets?
They are a royal people,
who penetrate mystery
and see with the spirit's eyes.

In illuminating darkness they speak out.

They are living, penetrating clarity.
They are a blossom blooming only
on the shoot that is rooted in the
flood of light.

Hildegard of Bingen, *Meditations with Hildegard of Bingen,*
trans. Gabriele Uhlein, O.S.F. (Rochester, Vt.: Bear & Company,
1983), p. 126. Used by permission.

"Are you the one who is to come?"

Knowing that no [one] can believe completely unless [they hear] the Good News
. . . our Lord revealed himself in answer to their questions by drawing attention
not so much to his words as to his deeds. *Go,* he said, *and tell John what you have
seen and heard: the blind receive their sight, the lame walk, the deaf hear and lepers
are cleansed, the dead are raised up, the poor have the good news preached to them.*
And yet these are still not the greatest of the signs which bear witness to the Lord:
the fullness of faith is in his cross, his death and his burial. This is why he adds:
Blessed is he who takes no offence at me. For the cross can give scandal even to the
elect. . . .

But what did you go out to see? A prophet? Yes, I tell you and more than a prophet.
. . . A great prophet indeed was he, in whom the whole line of prophets came to
an end. More in fact than a prophet, for many there were who hoped to see the

11

one of whom John prophesied, the one whom he saw with his own eyes, the one whom he himself baptized.

Ambrose of Milan (c. 339–397), *Commentary on the Gospel of St. Luke*, Book 5, in *A Word in Season: An Anthology of Readings from the Fathers*, vol.1, *Advent and Christmastide*, ed. Henry Ashworth, O.S.B. (Dublin: The Talbot Press, 1973), p. 37.

The meek and mild mediocrity of most of us stands in sharp contrast to that volcanic, upheaving, shaggy power of the prophets, whose descendants we were meant to be.

Thomas Kelly

The hope of the Seed

In this waiting time, creating Spirit,
we give you thanks for the new life,
the new world which rose up
from the Seed which died.

We thank you for the hope of the Seed.
We take encouragement that over many years
the life of the Seed has spread,
wending its way across the earth;
flourishing where it finds welcomed space;
greening;
bringing new life wherever it finds root.

Help us to be good gardeners;
to recognise Christ's Seed wherever it grows;
to learn how best to care for the Seed;
to work hard with patience, endurance and faith
throughout the seasons;
to experience the pleasure, challenge and delight
of the gardener
as we nurture Christ's greening of the whole earth.

Fiona Bennett, in *Kneelers: Prayers from Three Nations: Prayer Handbook Advent 2001–2002*, ed. Norman Hart (London: United Reformed Church, 2001), p. 13. © United Reformed Church 2001. Used by permission.

Present

On the flyleaf
of my confirmation present:
"To Wendy with love
from Nanna. Psalm 98."

I looked it up, eventually—
Cantate Domino.
I knew the first two verses
and skimmed the rest.

Thirty-five years afterwards,
at evensong on Day 19
the choir sings Nanna's psalm.
At last, I pay attention

to the words she chose.
O sing unto the Lord
a new song. Nanna,
it is just what I wanted.

Wendy Cope, *If I Don't Know* (London: Faber & Faber, 2001), p. 15.
Used by permission.

The signs of his presence

The signs of his presence
are blind people who can see,
the lame who walk again,
those whose skin diseases are cleared,
the deaf who can hear,
the dead who are brought back to life,
and the poor who have reason
for delighting in the good news they hear.

If these are the signs of his presence
and we are the ones who say he is coming,
what are we going to say

when they ask where he is?
What are we going to do
to justify our claim
that he is on his way?
Singing carols
with mince pies afterwards
is not enough.

Graham Cook (ed.), from "The sign of his presence," in *Exceeding our Limits: Prayer Handbook 1991* (London: United Reformed Church, 1991), Week 50, December 15. © Graham Cook. Used by permission.

Prayer

One: In the fertile darkness of soil,
         the green of life bursts out of its shell;
         in the fertilized darkness of womb,
         the flesh of life builds cell upon cell.

Many: **Those born in darkness**
         have seen life.

One: The closet may be a fertile place:
         creativity bursts out of a lonely hell,
         and from a closet fertilized with hope,
         the spirit leaps from a monastic cell.

Many: **Those born in darkness**
         have seen life.

One: Out of dark soil sprouts new life,
         from dark wombs springs embodied hope.
         Both stretch for the illumination
         of the cosmic kaleidoscope.

Many: **Those born in darkness**
         have seen life.

One: Dear God,

Many: **we seek your Word embodied**
         in life rooted in fertile darkness.

**In life stretching for illumination,
we await your transforming Word.**

Chris R. Glaser, from "Rite for Advent," in *Equal Rites: Lesbian and
Gay Worship, Ceremonies, and Celebrations,* ed. Kittredge Cherry and
Zalmon Sherwood (Louisville, Ky.: Westminster John Knox Press,
1995), pp. 77–78. © 1995 Westminster John Knox Press.
Used by permission of Westminster John Knox Press.

It has not pleased God to build either the congregation of Israel or the fellowship of the church on prophets. They are the warning, the correction, the voice in the wilderness.

Charles Williams

Fourth Sunday of Advent

Isaiah 7:10–16   Romans 1:1–7

Psalm 80:1–7, 17–19   Matthew 1:18–25

"... and named him Jesus"

The name of the virgin-born child is Jesus because, as the angel had explained, he was to save his people from their sins. And he who saves from sin will also rescue us from the mental and bodily weaknesses consequent upon it. "Christ", the anointed, is a word implying priestly or royal dignity. In the Old Testament both priests and kings are called christ, on account of their anointing with chrism or holy oil. They foreshadow the one who is true king and priest and who, when he came into the world, was *anointed with the oil of gladness above other kings.* From this anointing he is called Christ; those who share in that same anointing, that is, in his spiritual grace, are called christians. By his saving power, may he free us from our sins. As our high priest, may he reconcile us to God our Father. As our king, may he grant us the Father's eternal kingdom: for he is our Lord Jesus Christ, God living and reigning with the Father and the Holy Spirit till time flows into eternity. Amen.

> The Venerable Bede, from Homily 5 for Christmas Eve, in *A Word in Season: An Anthology of Readings from the Fathers for General Use,* vol. 1: *Advent and Christmastide,* ed. Henry Ashworth, O.S.B. (Dublin: The Talbot Press, 1973), p. 50.

The name of Jesus is in my mind as a joyful song, in my ear a heavenly music, and in my mouth sweet honey.

> Richard Rolle (1290–1349)

Incarnation

There is a time in our lives when we try to give shape to the mysteries, give them a precise or symbolic conceptual form. We make an effort to understand them, we read about them. As life goes on the shapes blur. Not because we understand less, but on the contrary, because we understand more. Struggling with our minds we defined *fides quaerens intellectum,* contemplating with faith, we penetrated. And thus we glimpsed that the hidden face of the mystery, the depth beneath its surface was much greater than what shows. We understood how little we understood. Not with a sense of frustration, but with the joy of knowing that we stand on the shore of a wide and mighty sea and can only hear its waves breaking on the beach: . . .

> These are but the fringes of his power
> and how faint the whisper that we hear of him!
> Who could comprehend the thunder of his might?
>
> (Job 26:14)

Luis Alonso Schökel, *Led by Hope: Spiritual Exercises for the Elderly*
(Slough: St. Paul Publications, 1991), pp. 65–66.

If you wish to know how such things come about, consult grace, not doctrine; desire, not understanding; prayerful groaning, not studious reading; the Spouse, not the teacher; God, not man; darkness, not clarity.

Bonaventure (1221–1274)

Someone comes!

Chorus:

> Someone comes to make things right,
> tomorrow, today, tonight.
> Jesus comes to make things right,
> tomorrow, today, tonight.

Angry people will shake hands,
they won't learn war any more,
they won't learn war any more.
Melt your guns and turn them into plows,
and don't learn war any more,
don't learn war any more.

Hungry people will be fed,
they won't be hurt any more,
they won't be hurt any more.

See the children playing in the street?—
they won't be hurt any more,
they won't be hurt any more.

Hurting people will be healed,
they won't be afraid any more,
they won't be afraid any more.
No-one's dirty or unclean,
so don't be afraid any more,
don't be afraid any more.

Someone's coming, coming soon,
we won't be alone any more,
we won't be alone any more.
God is with us, all the time,
we won't be alone any more,
we won't be alone any more.

> Brian Wren, in Susan Heafield (music) and Brian Wren (words), *We Can Be Messengers,* vol. 1: *Worship Songs: Christmas, Before and After* (Decatur, Ga.: Praise Partners Publishing, 2001), verses 1–4, p. 12. *We Can Be Messengers* is obtainable in USA from Hope Publishing Company, *hope@hopepublishing.com,* and in the UK from Stainer & Bell Ltd., *cwakefield@stainer.co.uk.* Used by permission.

A jubilee concert in Rome

The evening began with an Iranian Muslim women's ensemble singing verses from the Qur'an, and for the next two hours we were swept up in a celebration of music and dance that seemed to emanate from a different universe to the baroque extravaganza of the basilica next door. Here, the extravagance lay not in the brash proclamation of Rome's power frozen in marble and bronze but in the human body and voice—the female body and voice—transformed into a living icon of praise. Peruvian dancers, American sopranos, a Filipino choir, African, Polish and Romanian musicians, Korean women like bright butterflies in their national dress—that night the Vatican was truly catholic, and woman was truly incarnate. The evening ended with a group of young Italian ballet dancers, dressed in slinky costumes in the colours of the jubilee logo. As they writhed sinuously up the steps and arched their backs and raised their arms to the risen Christ,* I wanted to pinch myself. Could this possibly be happening on the Pope's doorstep? This was Eve risen, redeemed, beautiful, sexy, dancing where she should always have danced, in the heart of Christ's Church on earth.

*The Paul VI concert hall, where the concert was held, contains a vast bronze sculpture of the resurrection.

> Tina Beattie, *Eve's Pilgrimage: A Woman's Quest for the City of God*
> (London and New York: Burns & Oates, 2002), pp. 191–92.

A tentative hymn to/about Mary†

with asterisks (stardust)

> Mary, Mary, quite contrary,
> rebel, giving ear to God,
> earth-soprano,* singing freedom:
> Zion's song in "yes" and blood;
>
> earmarked Mary, world-affirming,
> in compliance giving birth,
> your defiance** gave us Jesus,
> Word-among-us, run to earth.
>
> Mary, mouthpiece of God's people,***
> Sister Chosen, giving voice,
> Ave Mary,**** Eve of Easter,
> Bibi Maryam,***** Sister Choice;
>
> Mary/Miram,****** ever-bearing
> life as hope for all to share,
> make us, women, men and children
> as expectant as you are!

> * Soprano comes from the same root as sovereign (sovrano—Italian), and has something to do with being high or supreme. Some traditions call Mary "Queen of Heaven". She is in a sense "prima donna", first lady—yet, as in a choir, she is first among equals; it takes contralto, tenor and bass to complete the whole. All the choir is (God-)parent to Jesus, who is the Child of humanity.

†Tune: STARDUST

** Mary wasn't just a compliant woman whom we often tend to glamorise by turning her into a somewhat ethereal figure, tall, slim and blonde, like a Swedish filmstar, dressed in immaculate (!) blue—Presbyterian blue—on a plinth in a niche with suitable back-lighting. Her acceptance of her role was very much an act of defiance: what will the neighbours have said, or the elders at the synagogue?

*** The Magnificat isn't exclusively Mary's own work. If there had been some Zealot copyright lawyer around at the time, he could have taken her to court for committing plagiarism. Almost all her song is quotation from the Old Testament. She makes herself a mouthpiece of the whole people of God; she becomes that "daughter of Zion" (see verse 1, line 4). There are only two original lines in the Magnificat: "My soul magnifies the Lord" (Luke 1:46) and "henceforth all generations shall call me blessed" (vs 48).

J. S. Bach with his uncanny sensitivity to the secondary layers of the bible, seems to have rumbled verse 48. In his version of the Magnificat he has the choir sing "omnes generations" (all generations) no less than 96 times! Mary's *own* words, as distinct from those she recalls and quotes, are future-orientated—she "remembers forward". How could it be otherwise? She was pregnant, for God's sake!

**** Ave Maria (Hail Mary). Read Ave backwards and you get Eva, which is how most European languages spell Eve . . . but of course eve is also the forerunner of the coming dawn.

***** Maryam (a two-syllable word, with the y pronounced as in Year) is the name whereby Mary is known among Muslims. Bibi is a term of veneration used for women saints and prophets.

****** Mary in Hebrew is Miriam, meaning "the rebellious one" (see verse 1, lines 1 and 2). Moses' sister Miriam led the women in a triumphant song-and-dance routine after Israel's liberating trek through the Red Sea (see verse 1, line 3).

CHRISTMAS, FIRST PROPER

Isaiah 9:2–7	Titus 2:11–14
Psalm 96	Luke 2:1–14 (15–20)

Christmas is for . . .

I've been to the pub. I had a couple of pints in Harlton at the Hare and Hounds, which were both bought for me, and then on to the Little Rose, Haslingfield, which was fantastic, vibrating with the Verve and the catch-all Christmas album: John Lennon, Slade, Wham, "Last Christmas I gave you my heart, but the very next day you gave it away." This is a Babysham Christmas, all the trimmings without the turkey, Bacchus in full flow. It is a pagan feast, the rituals are very different. Midnight Mass starts in forty-five minutes. I've been told one hundred times today that Christmas is for children. It's a dreadful let-out; it excuses adults completely from it. It is a time perhaps when we become like children. Is that so bad? It's a time when we are allowed to wonder. No wonder the Christmas cards take us back to the past. We are not hit with scenes of Oxford Street crushed to the corners; the toys are all wooden. It's innocence that we buy, a past innocence that we are all part of, or so we think: the time when we believed in Santa Claus and the lights on the tree were made of magic, Angel Gabriel was unchallenged, the carols sounded so sweet. We go to desperate lengths to recreate that holy day, that holiday. The story is the same—it's the same for a child as for an adult. You can believe it if you want to, believe it happened. God does not seek to control us.

> Peter Owen Jones, *Small Boat, Big Sea: One Year's Journey as a Parish Priest* (Oxford: Lion Publishing, 2000), p. 82.

The face of Christ

As we remember the coming of the Christ child, let us be aware that he may not come now in the form of a baby, but as a stranger, a beggar, a member of our family in distress, as an enemy, a soldier, someone who oppresses our people. . . . But these may be hiding the face of Christ. We must offer what is each person's basic

need—the need for acceptance, whoever we are and whatever we have done. . . .
We have to hold our doors open.

Quaker ministry spoken at Ramallah, Christmas 1992, in Janet
Morley, *Companions of God: Praying for Peace in the Holy Land*
(London: Christian Aid, 1994), p. 20.

Longing for the God of peace

Leader: Om Shalom, Om Shalom, Om Shalom

Silence: (We reflect on the Origin of our being
              and on the End to which we move)

Leader: Om Shalom, Om Shalom, Om Shalom

              As the hunted deer for the river longs
              For the God of Peace alone we sing
              Like a dry parched land athirst for rain,
              For the God of Peace we deeply yearn.
People: **Come, O come (2), Lord God of Peace,**
              Om Shalom (3)

Leader: Where can we find the peace we've sought?
              Too long we've planned, discussed, and fought;
              Blessed our children, beyond our feuds,
              They point in play to that world of peace.
People: **Come, O come (2), Lord God of Peace,**
              Om Shalom (3)

Leader: Given us now a clear peace sign
              Yet wrapped in peasant rags this Child;
              Here Peace breaks in, in love compels;
              O show us now your light of peace.
People: **Come, O come (2), Lord God of Peace,**
              Om Shalom (3)

From "Liturgy: Praying for Peace, Celebrating Peace," in *Worship in an
Indian Context: Eight Inter-Cultural Liturgies,* ed. Eric J. Lott (Bangalore:
United Theological College, 1986), p. 90. Used by permission.

Remembering the story

Putting it at its simplest, we might say that *Christians are those who remember the story of Jesus within the community of the church, in and for their own time and in their own lives.* "Remembrance" here has all the well-rehearsed connotations of the Greek *anamnesis,* encapsulating both the recollection of the past but also its making present, its re-membering or actualizing, in the here and now. Christians recall, repeat and rehearse the "old, old story", passed on from generation to generation, and, at the same time, reappropriate, retell, revise, refictionalize it in and for their own time. And these are not two separate activities, but one; for there is no way to recall and remember that is not at the same time a reshaping and a revising of what is received. Every act of remembrance is a complex process of selection, interpretation and arrangement of what has been received, in the light of the believing community's contemporary needs, experience and perceptions. This has been, from the beginning, the way in which the Jesus-story was both transmitted and renewed by Christians who perceived in its narrative possibilities endless applications to their own situations and lives.

Nicola Slee, "The Power to Re-member," in *Swallowing a Fishbone?
Feminist Theologians Debate Christianity,* ed. Daphne Hampson
(London: SPCK, 1996), p. 36.

The plastic angel

Our crèche set came complete with stable
    and a plastic angel.
Small, not at all to scale.
    the white-garbed creature with uncertain wings
        was obviously an afterthought,
            thrown in to complete the set,
                otherwise ceramic and hand-painted. . . .
Unless, of course, this angel was a last-minute substitute
    for one which was irresistible to the packer.
In that case, somewhere I have an irresistible ceramic angel,
    dressed gloriously in red,
        kneeling or flying on somebody else's coffee table
            even now
                as I unwrap the plastic angel.
If I could ever bring myself to throw away an angel,

it would be this one,
    this one with no redeeming features.
And yet, each year as I unwrap the plastic angel,
    I hesitate again to pitch this celestial messenger.
I'm reminded of my own lack of glory,
    my own plastic attempts at celebrating Christmas,
      my own feeble annunciations,
        and once again I place this bit of plastic
          over the stable.
If the plastic angel
    can get this far,
      perhaps there's a place in Bethlehem town
        for me.

Grace is the free, undeserved goodness and favour of God to humankind.

Matthew Henry (1662–1714)

Poor World (said I) what wilt thou do
To entertain this starry Stranger?
Is this the best thou canst bestow,
A cold, and not too cleanly manger?
Contend, ye powers of heaven and earth,
To fit a bed for this huge birth.

Richard Crashaw (1613–1649)

Christmas, Second Proper

Isaiah 62:6–12   Titus 3:4–7

Psalm 97   Luke 2:(1–7) 8–20

A time of glory and of peace

Every mother thinks her baby is the best in the world, but I knew mine was. It was as though the stars were singing that night, and the stable—that I would normally think was dirty and smelly with its steaming patches of manure—became like a palace. The starlight shone through the gaps in the wood, the breathing of the animals was like a soothing lullaby, and there was a manger there against the wall that would keep the baby safe from being trampled underfoot, like a little cot made just for him. Joseph wrapped up this tiny baby boy, perfectly formed, in a piece of white cloth, and they both fell asleep exhausted. I did not sleep. I was too excited. I kept on getting up to look at my baby, and from feeling so wretched and sorry for myself, I now knew how fortunate I was.

Towards dawn we had our first visitors—some poor people from the outlying countryside, who tiptoed in while the town was still asleep. They had been told to look for a baby wrapped up and lying in an animals' manger, but since no one else had been to see us it was odd that they knew. They knew the baby was going to save the people, and I told them he was going to be called Jesus, which means Saviour. They might have wondered how we knew, and we might have wondered how they knew, but we all knew our information was reliable. I will never forget the events of that night. It was a time of glory, and a time of peace.

Margaret Hebblethwaite, *Six New Gospels: New Testament Women Tell Their Stories* (London: Geoffrey Chapman, 1994), pp. 30–31.

Joy to the world

Leader: Joy to the world! Our Saviour is born!

People: **Joy to the earth! Our Saviour does reign!**

Leader: Emmanuel is with us.

People: **Christ dwells among us.**

Leader:	Wisdom comes from our God most high.
People:	**Light has gladdened the darkness.**

Leader:	Come, all you faithful people, worship the Messiah!
People:	**We gather together to behold and adore him.**

Leader:	Come, all you searching people, Love has been made manifest.
People:	**We raise our voices in praise and wonder.**

All:	**Gloria in excelsis Deo! All praise to the newborn Christ!**

Lisa Withrow, *Seasons of Prayer: Resources for Worship* (London: SPCK, 1995), p. 80. Used by permission.

Emmanuel

Star maker,
earth shaker,
power of the hurricane,
voice of the dove,
come to earth
to a blaze of angels,
called by compassion,
formed by love.

Joy Cowley, *Psalms for the Road* (Wellington, New Zealand: Catholic Supplies [N.Z.] Ltd., 2002), p. 23. Used by permission.

If you pray truly, you will feel within yourself a great assurance; and the angels will be your companions.

Evagrius of Pontus (c. 305–400)

Christmas lament

Ah, venerable Church!
With none of the simple joys of those shepherds
who came first of all
to worship around your crib!
With nothing left of the peace of your stable.

Fearing the coming of your kingdom,
tonight too Herod and his henchmen keep watch,
ready to lop off your young shoots,
keeping Christmas with glaring eyes.

And your disciples,
changing the colour of the Gospel
like a beaded dress displayed in a shop window,
the colour varying with the lighting,
with the enthusiastic mob,
and the Pharisees, today too,
all crowd around
you;

and like Zacchaeus perched in a tree,
one crow-like soul cries:
'On me and on all held in cursed bondage
turn, oh turn your eyes!'

> Ku Sang, *Wastelands of Fire,* trans. Anthony Teague (London and
> Boston: Forest Books, 1990), p. 49. © 1990 Ku Sang and Anthony
> Teague. Used by permission.

———

Be persuaded by me, all you who ardently and in all seriousness long for salvation: make haste, search persistently, ask ceaselessly, knock patiently, and continue until you reach your goal.

> Theognostos (fourteenth century)

———

A ruler for the poor

Luke's account of the sacrifice offered by Mary and Joseph (2:24) implies their lack of economic resources (cf. Leviticus 12:6–8). The story of the shepherds (2:8–20), though not necessarily requiring that Mary and Joseph be low in the social and economic scale, surely reveals Luke's intention to situate Jesus' birth in humble circumstances among the poor. In this context Jesus' birth in Bethlehem, "the city of David" (2:11), recognized as Messiah by shepherds, suggests not his birth into the honor and status of the royal line of the kings of Judah, but rather David's own social insignificance, as a shepherd boy in Bethlehem, before his rise to power. The

Messiah who is to be the ideal David, ruling righteously for the benefit of the poor (Isaiah 11:14), comes, like David himself, from the ranks of the poor, so that he may rule in solidarity with the poor. He is a king who meets not the expectations of the elite, but the hope of the poor for a ruler who will exalt the lowly and feed the hungry.

Richard Bauckham, *Gospel Women: Studies of the Named Women in the Gospels* (Edinburgh: T. & T. Clark; Grand Rapids: Wm. B. Eerdmans, 2002), p. 73.

CHRISTMAS, THIRD PROPER

Isaiah 52:7–10   Hebrews 1:1–4 (5–12)

Psalm 98   John 1:1–14

Word and word-bearer

The Word was made flesh, and not simply words, and yet the particular flesh in which the fullness of God was pleased to dwell was the flesh of our humanity. The oldest term in English for a human being is "reord-berend" or "word-bearer" and we are all the creatures of the flesh, especially the word-bearers. It is to human beings that the mystery and the gift of language has been entrusted. Our language is bound up not only with our knowledge of the world and ourselves but with our very being. If our being and our knowledge are corrupted and fallen, then by the same token so is our language, and if there is redemption for us in the depth of our being, then language too must be redeemed. What is not assumed is not redeemed, and therefore a part of the whole meaning of the incarnation is the story of the Word coming into his world as one who will learn and use, and in taking it up, *redeem language*. . . .

The story of how the Word of God came to redeem humanity begins not with speech but with silence. The first and deepest paradox of the incarnation is the self-emptying of Christ, the power of his powerlessness, the strength of his weakness. The seventeenth-century preacher Lancelot Andrewes seized upon the strange contradiction in terms with which the Word could be an infant: *verbum infans* for, of course, the Latin term *infans* means "without speech". And he exclaims with astonishment: "the Word without a word. The eternal word not able to speak a word". Just as our wounds are healed by his stripes, so our empty wordiness, hollow at the centre, is met and redeemed by Christ himself, becoming in his *infancy* a centre in which is hidden the Word that maintains the world, and *yet* a centre which has still to learn speech.

> Malcolm Guite, "Through Literature: Christ and the Redemption of Language," in *Beholding the Glory: Incarnation through the Arts*, ed. Jeremy Begbie (London: Darton, Longman & Todd; Grand Rapids: Baker Book House Company, 2000), pp. 33–34. Used by permission.

They sing for joy

What a god has now claimed his rule! He is as terrifyingly masculine as a warrior with sleeves rolled up for battle and as gently maternal as a carrier of a lamb. It is all there—for exiles. It includes the comfort of enormous power, with stress on *fort* (strengthen); it includes the comfort of nurture, with the stress on *com* (along with). Israel is in a new situation where singing is possible again. Have you ever been in a situation where because of anger, depression, preoccupation, or exhaustion you could not sing? And then you could? Change resulted from being addressed, called by a name, cared for, recognized, and assured. The prophet makes it possible to sing, and the empire knows that people who can boldly sing have not accepted the royal definition of reality. If the lack of singing is an index of exile, then we are in it, for we are a people who scarcely can sing. The prophet makes the hopefulness of singing happen again.

> Walter Brueggemann, *The Prophetic Imagination* (Minneapolis:
> Fortress Press, 2001), p. 71.

The kingdom comes indeed as a gift, but it comes also as a responsibility inviting urgent and active response from those to whom it is given. Salvation comes from God, but it is actualized in and through the struggle of the poor.

> George M. Soares-Prabhu

The light shines in the darkness

Look steadily at the darkness. It won't be long before you see the light. Gaze at things. It won't be long before you see the Word.

The Word became flesh; he came to dwell among us . . .

And stop those frantic efforts to change flesh back into words. Words, words, words!

> Anthony de Mello, S.J., *The Song of the Bird* (Anand, India: Gujarat
> Sahitya Prakash, 1982), pp. 28–29.

The Word made flesh

Christ Jesus, full of grace and truth,
you lived among us,
as a man of your people
and a man of your time.

You are the word made flesh.

When many distance themselves from the church,
help us to see that it may be
because the church has stopped being with the people,
because it has sought to be on good terms with the powerful.

Help your church to know that it can serve best
when it does not set itself apart,
when it feels as its own all that is human,
when it suffers with those who weep,
when it is happy with those who rejoice
and when it welcomes sinners.

Christ Jesus, full of grace and truth,
you are the word made flesh.
May the church serve in your likeness,
may it bring light in the darkness,
may it bring hope to those who have lost faith,
may it walk in your footsteps,
may it be love in deed.

Christ Jesus,
continue to become incarnate in all of us.

Francis Brienen, in *A Restless Hope: Prayer Handbook 1995*, ed. Kate
Compston (London: United Reformed Church, 1995), 29 October. ©
Francis Brienen. Used by permission.

———————————

You [Jesus Christ] are the Word of God humanified, and you are humanity deified.

Nicholas of Cusa (1401–1464)

———————————

First Sunday after Christmas

| Isaiah 63:7–9 | Hebrews 2:10–18 |
| Psalm 148 | Matthew 2:13–23 |

Once a year?

Christmas is over. Back to reality! We all know the feeling well enough.

The curled-up tangerine skin in the hearth, the drip of red candle grease on the mantelpiece, the daily quota of pine needles on the floor—all that is left to remind us rather sadly of a momentary escape from a humdrum routine.

And now these scattered remnants must be swept up, the glass balls and paper lanterns put away. Once a year is all very well, but you can't live with it for ever.

But is this what we *really* feel about Christmas?

A few days off in memory of a man from the past? A few days in which to glimpse what *his* sort of life could mean for us? A time to patch up family quarrels . . . to interrupt bombings? Just one or two days when the spirit of Jesus does play a part in our lives, when he really counts?

Yes—once a year is all very well, but you can't live with him for ever!

If this *is* what Christmas means, then, in fact, you don't believe in the Resurrection.

John A. T. Robinson, *But That I Can't Believe* (London: Fontana, 1967), p. 37.

Where is home?

When I met Elie Wiesel a second time, in April 1982, once again in his apartment, I wanted to speak with him about the subject of "*Heimat*"—"home." I asked him whether there was a place anywhere in the world where he felt at home. I was asking this question of someone who had survived Auschwitz, but I also put it to myself, hoping to receive from the conversation not so much answers as a better insight into the question of "being at home."

Elie Wiesel delineated three approaches to the subject, three basic aspects of possibly being at home. The first is that we should look for *Heimat* in time rather than space. The second is that to go back to one's own childhood is a manner of returning home. The third is that, for him, Jerusalem is home.

In our conversation, these three basic aspects were interwoven; they pervaded one another. "I feel at home in my city, in Jerusalem," was his spontaneous reply to my initial question. But right away he connected it with the recollection of his childhood in Eastern Europe. Wiesel felt at home in the time of his childhood in Romania; the time before the destruction of everything that could mean *Heimat* to an Eastern European Jew. In the words "Jerusalem," "my city," "Yes, Jerusalem," the first thing I discerned was a distancing from his present life in New York.

Dorothee Soelle, *Against the Wind: Memoir of a Radical Christian,*
trans. Barbara and Martin Rumscheidt (Minneapolis: Fortress Press,
1999), pp. 128–29.

A good portion of the evils that afflict humankind is due to the erroneous belief that life can be made secure by violence.

Leo Tolstoy (1828–1910)

In violence and travail

We give you thanks for the babe born in violence.

We give you thanks for the miracle of Bethlehem,
born into the Jerusalem heritage.

We do not understand why the innocents must be slaughtered;
we know that your kingdom comes in violence and travail.
Our time would be a good time for your kingdom to come,
because we have had enough of violence and travail.

So we wait with eager longing,
and with enormous fear,
because your promises
do not coincide with our favorite injustices.

We pray for the coming of your kingdom on earth
as it is around your heavenly throne.

We are people grown weary of waiting.

We dwell in the midst of cynical people,
and we have settled for what we can control.

We do know that you hold initiative for our lives,
that your love planned our salvation
before we saw the light of day.

And so we wait for your coming,
in your vulnerable baby
in whom all things are made new.

Amen.

Walter Brueggemann, *Awed to Heaven, Rooted in Earth: Prayers of Walter Brueggemann* (Minneapolis: Fortress Press, 2003), p. 149. © 2003 Augsburg Fortress. Used by permission.

What hope is there for innocence if it is not recognized?

Simone Weil

Witness

For a heroically long time, [Etty Hillesum] resisted the temptation to hate all Germans because of what many Germans were doing. But, finally, it became appropriate to hate. She found the guards at Westerbork bestial. She also felt that the position into which she and her fellow Jews were forced was horribly, hopelessly "twisted." Her descriptions of Westerbork inmates helping to load families, old people, and infants onto the doomed transport trains are ruthlessly candid and unbearably wrenching. She knew all too well that her survival would mean someone else's death, and the whole calculation seemed to her bitterly wrong. The means of staying alive had become utterly perverted, and perhaps the only way for her to save meaning was by accepting death.

Etty Hillesum lived at a time when the macrocosm of historical events almost completely crushed the microcosm of individual lives. It was her enormous act of resistance to reverse this order of importance, to assert that the microcosm of the soul can encompass the external world, and, in addition, hold infinite space.

Eva Hoffman, from the foreword to Etty Hillesum, *An Interrupted Life and Letters from Westerbork,* trans. Arnold J. Pomerans (New York: Henry Holt & Co., 1996), p. xii.

Agnus Dei: 2001

When the days grow longer, they come,
White as newness. Life and soul
Of the flock, unlike their dingy elders.

In a good year, grow stockier,
Turn into sheep. In a bad year
Leave the world in summer, behind screens,

Smoke, silence, smell of disinfectant.

This one comes with the very early lambs
Always. Doing the things lambs do,
Lord of the dance in the meadow.

He knows where he's going.

U. A. Fanthorpe, from *Queueing for the Sun* (Calstock,
Cornwall: Peterloo Poets, 2003), p. 91. © U. A. Fanthorpe 2003.
Used by permission.

Listen to the children

Listen to the children
singing at the manger,
faces full of wonder,
angels in disguise;
Listen to the story,
touch the edge of glory,
feel the breath of beauty,
tingle with surprise,
for in their wonder
Christ is meeting us today, and saying:

"Every hand that hurts the children,
every land that hates the children,
better take a heavy stone and jump into the sea.
I am in their loving, living,
I am in their crying, dying,
I am in their seeking, speaking,
Listen now to me. Listen now to me."

Listen to the children
huddled in the alley,
watching on the freeway
progress rushing by,
begging for a quarter,
killing for a dollar,
nothing in the future,
anger in their eyes . . .
and in their anger
Christ is meeting us today, and saying: "Every hand . . ."

Listen to the children,
thinking and exploring,
deeper than the ocean
higher than the skies.
Sit among the children
eager for an answer,
open-mouthed in wonder,
loving a surprise,
for in their seeking
Christ is meeting us today, and saying: "Every hand . . ."

Brian Wren, in Susan Heafield (music) and Brian Wren (words), *We Can Be Messengers: Worship Songs: Christmas, Before and After* (Decatur, Ga.: Praise Partners Publishing, 2001), pp. 32–34. *We Can Be Messengers* is obtainable in the USA from Hope Publishing Company, *hope@hopepublishing.com,* and in the UK from Stainer & Bell Ltd., *cwakefield@stainer.co.uk.* Used by permission.

SECOND SUNDAY AFTER CHRISTMAS

Jeremiah 31:7–14	Ephesians 1:3–14
Psalm147:12–20	John 1:(1–9) 10–18

What sort of Christ?

In his prose poem *Khristos* (1878), Turgenev dreams that he is in a village church together with the peasant congregation. A man comes to stand beside him: "I did not turn towards him, but immediately I felt that this man was Christ." However, when eventually he turns towards him he perceives "a face like everyone's face. A face like all men's faces . . . And the clothes on him like everyone else's." Turgenev is astonished: "What sort of a Christ is this then? . . . Such an ordinary, ordinary man." But he concludes: "Suddenly I was afraid—and came to my senses. Only then did I realize that it is just such a face—a face like all men's faces—that is the face of Christ."

Sergei Hackel, from "Some Russian Writers and the 'Russian Christ,'"
in *Eastern Churches Review* 10 (1978): p. 48.

Here is born for us a brother*

Here is born for us a brother,
born to share our testing days,
faithful, brimming with compassion,
worthy of increasing praise;
captives freeing, sickness healing,
Zion's straight and holy road,
fountain sparkling, life through dying,
our salvation, ark of God.

Ann Griffiths, from "Dyma Frawd a anwyd inni," trans. Alan Gaunt,
in *Hymns and Letters* (London: Stainer & Bell, 1999), p. 41. © 1997
Stainer & Bell Ltd. (Admin. in the USA and Canada by Hope
Publishing Co., Carol Stream, IL 60188.) All rights reserved.
Used by permission.

*Tune: HYFRYDOL.

Crossing frontiers

God has crossed the frontiers of divine life. God is not content for me to say only, "Forget me, I don't matter", because God's attentive love looks to me, assuring me that he is, to adapt the scriptural phrase, "not ashamed to be called my God", not ashamed to be who he is and to be identified as who he is in relation to me, even though I am a mess. Throughout the biblical story, God accepts identification in terms of those he works with—the God of Abraham, Isaac and Jacob, the Lord God of Israel, the one whose "body" is the community of Christian believers. There is no safe and pure self-identification for God except the mysterious affirmation of the divine freedom to be identified as the God who chooses a recalcitrant and mutinous people ("I will be what I will be", as Exodus 3:13 is best translated). So, as we are moved to say, "Look away from me to Christ, or to God", he says, "But *I* am free to go on looking to you." I discover myself as someone who is being made real by his attention to me; I live because he looks to me.

> Rowan Williams, *Ponder These Things: Praying with Icons of the Virgin*
> (Norwich: Canterbury Press, 2002), p. 12.

Hasten therefore to share in the Holy Spirit. He is with you when you call upon him; you can call upon him only because he is already present. When he comes in answer to your prayer, he comes with an abundance of blessings. He is the river whose streams give joy to the city of God.

> William of St. Thierry (1085–1148)

Becoming flesh

Do you remember that resurrection scene in Thornton Wilder's . . . play *Our Town?* . . . Emily Gibbs, who had died in childbirth in her mid-twenties, is allowed to leave her grave on the hill above Grover's Corners and return to life for one day. Against the counsel of others in the graveyard who tell her that the return will be too painful, she decides to come back for one day, and chooses her twelfth birthday.

The scene of her return opens in the kitchen, where her mother is busy fixing breakfast. Fourteen years have gone by. Emily pleads with Mama to look at her, just for a moment, as though she really saw her. Mama, however, is too busy.

This is the way the day unfolds. People are too busy to notice or to touch. Before long it is too much for her, and Emily cries out that she can't go on. It is too painful. . . . She pleads to be taken back up the hill to her grave. But first she takes one more look and says her goodbyes.

How sensual and bodily are her farewells! The divine yearning for the incarnational mystery is there. Emily says goodbye to the world, and to Grover's Corners, and to Mama and Papa. She bids farewell to clocks that are ticking and to Mama's sunflowers. She says goodbye to food and coffee and newly ironed dresses, to hot baths and sleeping and waking. She exclaims that the earth is just too wonderful for anyone to realize it.

James B. Nelson, *Body Theology* (Louisville, Ky.: Westminster/John Knox Press, 1992), pp. 195–96.

It is not over

    It is not over,
        this birthing.
    There are always newer skies
        into which
            God can throw stars.
    When we begin to think
        that we can predict the Advent of God,
        that we can box the Christ
            in a stable in Bethlehem,
    that's just the time
    that God will be born
    in a place we can't imagine and won't believe.
    Those who wait for God
        watch with their hearts and not their eyes,
            listening
                always listening
                    for angel words.

Ann Weems, *Kneeling in Bethlehem* (Philadelphia: Westminster Press, 1980), p. 85. © 1992 Ann Barr Weems. Used by permission of Westminster John Knox Press. Do not duplicate without written permission from Westminster John Knox Press, 100 Witherspoon Street, Louisville, KY 40202.

Dying to self is a progressive journey and I have come to believe that it is travelled only through praise.

Merlin R. Carothers

The baby had a birthday

The baby had a birthday—
we made the brandy sauce,
we drank his health
and spent our wealth
upon ourselves, of course.

We had a lovely party
and brightened up the place;
profusely strung
the tinsel hung—
you couldn't see his face.

Then when the feast was over,
and we'd run out of cheer,
we packed him in
the trimmings' tin
till Christmas time next year.

Cecily Taylor, in *Worship Live* no. 24 (London: Stainer & Bell, Autumn 2002), p. 12. © Cecily Taylor. Used by permission.

Epiphany

Isaiah 60:1–6

Psalm 72:1–7, 10–14

Ephesians 3:1–12

Matthew 2:1–12

BC:AD

This was the moment when Before
Turned into After, and the future's
Uninvented timekeepers presented arms.

This was the moment when nothing
happened. Only dull peace
Sprawled boringly over the earth.

This was the moment when even energetic Romans
Could find nothing better to do
Than counting heads in remote provinces.

And this was the moment
When a few farm workers and three
Members of an obscure Persian sect

Walked haphazard by starlight straight
Into the kingdom of heaven.

U. A. Fanthorpe, from *Christmas Poems* (Calstock, Cornwall: Peterloo
Poets, 2002). © U. A. Fanthorpe 2002. Used by permission.

"... and the stars"

On the fourth day God creates the stars, the signs of time. They are far more
ancient than we can imagine, yet for us they are markers of human times we need
to remember, days and years of significance.

Jesus is born in real human time, as St Luke reminds us, "when Quirinius was
governor of Syria" (Luke 2:2). God gives us the freedom of living in real time. The
events of our lives really happen. We can affect the course of this world and we are
affected by what happens around us. Through Mary, the star of Jesus rises over

the human world. The infant Jesus is linked to the royal house of David. He is the desire of nations, and therefore the judge of kings and governments and the refuge of all who have been exiled or injured in war or conflict. It is to him that the wise of this world come guided by a new star. In the nativity story they are represented by the three wise men, who are also seen as kings.

So . . . the challenge to us is to acknowledge that we have power to act on the world, to make meanings in our lives, to encounter the living God in the events and accidents of our existence. Time gives us access to truth and healing, "time for amendment of life" and the chance to forgive. In this process the wise men remind us that we need every ounce of our intelligence, skill and imaginative power to weave our experience into communicable meanings. At the same time the figure of Mary stands beside us as our companion and prophet of God's infinite and motherly care.

Angela Tilby, *Let There Be Light: Praying with Genesis* (London:
Darton, Longman & Todd), pp. 127–28.

God looks at the intention of the heart rather than the gifts he is offered.

Jean Pierre Camus (1582–1652)

Across the desert sands*

Across the desert sands,
Between the forest trees,
Through frozen wastes and fertile lands
And over swelling seas,
By villages and towns,
Rough path and winding road
By craggy peaks and rolling downs
I bear a precious load:

Gold of the world's wealth,
Incense for worship,
Myrrh meaning sorrow,
Love beyond telling.

*Tune: A PILGRIM CAROL.

A track that shepherds tread,
A half-remembered song,
A star that glimmers gold and red,
They're drawing me along,
And when the journey's done
I hope to meet my king
And lay before Him one by one
The gifts I come to bring:

Chorus

I've never seen the place,
No map describes the way,
But still I trust that by God's grace
I shall not go astray.
My Lord will show no scorn
Nor turn away from me,
But gladly take what I have borne
So far, so wearily:

Chorus

Now come, O come with me,
All you whose hearts are stirred,
Together we shall surely see
The light of God's own word,
And as we go we'll raise
With all our might and main
A pilgrim carol full of praise,
A tender, sweet refrain:

Chorus

Beckoning God

Beckoning God—
who called the rich to travel toward poverty,
    the wise to embrace your folly,
    the powerful to know their own frailty;
who gave to strangers
    a sense of homecoming in an alien land
and to stargazers
    true light and vision as they bowed to earth—
we lay ourselves open to your signs for us.

Stir us with holy discontent over a world
which gives its gifts to those
    who have plenty already
    whose talents are obvious
    whose power is recognized;
and help us
both to share our resources with those who have little
and to receive with humility the gifts they bring to us.

Rise within us, like a star,
and make us restless
till we journey forth
to seek our rest in you.

Kate Compston, in *Bread of Tomorrow: Praying with the World's Poor*,
ed. Janet Morley (London: SPCK/Christian Aid, 1992), pp. 53–54.
© Kate Compston. Used by permission.

Our lighted candles are a sign of the divine glory of the one who comes to dispel the dark shadows of evil and to make the whole universe radiant with the brightness of his eternal light. Our candles also show how bright our souls should be when we go to meet Christ.

Sophronius (d. c. 638)

Prayer

O God, the source of all insight,
whose coming was revealed to the nations
not among men of power
but on a woman's lap:
give us grace to seek you
where you may be found,
that the wisdom of this world may be humbled
and discover your unexpected joy,
through Jesus Christ. Amen.

Janet Morley, *All Desires Known* (London: SPCK, 1992), p. 7.
Used by permission.

FIRST SUNDAY AFTER EPIPHANY

(Baptism of the Lord)

Isaiah 42:1–9   Acts 10:34–43

Psalm 29   Matthew 3:13–17

On the *Baptism of Christ* by Piero della Francesca

That dove is beautifully shaped to match the shapes of the clouds in the sky. This gives stillness and calm to the energy of its hovering. Here is a mixture of activity . . . and rest. This combination is strong in Christ's body, in which the two are reconciled. Christ's head, chest, arms and hands are set in the stillness of prayer. . . . Below them, his hips are asymmetrically skewed—a suggestion of movement emphasised by the darkness of the background. It enables the walking tilt of his legs as he advances towards us. Yet the soles of his feet are set steadily in the stream. He stands. And he moves. Which? ". . . At the still point, there the dance is . . ." (T. S. Eliot, "Burnt Norton" II). Christ's feet are placed where the water of the stream changes from being a calm mirror of the hills above to a shallowness which lets us see its stony bed. According to the Gospels it was as Jesus came up from the water, in that crossing-over, that God declared him to be his only Son. It is a moment of definition, but also a moment of transition. In terms of the past, it recapitulates Israel's exodus. In terms of the future, it prophesies Christ's own passing from death to life. Although he is now as naked as he will be at his death, to which his baptism commits him, the pink cloak, which he has left with the angel nearest him, will clothe his resurrected body as he rises omnipotent from his tomb in Piero's fresco in the Town Hall at Borgo San Sepolcro, his sacrifice complete.

> John Drury, *Painting the Lord: Christian Pictures and Their Meanings*
> (New Haven, Conn., and London: Yale University Press and National
> Gallery Publications, 1999), pp. 88–89.

Gay and lesbian Christians know that God's spirit is not a tame dove but a wild goose, free of ecclesiastical attempts to control and confine it, that makes its home in the most unlikely places. The Spirit comes not in quiet conformity but demanding to be heard.

Elizabeth Stuart

Who are you?

When asked to introduce yourself to a group of people, how do you identify yourself after giving your name? I am a businessman, a housewife, a doctor, a baker? And if you are unemployed or unable to work, how do you feel about declaring this? Because we identify ourselves by what we do, we feel devastated when we are no longer capable of doing it, as though we had lost our very being.

You are not your occupation. You are not your achievements, you are not your failings, nor your health, wealth or status. All these things are connected with you, but are not you, for you do not cease to exist when these things disappear. Ultimately, who are you? . . .

You are a unique manifestation of God, who is closer to you than you are to yourself. This is the truth of your being, the glory and wonder of it.

Gerard W. Hughes, God of Compassion (London: CAFOD and
Hodder & Stoughton, 1998), pp. 63–64.

God's gift

God our Saviour
>you come to us
>in the unexpected mode and form
>of a persistent, suffering servant.

>Year after year, there's a crisis somewhere
>so that poor, homeless, illiterate, sick,
>hungry and exploited people suffer.
>Wars are fought and the innocent weep.

>Year after year our hearts ache for someone
>close to us who is desperate, feeling useless,
>marriage failing, troubles piling up,
>all seems hopeless.

Then we are surprised by your servant,
who brings justice, not by slogans
or the tramp of boots but by allowing himself
to be broken, his light dimmed.

Persistently and with endurance,
he shows that each person matters to you
that you are there
in every crisis and in each hurt.

It was to Jesus that your spirit came.
He is the servant, the Lamb of God,
and trusting him, we still have hope
in you our saviour.

By grace we have been saved through faith, the gift of God.

Tony Burnham, in *Say One for Me: Prayer Handbook 1990*, ed.
Graham Cook (London: United Reformed Church, 1990), January
14. © Tony Burnham. Text revised by author, and used by permission.

God has deified our nature, though not by turning it into himself, yet by making it his own inseparable habitation.

Richard Hooker

In one of our communities, there is a man called Pierre who has a mental handicap. One day someone asked him, "Do you like praying?" He answered, "Yes". He was asked what he did when he prayed. He answered, "I listen". "And what does God say to you?" "He says, 'You are my beloved son'."

Jean Vanier

Prayer

Dear Lord,
turn our religions inside out,
save them all from the modes of self glorification,
make servanthood the hallmark of their authenticity,

show all believing people
that the secret,
the source,
the origin
of all that's worth having and striving for
has already been modelled for us
in the self-sacrificing love of Jesus.

Leslie Griffiths, from "Nunc Dimittis," in *Touching the Pulse: Worship and Our Diverse World,* ed. Leslie Griffiths (London: Stainer & Bell, 1998), p. 82. © 1998 Stainer & Bell Ltd. Used by permission.

We do not know that at the centre of our being we find not ourselves but another, that our own identity is in another, that turning inwards and finding ourselves is to fall into the arms of another.

Ernesto Cardenal

SECOND SUNDAY AFTER EPIPHANY

Isaiah 49:1–7   1 Corinthians 1:1–9
Psalm 40:1–11   John 1:29–42

"Come and see"

The Kingdom of heaven was at hand, but [Andrew and Simon] did not know what was implied in that announcement. Their teacher had trained them to look forward to the One who was to come. Looking to that One means loving him. Loving him means following him.

A mysterious future rises up before their hearts as they follow him. They cannot formulate any anticipations about that future intellectually. They follow Christ, not as expecting something from him, but because he is himself. They do not know what to expect. Their very question shows it. "Rabbi, where are you staying?"

Yet he has nowhere on earth to lay his head. Truly to know this is the truest knowledge of his dwelling. . . . When he says . . . "Come and see," he says, "Come up here, and I will show you what must take place after this." If he calls us to himself in some earthly form, it is so that he may draw us to himself in his unchanging glory.

Richard Meux Benson, S.S.J.E., *The Followers of the Lamb*
(London: Longmans, Green, & Co., 1900), pp. 188–89
(language slightly modernized).

If God has called you, do not spend time looking over your shoulder to see who is following you.

Corrie ten Boom

Human freedom

Human freedom is the joy whereby human beings appropriate for themselves God's election. God has elected himself in his Son to be the God, Lord, Shepherd, Saviour, and Redeemer of humankind. Through his own election, he willed humankind to be his creatures, his partners, and his children, he, the God of the community of humankind, and we, the community of humankind, his people! Freedom is the joy whereby humankind acknowledges and confesses this divine election by willing, deciding, and determining themselves to be the echo and mirror of the divine act. Each individual is called to this commitment in the midst of the human community, not as the first disciple but as a follower in the visible and invisible footsteps of many; not as the only one but together with many known and unknown fellow Christians.

> Karl Barth, *The Humanity of God* (London: Collins, 1961; Fontana Library, 1967), p. 76 (translation slightly adapted).

The basis of the Christian community is not the family tie, or social or economic equality, or shared oppression or complaint, or mutual attraction . . . but the divine call. The Christian community is not the result of human efforts.

> Henri J. M. Nouwen

Receiving the gift

On the whole we are not very good at *receiving;* the Protestant work ethic has told us for many years now that dignity is earned, and it is far superior to earn than it is to receive. Indeed it seems a sign of deficiency or weakness in us if we need to receive from others. I travelled to Ballymeena and was taken round the town by a Presbyterian minister. He showed me seven of the Presbyterian churches in the town, and then he told me that he had met three of the Presbyterian ministers. When I registered some surprise that he had only actually met three of his own colleagues, he said, "Oh, it's really quite easy. You see, we're all strong enough anyway, we don't need each other."

> Myra Blyth, from "Exploration in Community: Why the Church?"
> in *Encounters: Exploring Christian Faith,* ed. Michael Mayne
> (London: Darton, Longman & Todd, 1986), p. 115. © Myra Blyth.
> Used by permission.

A hymn on being united in love*

Bless, and keep us, God, in your love united,
from your family never separated.
You make all things new as we follow after;
whether tears or laughter, we belong to you.

Blessing shrivels up when your children hoard it;
move us then to share, for we can afford it:
blessing only grows in the act of sharing,
in a life of caring; love that heals and grows.

Fill your world with peace, such as you intended.
Teach us to prize the earth, love, replenish, tend it.
God, uplift, fulfil all who sow in sadness,
let them reap with gladness, by your kingdom thrilled.

You renew our life, changing tears to laughter;
we belong to you, so we follow after.
Bless and keep us, God, in your love united,
never separated from your living Word.

The voice from the jukebox

I went into religion partly because I was not very good at dealing with the world.
I thought this was my unworldliness, but it was in fact my fear and incompetence.
In my innocence I confused spirituality with droopiness, and I imagined myself
with equally droopy colleagues, sighing blessings to each other.

I got a rude shock. Synagogue (and church) general meetings are not the
Communion of Saints, and an awful lot of religious business is concerned with
balance sheets, not blessings. At international meetings where the pace is hotter,
I got used to seeing clerics fingering calculators as expertly as their beads. You

*Suggested tune: FRANKFURTER SEGENSLIED.

have to be very competent to keep the show on the road—and I don't mean any disrespect.

This led to a crisis in my religious life. My religious organisation was a place where I gave blessings; this was after all what I was paid to do. But it was not a place where I seemed to receive any—at least not obviously. As my teacher tartly remarked when I complained to him, the congregation employed me to solve their problems. I didn't pay them to solve mine.

Blessings did come to me, but not from the place I had expected. They flowed into me from the worldly world I had rejected. A major source of ideas for sermons and spirituality came to me in airport lounges, bars, cafés (not always the genteel ones) and bus queues. To my astonishment the still, small voice of God spoke to me through the clamour of a juke-box.

I remember a song of Marlene Dietrich: "Where Have All the Flowers Gone?" she sang. Young girls had picked them. They had given them to their men. The men had gone to war, and got killed. Out of their graves flowers grew. Where had they gone, those flowers? Well, young girls had picked them. . . .

In a café in Germany I looked up and saw a young girl and a boy at the next table. A vase of flowers separated them. The full tragedy of Europe came home to me, and I knew the work I must do. So many people had to be reconciled to break that terrible repetition. God had spoken.

Lionel Blue, *Bright Blue: Rabbi Lionel Blue's Thoughts for the Day*
(London: British Broadcasting Corporation, 1985), pp. 11–12.
© Lionel Blue. Used by permission.

Daily change

A Eucharist which failed to look towards the transformation of the world and of the lives of the participants would be a contradiction in terms.

Whether I am celebrating Mass with a handful of Christians or on a more sizeable public occasion, I am always conscious that things are going to have to change, and I have always thought of education as being, in the widest sense, an agent of change. It is humiliating to see how slight change for good appears to be. In the conclusion to Rilke's poem "Archaic Torso of Apollo", he says simply, "You must change your life." The Ignatian preoccupation with daily change is of a piece with that.

Peter Steele, S.J., from "Unambiguous Commitment," in *Call and Response: Jesuit Journeys in Faith,* ed. Frances Makower (London: Hodder & Stoughton, 1994), p. 154.

Walking the way of Jesus

If you ask yourself what were the characteristics of the mind of Jesus, there are two in particular that it seems to me are quite crucial.

The first is that it was a mind that was massively concerned with specifics rather than universals. . . . He was a man with a burning obsession. His spiritual and mental energy was not diversified into the business of bringing light in whole areas of human ignorance. It was a burning obsession with the kingly rule of God—not as an academic thesis, but as promise and as presence and as judgment in the midst of life.

. . . The other characteristic of the mind of Jesus, which seems to me to be very relevant to this business of encountering others, is the fact that he had a "*crucified rather than a crusading mind*". The term is Kosuke Koyama's, who, being Japanese, was at the receiving end of the triumphalist tradition of the . . . western missionary enterprise—someone who was accustomed to being at the receiving end of the "crusading mind". . . .

The "crucified mind" . . . is a mind that is conscious of the mystery of the other person, that recognises the sovereignty of the rights of another person, of the authenticity of their inner suffering, and is very careful about making judgments. . . . The evolution of the crucified mind comes about because of a willingness to accept all the pain of human encounter, all its bane and blessing, all its joy and misery; to regret none of it except that which is futile, and to repent of none of it other than that which is sinful. And it is that kind of mind that characterises the Christian encounter with others.

Colin Morris, from "Encountering Others: The Politics of Belief," in
Encounters: Exploring Christian Faith, ed. Michael Mayne (London:
Darton, Longman & Todd, 1986), pp. 45–49. © Colin Morris. Used by
permission.

THIRD SUNDAY AFTER EPIPHANY

Isaiah 9:1–4   1 Corinthians 1:10–18

Psalm 27:1, 4–9   Matthew 4:12–23

Discipleship means joy

If we answer the call to discipleship, where will it lead us? What decisions and partings will it demand? To answer this question we shall have to go to him, for only he knows the answer. Only Jesus Christ, who bids us follow him, knows the journey's end. But we do know that it will be a road of boundless mercy. Discipleship means joy.

In the modern world it seems so difficult to walk with absolute certainty in the narrow way of ecclesiastical decision and yet remain in the broad open spaces of the universal love of Christ, of the patience, mercy and "philanthropy" of God (Titus 3:4) for the weak and the ungodly. Yet somehow or other we must combine the two, or else we shall follow the paths of men. May God grant us joy as we strive earnestly to follow the way of discipleship.

> Dietrich Bonhoeffer, *The Cost of Discipleship,* trans. R. H. Fuller, with
> some revision by Irmgard Booth (London: SCM Press, 1959), p. 32.

To come to Jesus or to follow him is to accompany him into the kingdom. Becoming a disciple is an alternative way of speaking about entering into the kingdom.

> Albert Nolan

Divisions

It's refreshing to realize that division was evident in the earliest of church writings, Paul's letters. The later-written Acts of the Apostles had it that the early Christians were all of "one heart and one soul, and . . . everything they owned was held in common" (Acts 4:32). But I've wondered if this retrospective depiction is the way things *should* have been in the early church rather than the way things actually *were*.

Even the story of Pentecost has struck me as an idyllic dream of the way the church *should* have begun—a dramatic turnaround, an inpouring of the Spirit that empowered early Christians to proclaim the gospel in the languages of strangers so the message could be taken all over the world. Maybe it gives today's church, so divided by language, culture, and belief, an impossible ideal.

. . . We should be glad for division and disagreement in whatever setting. It reveals God's restless Spirit at work. It marks the difference between a movement and fascism, between a church and a cult.

Thank you, God, for our divisions. They liven things up, and make us realize that we are alive, not yet "resting in peace." Thank you that we have beliefs, that we have passions, that we care enough to struggle. May our belief and passion and care for one another keep us together while we struggle for one another's blessings—as well as yours!

Chris Glaser, *Reformation of the Heart: Seasonal Meditations by a Gay Christian* (Louisville, Ky.: Westminster John Knox Press, 2001), pp. 158–59. © 2001 Chris Glaser. Used by permission of Westminster John Knox Press.

Safe in the hands of God

Safe in the hands of God who made me,
what can there be that I should fear?
God is my light and my salvation,
strong is his help when foes are near.

This I have prayed and will seek after,
that I may walk with God each day;
then will he give me his protection,
no trouble shall my heart dismay.

God of my life, my Lord, my master,
father and mother now to me:
come, shield me from the threat of evil,
open your hands and set me free!

Teach me your way and lead me onwards,
save me from those who do me wrong;

give me the grace to wait with patience,
help me to trust, hold firm, be strong.

Michael Perry, from *Psalms for Today* and *Songs from the Psalms,* ed.
David Iliff, Michael Perry, and David Peacock (London: Hodder &
Stoughton for Jubilate, 1990), no. 27B. © 1973 by Jubilate Hymns,
Ltd. © 1996 Mrs. B. Perry (admin. for USA by Hope Publishing
Company, Carol Stream, IL 60188). All rights reserved. Used by
permission.

Addressed to God

Where then did I find you to be able to learn of you? . . . Your best servant is the
person who does not attend so much to hearing what he himself wants as to willing what he has heard from you.

Late have I loved you, beauty so old and so new; late have I loved you. And see,
you were within and I was in the external world and sought you there, and in my
unlovely state I plunged into those lovely created things which you made. You
were with me, and I was not with you. The lovely things kept me far from you,
though if they did not have their existence in you, they had no existence at all. You
called and cried out loud and shattered my deafness. You were radiant and
resplendent, you put to flight my blindness. You were fragrant, and I drew in my
breath and now pant after you. I tasted you, and now I feel nothing but hunger
and thirst for you. You touched me, and I am set on fire to attain the peace which
is yours.

Augustine of Hippo, *Confessions,* trans. Owen Chadwick (Oxford:
Oxford University Press, 1991), 10.37–38, p. 201.

After/Word: Indiana

Longing for the light
persists. In that other country,*
that dream-clad edge of sea
stretching back to India,
even the limestone walls
fed back the brightness,
even the dullest of trees

*The author recalls time spent in Western Australia.

startled into bushy blooms—
the banksia erect,
the stamens of the bottle-brush
a spun galaxy of red.

Some mornings a rooster
not yet broken to urban life
saluted those hills of sand,
and sometimes I walked
the streets of that town
alight with gladness, as though
I had already crossed the border
where only light exists.

Words came back: *amo,*
amas, amat, that old conjugation,
and I wondered if the verb
could be objectless, intransitive.
I wondered how it came to be
that past the middle of my life,
I walked alone in brazen light
and parsed the words for love.

Sonia Gernes, *A Breeze Called the Fremantle Doctor* (Notre Dame,
Ind.: University of Notre Dame Press, 1997), p. 174. © Sonia G.
Gernes 1997. Used with permission.

A "story-shaped" spirituality

Even though Matthew places great emphasis on spirituality as obedience to the
will of God as taught by Jesus, it is crucial to draw a lesson from the gospel genre
which Matthew has used, and to point out in consequence that Matthean spirituality is story-shaped not Torah-shaped. Matthew's gospel contains commandments and community rules, but it cannot be reduced to them. Rather, it is
"messianic biography", and spirituality is a personal response—both at the individual and at the corporate levels—to that biography. Wayne Meeks puts this well:
"Matthew makes that story part of the grammar of Christian ethics. The commandments are not separable from the commander, the teachings from the

teacher. Discipleship is 'following' the person identified in the story, who, raised from the dead, goes on leading the community."

A corollary of this is that there is a sense in which spirituality, according to Matthew, is not given. It remains something to be worked out and to be worked at. What is given is the story of the messiah and of the breaking into the present of the kingdom of heaven. . . .

What is given also, and most importantly, is the promise of the ever-abiding presence of Jesus (28:20). But discerning that presence is not a matter immune from doubt. Even when the risen Lord appears to the Eleven, Matthew tells us that "some doubted" (28:17). That is why faith, child-like humility, a spirit of generous forgiveness, and a reluctance to be judgemental are all necessary. It is why criteria for testing the words of prophets claiming to speak in the name of the Lord are needed, as well. Entering the narrow gate and going the hard way are ventures as fraught with difficulty and temptation for the follower of Jesus as they were for Jesus himself.

Stephen C. Barton, *The Spirituality of the Gospels* (London:
SPCK, 1992), pp. 28–29.

Today*

> Where does our salvation start?
> Where else but here in the human heart!
> We need not wait until all is proved
> before we know we are known and loved.
> The door is open, the table spread:
> Come unto me, the Saviour said.
>
> Lord, we come! like those of old
> some slow to follow, some overbold,
> today's disciples, our service flawed
> by sins and faults, by tasks ignored.
> The door is open, the table spread:
> You are my friends, the Saviour said.
>
> We, your Church, confess our blame:
> we let survival become our aim.

*Suggested tune: FOYE.

The times are hard, the tide is out;
we feed the hungry on crusts of doubt.
The door is open, the table spread:
Where is your faith? the Saviour said.

Lord, we come, your People still;
renew us in spirit to do your will,
to feed the hungry and end the strife
that makes a hell of our common life.
The door is open, the table spread:
Love one another, the Saviour said.

Fred Pratt Green, from *Partners in Creation: The Hymn Texts of Fred Pratt Green*, comp. Bernard Braley (London: Stainer & Bell; Carol Stream, Ill.: Hope Publishing Company, 2003), no. 96, p. 104.

To be alive to the reality of God is to be aware of his glorious foolishness, and of the infinite sufferings which make him the Father and friend of all the fools of love.

John Austin Baker

Fourth Sunday after Epiphany

Micah 6:1–8	1 Corinthians 1:18–31
Psalm 15	Matthew 5:1–12

Justice, love, humility

Act justly. What exactly does that mean? I don't know, but to treat others as we would have them treat us is a very good guideline in all our dealings. . . . The most important and effective work any of us can do for the promotion of justice is to start on the roots of injustice within ourselves.

Love tenderly. Do you ever feel your life is blighted because you have never been sufficiently loved? . . . If we can turn our attention to our need to love, ignoring that fact that we feel that we ourselves are unloved, the effect can be amazing and we can find a great load falling from us.

Walk humbly before your God. Humility derives from the Latin word "humus" meaning the earth. Humility is about seeing the truth of things, seeing ourselves in perspective, so that we are no longer the centre of the universe, but an element in its dance, with God as the choreographer.

Gerard W. Hughes, *God of Compassion* (London: CAFOD and
Hodder & Stoughton, 1998), pp. 53–54.

What does the Lord require?*

What does the Lord require
for praise and offering?
What sacrifice, desire
or tribute bid you bring?
  Do justly;
  love mercy;
walk humbly with your God.

Rulers of earth, give ear!
should you not justice know?

*Tune: SHARPTHORNE.

Will God your pleading hear,
while crime and cruelty grow?
    Do justly . . .

Masters of wealth and trade,
all you for whom men toil,
Think not to win God's aid
if lies your commerce soil.
    Do justly . . .

Still down the ages ring
the prophet's stern commands:
to merchant, worker, king,
he brings God's high demands:
    Do justly . . .

How shall our life fulfil
God's law so hard and high?
Let Christ endue our will
with grace to fortify.
    Then justly,
    love mercy;
walk humbly with your God.

Words by Albert F. Bayly (1901–84). © Oxford University Press 1988.
Reproduced by permission.

Shaker testimony

In their everyday life Believers have labored with hands and hearts and minds in the glory of our Father Mother God by attending to every gift in its season and so enriching their own lives and those of countless others. Through their religious consecration they have always sought to share freely with all the spiritual tradition that is their heritage from Mother Ann and the Elders with her, and all the first Parents in the Gospel, and continuing down through the several thousand Believers over the last two hundred years. This Shaker heritage has its never-ceasing source in the true evangel which our beloved Jesus Christ taught, especially as witnessed in the Beatitudes: *Blessed are the poor in spirit, the meek, for theirs is heaven and earth.*

Eldress Gertrude M. Soule, from the preface to *The Shakers: Two Centuries of Spiritual Reflection,* ed. and intro. by Robley Edward Whitson (Ramsey, N.J.: Paulist Press, 1983), p. xiii.

The more we live and try to practise the Sermon on the Mount, the more shall we experience blessing.

David Martyn Lloyd-Jones

The scandal of Christ

Christians on the whole are very ordinary people. That this should be so is itself extraordinary, for of all the world religions Christianity is by far the most extraordinary—"impossible" and "absurd" as Tertullian said without any exaggeration at all, a "scandal" to the Jews and sheer "feeble-mindedness" (*moron*) to the Greeks. *Moron,* it may be said, translated in most English versions as "folly" or "foolishness", is a quality applied to children (in modern Greek a *moron paidhi* means simply a very small child) and, at least by Euripides, to women, regarded by the Greeks as a pretty scatterbrained lot. Yet St Paul is bold enough to apply the term to God himself—a childish, womanish, feebleminded God then, which surely should give us pause to think.

R. C. Zaehner, *The City within the Heart* (London: Unwin Paperbacks, 1980), p. 57.

There is inexhaustible meaning in the statement that God has chosen the foolish things of the world to put to shame them that are wise, and the weak things to confound those that are strong, but there is all the difference in the world between believing that and supposing that God takes delight in immaturity, incompetence, wishy-washiness and muddle.

J. H. Oldham

Honouring Christ

Do you want to honour the body of Christ? Then do not despise his nakedness. Do not honour him here [in church] clothed in silk vestments and then ignore him, naked and frozen in the street. Always remember that he who said, "This is my body", and gave effect to his word, also said, "I was hungry and you gave me no food", and "inasmuch as you did not do it to one of these, you did not do it to me". The body of Christ needs no clothing in the first sense but only [the worship of] a pure heart. But in the second case it needs clothing and all the care we can lavish upon it.

. . . Imagine that Christ is that tramp, that stranger who comes in need of a bed for the night. You turn him away and then start laying carpets on the floor, draping the walls, hanging lamps on silver chains from the capitals of the columns. Meanwhile the tramp is arrested and put in prison, but you never give him a second thought.

. . . No one was ever condemned for not beautifying Christ's house, but those who neglect their neighbour were threatened with hell fire and eternal punishment with devils. Beautify this house if that is what you want to do, but never neglect your brother or sister in need. They are temples of infinitely greater value.

John Chrysostom, from *Homily 15 on the Gospel according to St. Matthew*, 4, in *Spiritual Classics from the Early Church*, comp. and intro. Robert Atwell (London: National Society/Church House Publishing, 1995), pp. 111–12.

Celebration

In the celebration that embraces the exile and outcast,
in the joy that sings of freedom at last,
we worship the God of justice and peace,
we praise the God of freedom and joy,
we adore the God of love and new life,
we bless the God of reconciliation and healing,
we glorify the God of harmony and bliss.
We add our voice to the music of God,
we fall silent in the presence of Mystery,
in wonder and awe and love,
the Mystery that is the Source of our being

and the God of our belonging,
beautiful, utterly holy, glorious light,
unbounded love. Alleluia! Alleluia!

Jim Cotter, from *Towards the City: A Version of Psalms 101–150*
(Sheffield: Cairns Publications, 1993), prayer after Psalm 147.
Used by permission.

Peace

Peace between neighbours,
Peace between kindred,
Peace between lovers,
In love of the King of life.

Peace between person and person,
Peace between wife and husband,
Peace between woman and children,
The peace of Christ above all peace.

Bless, O Christ, my face,
Let my face bless every thing;
Bless, O Christ, mine eye,
Let my eye bless all it sees.

From *Carmina Gadelica: Hymns and Incantations,* collected by
Alexander Carmichael, selected and arranged by John MacInnes
(Edinburgh: Floris Books, 1992), p. 280.

FIFTH SUNDAY AFTER EPIPHANY

Isaiah 58:3–9a (9b–12)	1 Corinthians 2:1–12 (13–16)
Psalm 112:1–9 (10)	Matthew 5:13–20

Learning to see

If we spend our energies searching the "heavens" and "spiritual things," trying to rise above the clutter of our daily lives, we will not find the God whom Jesus loved. No. We must learn to see that to be the salt of the earth, flavorful and tasty; to be the light of the world, not hidden but rather illuminating God's presence in the world, is to be epiphanies ourselves. We are called in this season to be bright manifestations of the power of God in history. Our vocation is to join Jesus and many others in giving God a voice, giving God an embodied life on earth. By the power of the Spirit which we witness in the life, death, and resurrection of Jesus, to be the salt of the earth and the light of the world is to be "in Christ," the active cooperative movement between divine and human being on this earth. As we learn to see sacredly, we will know where we are called to be and what we are called to do. We will find ourselves able to believe in both God and ourselves as empowering friends, *compañeras/os,* and helpmates.

> Isabel Carter Heyward, from "Learning to See," in *Speaking of Christ:*
> *A Lesbian Feminist Voice* (New York: The Pilgrim Press, 1989), p. 51.

God's ways are always truth and justice and mercy.

> Yves Congar

God in hiding*

Rabbi Barukh's grandson was upset because his playmate didn't bother to look for him when they were playing hide-and-seek. The grandfather, with tears in his eyes, told him that God says the same thing: "I hide, but no one wants to seek me." The story is told by Martin Buber in Tales of the Hasidim: The Early Masters *(New York: Schocken Books).*

*Suggested tune: KRYPTOS.

66

God in hiding, we will seek you;
we will cross the thorny ground,
where you wait among the shadows,
playmate longing to be found;
we will risk ourselves with Jesus,
learn from him hope's searching ways,
follow him through deepest darkness,
dare with him, life's tangled maze.

Jesus searched the dark before us,
grieving in Gethsemane;
crossing death's abyss to find you
through the gloom of Calvary.
You were calling from the darkness,
urging him to brave love's night;
you were waiting to receive him
in your resurrecting light.

Still your Spirit, hiding in us,
urges us to seek and know
your persistent, wounded presence
where we hardly dare to go.
Though earth's sorrows overwhelm us,
as we long to see your face,
we will love you in our neighbours,
find, with them, your hiding place.

Salt and light

Much more important is God's call to me to be "salt and light" in the place and in the situation into which he has put me. This involves a constant struggle to maintain standards of honesty and integrity in an environment where lies, deceit and politics are commonplace. What do you do for example, when a customer pays an invoice twice in error and your company decides to say nothing: or when a supplier demands payment on an overdue account and your cash-flow means that he won't be paid for some time yet? Tell him the cheque is in the post? Issues like these are commonplace for many of us and they are often not that clear cut. A steadfast refusal to get involved with office politics has been a further issue that I have had to address. I know of several Christians whose careers have suffered because they have abstained from such activities.

> Malcolm Claydon, from "Christians Speaking," in *Touching the Pulse:
> Worship and Where We Work*, ed. Bernard Braley (London: Stainer &
> Bell, 1996), no. 90, p. 57.

Economic transformation

Those who engage with the business of economic transformation, which is the opening of the world to justice and the freeing of the world to a future of hope, are in my view doing work that is not just good but sacred: they share in the dynamic of life towards grace and the redeeming of its mortgages.

And that dynamic has its roots in the universe's gracious beginning in freedom, the gracious restoration of that freedom in Jesus Christ, and the offer of life in the freedom of the Spirit. So I believe; and if the language in which I express that belief is indeed the language of the Christian community, that is because I know no other in which to express my further conviction: that the work of redemption, of unmortgaging the future, is work of ultimate significance, of importance beyond measure, and sustained by the resources of grace it needs.

> Peter Selby, *Grace and Mortgage: The Language of Faith and the Debt
> of the World* (London: Darton, Longman & Todd, 1997), p. 168.

Salt and light (2)

The guarantee of the permanence of the community of faith resides in the imperishable quality of salt.

"You *are* the salt"—not: You should be the salt! It is not for the disciples to decide whether they are or are not to be salt. Nor is any appeal made to them to become the salt of the earth. They are that salt, whether they want to be or not, in the power of the call they have encountered. You *are* the salt—not: You have the salt. It would be an unwarranted abbreviation were one to follow the Reformers and equate the disciples' message with the salt. What is meant is their entire existence insofar as it is grounded anew through Christ's call to discipleship, this existence of which the Beatitudes speak. Those who have been called by Jesus and stand in his discipleship are, through precisely that call, the salt of the earth in their entire existence.

. . . The same one who says of himself in direct speech, "I am the light," says to his disciples in direct speech: You are the light in your entire lives insofar as you abide in my call. And because you are the light, you can no longer remain hidden, whether you want this or not. . . . They must now be what they are, or they are not followers of Jesus. Those who follow are the visible community of faith. Their act of following, of discipleship, is a visible activity singling them out from the world—or it is not discipleship. And this discipleship is as visible as light in the night, as a hill on the plain.

Dietrich Bonhoeffer, from "The Sermon on the Mount: Matthew 5,"
in *The Cost of Discipleship*, trans. Douglas W. Stott, in Dietrich
Bonhoeffer, *Meditations on the Cross*, ed. Manfred Weber (Louisville,
Ky.: Westminster John Knox Press, 1998), pp. 81–83.

Cry the gospel with your whole life.

Charles de Foucauld

Sixth Sunday after Epiphany

Deuteronomy 30:15–20	1 Corinthians 3:1–9
Psalm 119:1–8	Matthew 5:21–37

A lesson

I learned again that God is everywhere. He resides in Arks and on altars, as any worshipper knows through experience. But if you seek Him, you find Him, in boardrooms and bedrooms, in Hymns Ancient or in Juke-box Modern, in discos or pubs. In God, distinctions between rich and poor, slave and free, Jew and Greek, or German or Arab for that matter, don't matter. You can learn this from the spirituality of Paul, or it can be deduced from the lowest common denominator of human experience—a shared hangover.

I learned that God is my eternal home—He is not my life sentence in gaol. So why do we try to limit God? It is because He is so vast, and the distance that separates us so daunting. We get tired of straining upwards so that He can reach us. We cop out and try to make Him smaller and lower, so that we can reach Him— a deity just the right height for a cage or a kennel. But the world shows us how foolish that is. My liturgy asks a great question: "Where is the place of God's glory?" I understood afresh the answer. "Blessed is the Lord, whose glory is revealed in every place!"

> Lionel Blue, *Bright Blue: Rabbi Lionel Blue's Thoughts for the Day*
> (London: British Broadcasting Corporation, 1985), pp. 86–87. ©
> Lionel Blue. Used by permission.

It is cynicism and fear that freeze life; it is faith that thaws it out, releases it, sets it free.

> Harry Emerson Fosdick

Hebrew song

For we are Your people and You are our God.
We are Your children and You are our father.

We are Your servants and You are our master.

We are Your community and You are our portion.

We are Your inheritance and You are our destiny.

We are Your flock and You are our shepherd.

We are Your vineyard and You are our keeper.

We are Your work and You are our creator.

We are Your beloved and You are our friend.

We are Your own and You are our nearest.

We are Your people and You are our king.

We are the people known to You and You are the God made known by us.

> From *Forms of Prayer for Jewish Worship,* vol. III, *Prayers for the High Holydays* (London: Reform Synagogues of Great Britain, 1985), p. 331. © Reform Synagogues of Great Britain. Used by permission.

On Psalm 119

This poem is not, and does not pretend to be, a sudden outpouring of the heart. . . . It is a pattern, a thing done like embroidery, stitch by stitch, through long, quiet hours, for love of the subject and for the delight in leisurely, disciplined craftsmanship.

Now this, in itself, seems to me very important because it lets us into the mind and mood of the poet. We can guess at once that he felt about the Law somewhat as he felt about his poetry; both involved exact and loving conformity to an intricate pattern. This at once suggests an attitude from which the Pharisaic conception could later grow but which in itself, though not necessarily religious, is quite innocent. It will look like priggery or pedantry (or else like a neurotic fussiness) to those who cannot sympathise with it, but it need not be any of these things. . . . "O that my ways *were* made so direct that I *might* keep thy statutes!" (5). At present they aren't, and he can't. But his effort to do so does not spring from servile fear. The Order of the Divine mind, embodied in the Divine Law, is beautiful. What should [anyone] do but try to reproduce it, so far as possible, in [their] daily life?

> C. S. Lewis, *Reflections on the Psalms* (London: Geoffrey Bles, 1958), pp. 58–59.

Ordinary people

The Bible is filled with the companionship of the confused and seeking, men and women made of the most ordinary stuff who often fail to understand, who make mistakes, whose humanity is transparent, but who encounter the living God and whose lives thereby are changed. When Paul says that he regards no one any longer from a merely human point of view, he means that in Christ the limitations of the human perspective are overcome. People are not taken out of this life, but are given strength and power and purpose to live in it.

> Peter J. Gomes, *The Good Book: Reading the Bible with Mind and Heart* (New York: William Morrow & Company, Inc., 1996), p. 187.

I have a growing sense that the models for relationships in community that the church has offered us—models of self-sacrifice, servanthood, and harmonious/homogeneous unity—are neither healthy nor viable. I suspect that these models are in many ways models of exploitative and abusive relationships.

> Rita Nakashima Brock

Come, teach us*

Come, teach us, Spirit of our God,
    the language of your way,
    the lessons that we need to live,
the faith for every day.

Excite our minds to follow you,
    to trace new truths in store,
    new flight paths for our spirit space,
new marvels to explore:

Engage our wits to dance with you,
    to leap from logic's base,
    to capture insight on the wing,
to sense your cosmic grace:

Inspire our spark to light from you,
    to catch creation's flair,

*Tune: PITYOULISH.

new artistry to celebrate,
new harmonies to dare:

Delight our hearts to worship you,
   to learn compassion's code,
   to live in context of your love,
great teacher who is God!

Seventh Sunday after Epiphany

Leviticus 19:1–2, 9–18
Psalm 119:33–40

1 Corinthians 3:10–11, 16–23
Matthew 5:38–48

A hymn to imperfection

Hey! Let's celebrate weakness!
Yes! You know!
Weakness as in failure!
Let's celebrate the slips and slops,
the drops and falls and oh-ohs
that teach us wisdom
and compassion
and patience
and humour
and understanding
of what it means to be
not a human being
but a human becoming.
Let us celebrate
all those opportunities for growth
that were ours yesterday and today.
Let's celebrate for ourselves.
Let's celebrate for each other.
And while we are at it,
let us give thanks
for the mistakes
we will make tomorrow.
If we find them painful
or a bit embarrassing
we can remember that perfection
means having no room
for improvement,
no need for anyone else,

and who wants that?
Let us be grateful,
oh so deeply grateful,
that God is still shaping us.

Joy Cowley, *Psalms for the Road* (Wellington, New Zealand: Catholic
Supplies [N.Z.] Ltd., 2002), pp. 44–45. Used by permission.

Ironic though it may seem, I doubt that the world will ever take Christians seriously again until they are prepared to become fools for Christ's sake.

Colin Morris

This child of God

The king gave Bishop Aidan a first-class horse to help him get across rivers, or to respond to some urgent need. Aidan's practice was normally to walk everywhere, and sometime later he met a beggar who asked for his help. Without a second thought, Aidan got off and gave him the horse with all its royal harness, for he was unfailingly kind and generous to the destitute.

The king heard of this, and as they were going in for a meal he accosted him: "My Lord Bishop, why have you given away our royal horse which was intended for your use? We have many less valuable beasts, which would have been good enough for a poor man. And I chose that one specially for you!"

Aidan replied without any hesitation: "My Lord King, what are you saying? Surely this foal of a mare is not more valuable to you than this child of God?"

They went in to eat, and the bishop sat down while the king warmed himself with his soldiers in front of the fire. Suddenly he recalled the bishop's rebuke. He threw down his sword, and ran and knelt at the bishop's feet to beg forgiveness: "I will never judge how you use my money in the care of God's children!"

The Venerable Bede, *Ecclesiastical History of the English People,* trans.
Douglas Dales (Norwich: The Canterbury Press, 2001), p. 129.

We have forgotten that to be radical means simply to go to the root of things.

Rubem Alves

True virtue

There is a general and particular beauty. By a particular beauty, I mean that by which a thing appears beautiful when considered only with regard to its connection with, and tendency to, some particular things within a limited, and as it were a private sphere. And a general beauty is that by which a thing appears beautiful when viewed most perfectly, comprehensively and universally, with regard to all its tendencies, and its connections with every thing to which it stands related. The former may be without and against the latter. As a few notes in a tune, taken only by themselves and in their relation to one another, may be harmonious, which, when considered with respect to all the notes in the tune, or the entire series of sounds they are connected with, may be very discordant, and disagreeable. That only, therefore, is what I mean by true virtue, which, belonging to the heart of an intelligent being, is beautiful by a general beauty, or beautiful in a comprehensive view, as it is in itself, and as related to every thing with which it stands connected. And therefore, when we are enquiring concerning the nature of true virtue—wherein this true and general beauty of the heart does most essentially consist—this is my answer to the enquiry:

   True virtue most essentially consists in *benevolence to being in general.* Or perhaps, to speak more accurately, it is that consent, propensity and union of heart to being in general, which is immediately exercised in a general good will.

> Jonathan Edwards, *The Nature of True Virtue* (Ann Arbor: University
> of Michigan Press; Rexdale: John Wiley & Sons, 1960), pp. 2–3.

A rabbi reflects on the Jewish law

Halakhah revolves around two poles: the legal, that is, specified and detailed rules of behavior, and the relational, that is, the yearning to give expression to the intimate covenantal relationship between God and Israel. Both these poles have shaped *halakhic* thought and practice. The legal pole, the tendency to fix formulations for conduct, may reflect the yearning and need of human beings for order and predictability in relationships. The way is given. The task of the covenantal Jew is merely to respond. On the other hand, the covenantal pole emphasizes that *halakhah* is not only a formal system concerned with rules of procedure but also an expressive system grounded in the love relationship symbolized by God's invitation to Israel to become his covenantal community. The understanding of *halakhah* as a covenantal relational experience guards against the mistaken notion that a dynamic living relationship with God can be structured exclusively by fixed and permanent rules. The need for order must not be at the expense of spontaneity, personal passion, novelty, and surprise. One committed to the *halakhic* system can meet God in new ways. The perennial problem that one faces in living by *halakhah* is how to prevent the covenantal relational pole from being obscured by the massive, seemingly self-sufficient legal framework.

David Hartman, from "Halakhah," in *Contemporary Jewish Religious Thought,* ed. Arthur A. Cohen and Paul Mendes-Flohr (New York: The Free Press, a division of Macmillan; London: Collier Macmillan, 1972), p. 310.

A song of light*

> May the anger of Christ be mine,
> when the world grows hard and greedy;
> when the rich have no care for the poor,
> when the powerful take from the needy.
>
> *Refrain:*
> *In a world of restless change*
> *standing for love and faith and justice;*
> *in a dark, confusing time*
> *bearing the light, the shining light of Christ.*
>
> May the pity of Christ be mine,
> when the outstretched hand's not taken,
> when the jobless stand in line,
> when the lonely live forsaken.
>
> *Refrain*
>
> May the love of Christ be mine
> for the anguished, for the ailing,
> for the frail disabled life,
> for the fallen, for the failing.
>
> *Refrain*

*Tune: EATON.

May the actions of Christ be mine,
bringing hope, bringing new direction;
making peace in a warring time,
offering welcome, not rejection.

Refrain

Colin Gibson, *Reading the Signature: New Hymns and Songs*
(Carol Stream, Ill.: Hope Publishing Company, 1997), p. 13. © 1994
Hope Publishing Company, Carol Stream, IL 60188.

Augustine speaks to his God

At one time we were moved to do what is good, after our heart conceived through your Spirit. But at an earlier time we were moved to do wrong and to forsake you. But you God, one and good, have never ceased to do good. Of your gift we have some good works, though not everlasting. After them we hope to rest in your great sanctification. But you, the Good, in need of no other good, are ever at rest since you yourself are your own rest.

Augustine of Hippo, *Confessions,* trans. Owen Chadwick (Oxford and
New York: Oxford University Press, 1991), p. 304.

Christ appeared not as a philosopher or a wordy doctor, or noisy disputer, or even as a wise and learned scribe, but he talked with people in complete simplicity, showing them the way of truth in the way he lived, his goodness and his miracles.

Angela of Foligno (1248–1309)

Eighth Sunday after Epiphany

Isaiah 49:8–16a	1 Corinthians 4:1–5
Psalm 131	Matthew 6:24–34

Poverty that frees

I began to see poverty as a way to freedom, a letting go of all those securities which make me feel safe but which are, in fact, barriers to true freedom. The greatest barrier is a conviction of our own rightness and righteousness. As the truth dawned on me, I became less afraid of questions and challenges, less anxious to "help" people and more content to be with them. It was like learning to swim. I began to learn that I could float when out of my depth. I now thought of poverty as a kind of swimming exercise, a practice which enables us to let go of the rail of our own security and certainty so that we can learn to float in God.

Gerard W. Hughes, *In Search of a Way: Two Journeys of Spiritual Discovery* (London: Darton, Longman & Todd, 1986), p. 57.

Abandoned to faith

O God, before whose face
we are not made righteous
even by being right:
free us from the need
to justify ourselves
by our own anxious striving,
that we may be abandoned
to faith in you alone,
through Jesus Christ. Amen.

Janet Morley, *All Desires Known* (London: SPCK, 1992), p. 24.
Used by permission.

The problem with anxiety

In our age everything has to be a "problem." Ours is a time of anxiety because we have willed it to be so. Our anxiety is not imposed on us by force from outside. We impose it on our world and upon one another from within ourselves.

Sanctity in such an age means, no doubt, travelling from the area of anxiety to the area in which there is no anxiety or perhaps it may mean learning, from God, to be without anxiety in the midst of anxiety.

Fundamentally, as Max Picard points out, it probably comes to this: living in a silence which so reconciles the contradictions within us that, although they remain within us, they cease to be a problem.

Contradictions have always existed in the human soul. But it is only when we prefer analysis to silence that they become a constant and insoluble problem. We are not meant to resolve all contradictions but to live with them and rise above them and see them in the light of exterior and objective values which make them trivial by comparison.

Thomas Merton, *Thoughts in Solitude* (London: Burns & Oates, 1958, 1975), pp. 82–83.

Put your books and your formulas aside; dare to abandon your teacher whoever your teacher may be and see things for yourself. Dare to look at everything around you without fear and without formula and it won't be long before you see.

Anthony de Mello

We shall go out*

We shall go out with hope of resurrection,
We shall go out, from strength to strength go on,
We shall go out and tell our stories boldly,
    Tales of a love that will not let us go.
We'll sing our songs of wrongs that can be righted,
We'll dream our dream of hurts that can be healed,
We'll weave a cloth of all the world united
    Within a vision of a Christ who sets us free.

*Tune: LONDONDERRY AIR, traditional Irish.

We'll give a voice to those who have not spoken,
We'll find the words for those whose lips are sealed,
We'll make the tunes for those who sing no longer,
    Vibrating love alive in every heart.
We'll share our joy with those who are still weeping,
Chant hymns of strength for hearts that break in grief,
We'll leap and dance the resurrection story
    Including all within the circles of our love.

June Boyce-Tillman, in *Reflecting Praise*, ed. June Boyce-Tillman and
Janet Wootton (London: Stainer & Bell and Women in Theology,
1993), No. 82. © 1993 Stainer & Bell Ltd. (Admin. in the USA and
Canada by Hope Publishing Co., Carol Stream, IL 60188.)
All rights reserved. Used by permission.

Gazing

The difficulty we often have in simply looking at a painting . . . is a testimony not
only to the grip our preoccupations and anxieties have upon us, but also to our
fear of being changed. It is as if we know deep down only too well that contemplation is transforming. I often think in this connection of a passage in a letter
written by the German poet Rainer Maria Rilke in 1907 to his wife Clara, who was
a sculptor. "Gazing is such a wonderful thing, about which we know little; in gazing we are turned completely outward, but just when we are so most, things seem
to go on within us, which have been waiting longingly for the moment when they
should be unobserved." And at the end of his famous poem contemplating the
torso of an ancient statue of Apollo, the poet addresses himself, "There is no part
that does not see you. You must change your life. This strange shift, in which it
seems as though the work of art is looking at us searchingly, rather than we looking at it, and that it is inviting us to change, is one which all lovers of art will recognize from their experience."

Martin L. Smith, *The Word Is Very Near You: A Guide to Praying with
Scripture* (Cambridge, Mass.: Cowley Publications, 1989), pp. 130–31.

My God and my all!

Francis of Assisi (1182–1226)

LAST SUNDAY AFTER EPIPHANY

Exodus 24:12–18
Psalm 2

2 Peter 1:16–21
Matthew 17:1–9

Today's transfiguration

I watch the sky receive
today's transfiguration;
and vision, glory, hope,
all that this world cannot yet see
is nearly touchable.
And yet, that valley there, Jezreel,
its sheen of beauty biblical in scope,
was once a name of blood,
like Auschwitz, like Shatilla.
And when you met your friends
there on the plain,
no longer bathed in light,
you found them wrestling
with demons they couldn't just dismiss
because they wanted to.
O Jesus, we believe;
help thou our unbelief.

Janet Morley, *Companions of God: Praying for Peace in the Holy Land*
(London: Christian Aid, 1994), p. 53. © Christian Aid and Janet
Morley. Used by permission.

Mysteries are not dark shadows, before which we must shut our eyes and be silent. On the contrary, they are dazzling splendours, with which we ought to sate our gaze.

A Carthusian

Being Christs to one another

Who then can comprehend the riches and the glory of the Christian life? It can do all things and has all things and lacks nothing. It is lord over sin, death, and hell, and yet at the same time it serves, ministers to, and benefits all. But alas in our day this life is unknown throughout the world; it is neither preached about nor sought after; we are altogether ignorant of our own name and do not know why we are Christians or bear the name of Christians. Surely we are named after Christ, not because he is absent from us, but because he dwells in us, that is, because we believe in him and are Christs to one another and do to our neighbours as Christ does to us.

Martin Luther, from *Treatise on Christian Liberty,* trans. John
Dillenberger in *Martin Luther: Selections from His Writings*
(New York: Doubleday, 1961), p. 76.

Wholeness does not consist in removing a present source of travail; it demands a complete transformation of the person's attitude to life, which in turn is an outward sign of a transfigured personality.

Martin Israel

Bird of Paradise

Driving last year in the red wilderness of Australia's Great Sandy Desert, again and again I was surprised by the sudden arrival of a flock of budgerigars, flying in perfect formation. Startled at the sight of the truck, they would turn, the sun would flash on their emerald wings, and then the vision would be gone. Jung, I remembered, said that the moments the eternal erupted into the transitory had been the best moments of his life. George Herbert, writing about prayer, notes the same eruption:

The Milkie Way, the Bird of Paradise,
Church bels beyond the Starres heard, the Soul's Blood,
The Land of Spices, something understood.

Monica Furlong, *Bird of Paradise: Glimpses of Living Myth* (London:
Mowbray, 1995), p. 1.

Prayer

Prayer the Church's banquet, angels' age,
>God's breath in man returning to his birth,
>The soul in paraphrase, heart in pilgrimage,
The Christian plummet sounding heav'n and earth;
Engine against th' Almighty, sinners' tower,
>Reversèd thunder, Christ-side-piercing spear,
>The six days' world transposing in an hour,
A kind of tune, which all things hear and fear;
Softness, and peace, and joy, and love, and bliss,
>Exalted manna, gladness of the best,
>Heaven in ordinary, man well dressed,
The milky way, the bird of Paradise,
>Church-bells beyond the stars heard, the soul's blood,
>The land of spices; something understood.

George Herbert, "Prayer (I)," from *The Temple* (1633), text as in *George Herbert and Henry Vaughan,* Oxford Authors Series, ed. Louis L. Martz (Oxford and New York: Oxford University Press, 1986), p. 44.

Baptized by the morning

Risen Lord Jesus,
as the rising sun
baptizes trees and shrubs
in rippling light,
let me be baptized
by your resurrection light.

May I
trust in you above all else,
hope in you above all other goals,
seek you in all things,
find you in every situation,
meet you among all people,
know you over everything—

And love you with adoration
beyond
beyond
beyond all telling.

Bruce Prewer, from *Australian Accents,* by Bruce D. Prewer and Aub
Podlich (Adelaide: Lutheran Publishing House [now Openbook
Publishers], 1988), p. 63. Used by permission.

Conversation with the abbot

How to dispel the passions that make us manipulate instead of worship? Well, the first thing to realize is that you *are* the glory of God. In Genesis you can read: "Yahweh God fashioned man of dust from the soil. Then he breathed into his nostrils a breath of life, and thus man became a living being" (Genesis 2:7). We live because we share God's breath, God's glory. The question is not so much, "How to live for the glory of God?" but, "How to live who we are, how to make true our deepest self?"

With a smile John Eudes said, "Take this as your koan: 'I am the glory of God.' Make that thought the center of your meditation so that it slowly becomes not only a thought but a living reality. You are the place where God chose to dwell, you are the *topos tou theou* (God's place) and the spiritual life is nothing more or less than to allow that space to exist where God can dwell, to create the space where his glory can manifest itself. In your meditation you can ask your self, 'Where is the glory of God? If the glory of God is not there where I am, where else can it be?'"

Henri J. M. Nouwen, *The Genesee Diary: Report from a Trappist
Monastery* (New York: Doubleday, 1981; Image ed. 1989), pp. 70–71.

Peace song*

How many wars will devastate the earth
before we live in harmony?
How many battlefields will run with blood

---

*'I will write peace on your wings, and you will fly over the world' (words written on the paper birds [cranes] which Sadako Sasaki, child victim of atomic radiation in Hiroshima, made before she died). August 6 is Hiroshima Day, and also the feast of the Transfiguration.

before the killing stops?
How many young men and women will die
before the world comes of age?
The answer is in the cranes that fly for peace.
The answer is in the paper cranes.

How many captives will languish in gaol
before their strong protests are heard?
How many governments will ignore human need
before they are overthrown?
How many babies will be born deformed
before all testing is banned?
The answer is in the cranes that fly for peace.
The answer is in the paper cranes.

How many children will fold paper cranes
before we learn to live in love?
How many birds of hope will spread their wings
before all nations unite?
How many peace towers will children erect
before their message is heard?
The answer lies in our faithfulness to Christ
who calls us all to pray and work for peace.

Jean Mortimer, in *Exceeding Our Limits: Prayer Handbook 1991*
(London: United Reformed Church, 1991), August 4.
Used by permission.

ASH WEDNESDAY

Joel 2:1–2, 12–17
Psalm 51:1–17

2 Corinthians 5:20b–6:10
Matthew 6:1–6, 16–21

We have to desire God

We cannot assume that prayer just happens. It is a life, a relationship, a sending and a receiving, a longing and a providing. It is often difficult to distinguish prayer from life.

You cannot turn on prayer like a tap and expect anything to come out of it if there has been no connecting up of the tap with the main supply. Day after day we have to maintain that connection with the source of prayer, which is the Holy Spirit of God. That is not to say that if, after long years of neglect, we turn back to the source in heartfelt prayer the supply will not be instantly available, but the will to turn to God gets weaker and weaker, and the will in prayer is all important. Will is rather a cold word; we associate it with "iron" and Victorian public schools, but it has an important place in the vocabulary of prayer, as the strength with which we commit ourselves to the love of God.

Desire is perhaps a better word. We have to desire God to begin in prayer. There has to be some sort of spark within us which begins that process, which the Holy Spirit can then fan into flame. The very beginning of prayer is a joining of desires, and like human love it is a great mystery how attraction begins. We can only search into our own hearts to see how that miracle was wrought in our own lives. We can uncover the means by which prayer, which is the desire to be with God, took hold of our lives. Prayer is a process of communing: it is best held in a total relation, with all that we do and all that we are, gently, through life. I say gently because to snatch for it is often to miss it.

David Scott, *Moments of Prayer* (London: SPCK, 1997), p. 12.

The new song

Be faithful to the new song
thrusting through your

earth like a daffodil.
Be flexible
and travel with the rhythm.

Let your mind
be bent by what is coming:
making is
a way of being made
and giving birth

a way of being born.
You are the child
and father of a carol,
you are not
the only maker present.

How you make
is how you will be made.
Be gentle to
the otherness you carry,
broken by

the truth you cannot tell yet.
Mother and be
mothered by your burden.
Trust, and learn
to travel with the music.

Sydney Carter, *The Two-Way Clock: Poems* (London: Stainer & Bell, 2000), pp. 67–68. © 1974 Stainer & Bell Ltd. Used by permission.

Often nothing requires more courage than admission of fault. The disturbance that repentance evokes in our personal and collective psyches is so jarring that we tend to exhaust every other available dynamic before we succumb. We dread the bald admission of our wrong-doing!

Joan Puls

Where your treasure is . . .

The heart of the matter is, you should never belong fully to something that is outside yourself. It is very important to find a balance in your belonging. You should never belong totally to any cause or system. Frequently, people need to belong to an external system because they are afraid to belong to their own lives. If your soul is awakened then you realize that this is the house of your real belonging. Your longing is safe there. Belonging is related to longing. . . . Longing is a precious instinct in the soul. Where you belong should always be worthy of your dignity. You should belong first in your own interiority. If you belong there, and if you are in rhythm with yourself and connected to that deep, unique source within, then you will never be vulnerable when your outside belonging is qualified, relativized or taken away. You will still be able to stand on your own ground, the ground of your soul where you are not a tenant, where you are at home. . . . "Where your treasure is, there is your heart also."

> John O'Donohue, *Anam Cara* (London: Bantam Books, 1999),
> pp. 181–82.

Among the attributes of God, although they are all equal, mercy shines with even more brilliance than justice.

> Miguel de Cervantes (1547–1616)

Christians

For Christians are not distinguished from the rest of humankind either in locality or in speech or in customs. For they dwell not somewhere in cities of their own, neither do they use some different language, nor practise an extraordinary kind of life. Nor again do they possess any invention discovered by any intelligence or study of ingenious men, nor are they masters of any human dogma as some are. But while they dwell in cities of Greeks and barbarians as the lot of each is cast, and follow the native customs in dress and food and the other arrangements of life, yet the constitution of their own citizenship, which they set forth, is marvellous, and confessedly contradicts expectation. They dwell in their own countries, but only as sojourners; they bear their share in all things as citizens, and they endure all hardships as strangers. Every foreign country is a homeland to them, and every homeland is foreign. . . . Their existence is on earth, but their citizenship is in heaven. They obey the established laws, and they surpass the laws in their own lives. They love everybody, and they are persecuted by everybody. They are ignored, and yet they are condemned. They are put to death, and yet they are endued with life. They are in beggary, and yet they make many rich. They are in want in all things, and yet they abound in all things. . . . In a word, what the soul is in a body, this the Christians are in the world.

> *The Epistle to Diognetus* (early Christian document), from sections
> 5 and 6, in J. B. Lightfoot, *The Apostolic Fathers* (London: Macmillan
> & Co., 1891), pp. 253–54, translation slightly modernized.

A time of *kairos*

Kairos is a particular type of time. Unlike *chronos,* or time that can be counted and counted upon with watches and calendars, *kairos* is a special time of crisis or particular opportunity. Thus at the beginning of Jesus' ministry, Mark 1:15 says, "The time [*kairos*] is fulfilled, and the kingdom of God has come near; repent, and believe in the good news." In Jesus' preaching the promises of the prophets are fulfilled and the year of Jubilee is at hand. This special moment presents a crisis of discernment and decision to accept the good news of the advent of God's new household. As Paul put it in 2 Corinthians 6:2, "Now is the acceptable time [*kairos*]; see, now is the day of salvation!"

This appointed time of decision making has always been a part of the biblical message and of theological interpretation of the meaning of eschatology, or the end or purpose of life and history. It also comes to the fore as a description of contemporary events whenever there is a great crisis in which a decision must be made. In our time the *kairos* appears in the worsening crises of oppression, poverty, injustice, and ecological disaster that confront us on every side. How are we to interpret these signs of the times and how are we to respond?

> Letty Russell, *Church in the Round: Feminist Interpretation of the
> Church* (Louisville, Ky.: Westminster/John Knox Press, 1993), p. 80.

Just visiting

In the last century, a tourist from the States visited the famous Polish rabbi, Hofetz Chaim.

He was astonished to see that the rabbi's home was only a simple room filled with books. The only furniture was a table and a bench.

"Rabbi, where is your furniture?" asked the tourist.

"Where is yours?" said Hofetz.

"Mine? But I'm passing through. I'm only a visitor here."

"So am I."

Anthony de Mello, S.J., *The Song of the Bird* (Anand, India: Gujarat Sahitya Prakash, 1982), p. 156.

First Sunday in Lent

Genesis 2:15–17; 3:1–7   Romans 5:12–19
Psalm 32   Matthew 4:1–11

To live facing despair

The desert is the home of despair. And despair, now, is everywhere. Let us not think that our interior solitude consists in the acceptance of defeat. We cannot escape anything by consenting tacitly to be defeated. Despair is an abyss without bottom. Do not think to close it by consenting to it and trying to forget you have consented.

This, then, is our desert: to live facing despair, but not to consent. To trample it down under hope in the Cross. To wage war against despair unceasingly. That war is our wilderness. If we wage it courageously, we will find Christ at our side. If we cannot face it, we will never find him.

Thomas Merton, *Thoughts in Solitude* (London: Burns & Oates, 1958, 1975), pp. 22–23.

The devil never tempts us with more success than when he tempts us with a sight of our own good actions.

Thomas Wilson (1663–1755)

Revise our taking

You, you giver!
You have given light and life to the world;
You have given freedom from Pharaoh to your people Israel;
You have given your only Son for the sake of the world;
You have given yourself to us;
You have given and forgiven,
    and you remember our sin no more.
And we, in response, are takers:
    We take eagerly what you give us;

we take from our neighbors near at hand as is acceptable;
we take from our unseen neighbors greedily and acquisitively;
we take from our weak neighbors thoughtlessly;
we take all that we can lay hands on.
It dawns on us that our taking does not match your giving.
In this Lenten season revise our taking,
> that it may be grateful and disciplined,
> even as you give in ways generous and overwhelming.
Amen.

Walter Brueggemann, *Awed to Heaven, Rooted in Earth: Prayers of Walter Brueggemann* (Minneapolis: Fortress Press, 2003), p. 154. © 2003 Augsburg Fortress. Used by permission.

Necessary temptation

At the Friday night dances after the game in my hometown, I always sensed that the regular preaching against dancing was wrong. Ostensibly the proscription against dancing went all the way back to this story in Genesis. Dancing would inevitably lead to sexual stimulation, and thus to the temptation of sexual love outside of marriage. But pragmatically, I knew that those couples dancing enthusiastically to the latest rock 'n' roll were much less likely to be tempted than the couples wrapped in each other's arms in parked cars just outside the building.

But the proscription and the fears were based in both a misinterpretation of this passage at the very beginning of the biblical story, and in the assumption that sexual sins were the highest order of sin. Adam and Eve's sin is disobedience; the temptation is pride—to be like a god.

. . . Sometimes the church's method is not to teach us to be responsible for our lives and behavior, but instead the elimination of temptation itself. . . . We are given not only life by God, but also the responsibility of choice. We are responsible for our choices and behaviors whatever the consequences. We should neither be made the scapegoats for others' temptations, nor blame others for our own. We can begin by considering Eve's temptation and sin, then reflect on what our own response might be.

Mary Zimmer, from "Eve: Necessary Temptation," in *Sister Images: Guided Meditations on the Stories of Biblical Women* (Nashville: Abingdon Press, 1993), pp. 95–96, 98. Used by permission.

Another view on Genesis 3

Rabbi Jonathan Magonet writes:

> It is as if God, like an overprotective father, had accidentally achieved the very thing He wanted to avoid. By trying to keep the children from the pain of knowledge, God led them to seek it; in trying to keep them in the Garden of Eden, in the paradise of childhood, God had given them the impetus to step outside—and once outside, there was no way back.

Magonet goes on to interpret the expulsion as a moment of liberation, when "God cut the strings of the puppets and let them walk erect upon the earth."

Another Jewish scholar, Tikva Frymer-Kensky, offers a similar interpretation. She sees the eating of the fruit of the tree of knowledge as symbolizing the moment when humankind broke free of the tyranny of the pagan gods and accepted moral responsibility for a world in which we must live without recourse to divine intervention. Thus, in Frymer-Kensky's reading, Eve is a Promethean figure who "wrests knowledge from the realm of the divine, takes the first step towards culture, and transforms human existence."

. . . Such readings invite us to think differently about the nature and origins of sin. If the story of Adam and Eve in the garden represents the acquisition of moral knowledge and thus the maturing of humankind, then the first immoral act is not the eating of the fruit (one cannot be immoral before knowing good and evil), but the murder of Abel. This signifies the moral failure of humankind and the descent into violence and death.

Tina Beattie, *Eve's Pilgrimage: A Woman's Quest for the City of God*
(London and New York: Burns & Oates, 2002), pp. 45–46,
quoting from Jonathan Magonet, *A Rabbi's Bible* (London:
SCM Press, 1991), p. 114.

When our first parents were driven out of Paradise, Adam is believed to have remarked to Eve: "My dear, we live in an age of transition."

William Ralph Inge

I am tempted

In the wilderness

I am tempted
to feed on my grievance,

to protest,
to seek power.

But I will listen to the Word of God:
'Love me,
love your neighbour,
love your enemy.'

I am tempted
to say from the heights of religion,
'See how free *I* am'—
playing on the virtue of my salvation.

But I will not tempt God.
I will journey with others,
that we might find wholeness.

I am tempted
to 'mother',
to 'bewitch',
to use others' needs,
to claim power over them.

But I would worship God—only—
the One who holds together
human distortion and love,

that we might grow.

Mary Robins, *Desert Flowers: A Journey into the Feminine in Women,*
Men, and God (Sheffield: Cairns Publications, 1990), p. 90.
© Mary Robins 1990. Used by permission.

Save us, O Lord, from the snares of a double mind. Deliver us from all cowardly neutralities. Make us to go in the paths of thy commandments, and to trust for our defence in thy mighty arm alone; through Jesus Christ our Lord.

Richard Hurrell Froude (1803–1836)

SECOND SUNDAY IN LENT

Genesis 12:1–4a	Romans 4:1–5, 13–17
Psalm 121	John 3:1–17

The beckoning Spirit

Always the breath—the wind—of the Spirit is moving. We know it by its effect. We have no need to ask for its authentication. Is it Protestant? Is it Catholic? Where the fruit of the Spirit is apparent, there the Spirit is at work. We should place ourselves in its course that we may be carried by its impulse, even though this leads us to association with strange comrades. . . . For whatever promotes . . . love and joy and peace has its source in that divine love which sent the Son into the world, not to judge the world, *but that the world may be saved through him.*

William Temple, *Readings in St. John's Gospel* (London: Macmillan, 1939), p. 49.

Just as birth does not take place without nine months of intensive preparation, so spiritual rebirth can only take place when we are ready for it and our time has come. It is as dangerous to try to force it as it is to induce a premature birth.

Hugh Montefiore

Embark with Christ

Adventure yourselves with [Christ]; cast yourselves upon his Righteousness, as that which shall bring you to God: as a poor captive exile, that is cast upon a strange land, a land of robbers and murderers, where he is ready to perish, and having no hope, either of abiding there, or escaping home with life: do you likewise; you are exiles from the presence of God, and fallen into a land of robbers and murderers: your sins are robbers, your pleasures are robbers, your companions in sin are robbers and thieves: if you stay where you are, you perish, and escape home of yourselves you cannot: Christ offers, if you will venture with him, he will bring you home, and he will bring you to God.

John Wesley, from "Wesley's Covenant Service, Directions for Renewing Our Covenant with God (1780)," in *John and Charles Wesley: Selected Writings and Hymns,* ed. Frank Whaling (Ramsey, N.J.: Paulist Press; London: SPCK, 1981), p. 135.

There is never an act of faith without risk.

Eric James

On the Benedictine Rule

Most important of all, perhaps, is the Prologue's insistence that this rule is not being written by a spiritual taskmaster who will bully us or beat us down in a counterfeit claim to growing us up but by someone who loves us and will, if we allow it, carry us along to fullness of life. It is an announcement of profound importance. No one grows simply by doing what someone else forces us to do. We begin to grow when we finally want to grow. All the rigid fathers and demanding mothers and disapproving teachers in the world cannot make up for our own decision to become what we can by doing what we must.

In [the] very first paragraph of the rule Benedict is setting out the importance of not allowing ourselves to become our own guides, our own gods. Obedience, Benedict says—the willingness to listen for the voice of God in life—is what will wrench us out of the limitations of our own landscape. We are being called to something outside of ourselves, something greater than ourselves, something beyond ourselves. We will need someone to show us the way: the Christ, a loving spiritual model, this rule.

Joan Chittister, *The Rule of Benedict: Insights for the Ages* (New York: Crossroad Publishing Company; Middlegreen, Slough: St. Pauls, 1992), p. 20.

Live with questions

I would like to beg you . . . to have patience with everything that is unsolved in your heart and to try to cherish the questions themselves like closed rooms and like books written in a very strange tongue. Do not search now for the answers, which cannot be given you because you could not live them. It is a matter of living everything. *Live* the questions now. Perhaps you will then gradually, without noticing it, one distant day live right into the answer.

Rainer Maria Rilke, *Letters to a Young Poet,* trans. Reginald Snell
(London: Sidgwick & Jackson, 1945), p. 21.

Diary entry 1925

November: Mother sent me some of my high school books (now that I have a place of my own to keep them in) and the other day I came across these words, written on a faded slip of paper in my own writing. I do not remember writing them.

"Life would be utterly unbearable if we thought we were going nowhere, that we had nothing to look forward to. The greatest gift life can offer would be a faith in God and a hereafter. Why don't we have it? Perhaps like all gifts it must be struggled for. 'God, I believe' (or rather, 'I must believe or despair'). 'Help thou my unbelief.' 'Take away my heart of stone and give me a heart of flesh.' "

I wrote the above lines when I felt the urgent need for faith, but there were too many people passing through my life—too many activities—too much pleasure (not happiness).

I have been passing through some years of fret and strife, beauty and ugliness, days and even weeks of sadness and despair, but seldom has there been the quiet beauty and happiness I have now. I thought all those years that I had freedom, but now I feel that I had neither real freedom nor even a sense of what freedom meant.

And now, just as in my childhood, I am enchained, tied to one spot, unable to pick up and travel from one part of the country to another, from one job to another. I am enchained because I am going to have a baby. No matter how much I may sometimes wish to flee from my quiet existence, I cannot, nor will I be able to for several years. I have to accept my quiet and stillness, and accepting it, I rejoice in it.

Dorothy Day, *Selected Writings: By Little and By Little,* ed. Robert
Ellsberg (Maryknoll, N.Y.: Orbis Books, 1983, 1992), pp. 21–22.

"Move," says the Spirit*

"Move," says the Spirit,
"and respond and grow.
Leave the past behind you,
there's yet more to know."

*Tune: Wylam (see *Worship Live,* as above).

"Move," says the Spirit,
"and begin to love.
You have worth and value
to the Lord above."

"Move," says the Spirit,
"to the rhythm of life.
Work for peace and justice
and an end to strife."

"Move," says the Spirit,
"be alert and speak.
Give God's gracious message
to the poor and weak."

"Move," says the Spirit,
"at your Lord's command.
He gives strength and power
for the work in hand."

Joyce M. Firth, in *Worship Live* no. 13 (London: Stainer & Bell, Spring 1999), p. 14. © Joyce M. Firth. Used by permission.

Prayer

God, take me by Your hand, I shall follow You dutifully, and not resist too much. I shall evade none of the tempests life has in store for me, I shall try to face it all as best I can. But now and then grant me a short respite. I shall never again assume, in my innocence, that any peace that comes my way will be eternal. I shall accept all the inevitable tumult and struggle. I delight in warmth and security, but I shall not rebel if I have to suffer cold, should You so decree. I shall follow wherever Your hand leads me and shall try not to be afraid. I shall try to spread some of my warmth, of my genuine love for others, wherever I go. But we shouldn't boast of our love for others. We cannot be sure that it really exists. I don't want to be anything special, I only want to try to be true to that in me which seeks to fulfill its promise.

Etty Hillesum, *An Interrupted Life: The Diaries, 1941–1943* and *Letters from Westerbork,* trans. Arnold J. Pomerans (New York: Henry Holt & Company, 1996), p. 63.

THIRD SUNDAY IN LENT

Exodus 17:1–7   Romans 5:1–11

Psalm 95   John 4:5–42

A reservoir

There is a reservoir in my neighborhood that is part of the Louisville Water Company. I am one of the regular walkers around its perimeter. On the way back from my walk, I often sit by a fountain along Frankfort Avenue. When the morning or late afternoon sun hits the water drops, they sparkle with light. So the fountain has become an icon for me of the "inner spring of water always welling up" of which Jesus speaks in John 4. I go to the fountain to ask God the how and why questions of my life.

The Samaritan woman, or the woman at the well, was a woman of questions. She asked the socially taboo question of why Jesus, as a Jew, would speak to her, a Samaritan and a woman. She asked the pragmatic question about where Jesus might get a bucket for the promised living water. And by way of argument, she asked the theological question about where the spirit of God resides. The Samaritan woman has been judged as a cantankerous and stubborn person, but her persistent, even sarcastic, questions bring her to the realization that she is known by this man at the well. She finds her Messiah through her questions.

> Mary Zimmer, from "The Samaritan Woman: Living Water," in *Sister Images: Guided Meditations from the Stories of Biblical Women* (Nashville: Abingdon Press, 1993), p. 44. Used by permission.

Like the Samaritan woman, contemporary women thirst for living water. They stand at the well, hoping to draw life from ancient traditions. They long to discover their own inner wells, to meet God within, as source of their wisdom, power, creativity and strength.

> Kathleen Fischer

Seeing

In a remarkable book [*All Hallows Eve*] the English author Charles Williams shows us a girl who has just been killed in a plane crash. Her soul released from her body discovers a new world which she never saw before, she has just entered the invisible world which is now the only reality to her. She cannot see the visible world with the eyes of her soul. At one point she finds herself beside the Thames. She had seen it before as a foul stretch of filthy water, a refuse dump for London. But because she is now out of her body and does not relate everything to herself, she *sees* the Thames for the first time. She discovers it as a fact, a great river flowing through a great city. Its waters are dirty and opaque, they carry London's refuse to the sea. But this is as it should be, this is their proper role and they are authentic. And when she sees them as they are and accepts them, without emotion or physical repulsion because she can no longer feel disgust for them, no longer having a body to bathe in them or lips to drink from them, she sees the depths of the waters. They become less and less opaque. And at last they become transparent. This transparency increases until at the heart of the waters she sees a luminous thread which is the primordial water, as God created it, and at the heart of this primordial water, a yet more luminous thread, which is the marvellous water that Christ offered the Samaritan woman.

Through her disembodiment, the dead girl has been able to see things she was formerly blind to. The same is true of us. If we could become detached from ourselves and gain the inner freedom which the Fathers called "apathy", that is to say the absence of passion, we could see things more and more luminously. We could also see the splendour of God's presence in this dark and opaque world. We could see grace active everywhere and in all things.

Anthony Bloom (Metropolitan Anthony) in Metropolitan Anthony
and Georges Lefebvre, *Courage to Pray,* trans. Dinah Livingstone
(London: Darton, Longman & Todd; Crestwood, N.Y.: St. Vladimir's
Seminary Press, 1984), pp. 10–11.

As dry flour cannot be united into a lump of dough, or a loaf, but needs water, so we who are many cannot be made one in Christ Jesus without the water that comes from heaven.

Irenaeus (130–202)

Sinking wells

Come to the waters,
all you who are thirsty:
children who need water
free from diseases,
women who need respite
from labour and searching,
plants that need moisture
rooted near the bedrock,
find here a living spring.
O God, may we thirst
for your waters of justice,
and learn to deny no one
the water of life.

Janet Morley, in *Dear Life: Praying through the Year with Christian
Aid,* comp. Janet Morley, Hannah Ward, and Jennifer Wild (London:
Christian Aid, 1998), p. 78. © Christian Aid and Janet Morley.
Used by permission.

"Go and tell"

To "go and tell" is to preach the Gospel. At two crucial and dramatic points Jesus chose women for his own self-revelation and sent them to spread the Word, to preach the gospel.

The first woman who "goes and tells" is the woman at the well. By first-century social customs it is amazing that Jesus readily discussed religion at a chance meeting with a woman. It suggests his readiness to accept an average person as an intelligent human being. Beyond that, this woman of Samaria is the first person to receive the message that Jesus is the expected one, the Messiah. Jesus discusses spiritual matters with her, explaining that he has "living water" to offer, and then reveals to her that he is the Messiah.

. . . This woman was not just any woman. To begin with, she had three strikes against her. She had a low assigned status *as a woman* in the culture and religion of the first century. She had a low assigned status *as a Samaritan*—a kindred people whom the Jews despised. She had a third low status as a woman *whose lifestyle was suspect.*

How can we explain that Jesus chose for his critical message to the community such a negative-value person? A woman, a Samaritan, a sinner. It is easy to see that because these three negatives are frequently so entrancing to the preacher or interpreter it is difficult to get past them to see the woman as a person. . . . [Yet] we see a person who is responsive to verbal exchange, sharp, skeptical, quick to see meaning—and a person who is open to Jesus' self-declaration.

. . . Jesus gave the woman a message bombshell. He knew it would motivate her to preach. It acted as a spiritual "call" within her. She went forth immediately to tell a message—and the message got through. *She was the medium.* She left her water pot to go and tell. She left her woman-job for her preacher-job. Her culturally assigned status gave way to her Jesus-assigned status—one who is worthy to go and tell.

Rachel Conrad Wahlberg, *Jesus According to a Woman,* rev. ed.
(New York/Mahwah: Paulist Press, 1986), pp. 85–90.

"A draught from the water-springs of life will be my free gift to the thirsty."

Revelation 21:6b, New English Bible

God's free gift

What the disciples were able to experience [in the presence of the risen Jesus] was the wholly, gratuitously other, . . . made present to them as a giving back of someone familiar. Not someone from this side gone there, but someone from there given in a wholly new way, that was yet a continuation of the way they had sensed him as being given while he was with them before his death. This meant that the wholly, gratuitously, utterly other was no longer simply strange, but, without ceasing to be other, was a presence of recognizable, familiar, love for them. This was the beginning of the recasting of the disciples' perception of God, the wholly "other", in terms of Jesus, the risen Lord.

. . . Furthermore, the irruption of the gratuitous "other" happened within the disciples' frame of reference. They were frightened, ashamed, muddled, disappointed; the irruption didn't depend on them being in the "right" mood. And it happened as *forgiveness.* This is the second great category of the experience of the resurrection. Part of the utterly gratuitous other is that it is entirely outside any system of retribution and desert, and is therefore experienced by us as loosing us from being tied in to the "customary" other. The gratuitous other quite undermines all things that do not depend on gratuity, both our wounded relationships, and our virtues, which involve elements of protection and security. It is both as forgiveness of our sins and complete restructuring of our virtues that the gratuitous other reaches us.

James Alison, *Knowing Jesus* (London: SPCK, 1993), pp. 15, 16.

Prayer

Most loving God, you brought forth from the rock a spring of living water for your thirsty people: bring forth from the hardness of our hearts sincere tears of repentance, that we may be able to weep for our sins and obtain by your mercy their forgiveness. Listen graciously to our prayers, and deliver our hearts from all temptation by evil thoughts, that we may become the dwelling-place of your Holy Spirit, through Christ our Lord. Amen.

From *Regularis Concordia* (970), in *Christ the Golden-Blossom:
A Treasury of Anglo-Saxon Prayer,* ed. and trans. Douglas Dales
(Norwich: The Canterbury Press, 2001), pp. 16–17.

FOURTH SUNDAY IN LENT

| 1 Samuel 16:1–13 | Ephesians 5:8–14 |
| Psalm 23 | John 9:1–41 |

To follow wherever God may lead is to see God, whose passing by is a sign of God's presence for the one who follows.

Gregory of Nyssa

Following the Son of David

Psalm 23 is used in all rites of passage but it offers an especially illuminating insight into baptism. Its influence on the iconography of baptisteries can be traced from the painting of the Good Shepherd beside the font of the third-century Syrian house-church at Dura Europos to Victorian stained glass.

At the outset of the psalm we meet "my shepherding Lord" . . . , moving the flock on to waters which are safe, clear and accessible. The intensive form of the verb "revive" suggests that the shepherd is always looking out for our welfare, repeatedly turning us in the right direction; a reminder that baptism is only the beginning of a journey on which we shall be challenged again and again to follow Christ's lead. In a nomadic economy where pastures are over-grazed and water-courses change with the seasons, sheep cannot always remain in the same place or they die—a truth lost on some stalwart Christians! The paths of righteousness are not just correct moral rules to keep but ways that will engender justice for the whole community. The derivation of the word "paths" (maʿggle) from "round" (ʿagol) implies a liturgical procession which would have been led by the anointed sovereign with crook and staff (orb and sceptre) showing God's authority. By our baptism we share in that royal priesthood and join in the same walk with Christ.

> Lord, you are my shepherd;
> there is nothing I shall want.
> Fresh and green are the pastures

where you give me repose.
Near restful waters you lead me,
to revive my drooping spirit.

You guide me along the right path;
you are true to your name.
If I should walk in the valley of darkness
no evil would I fear.
You are there with your crook and your staff;
with these you give me comfort.

You have prepared a banquet for me
in the sight of my foes.
My head you have anointed with oil;
my cup is overflowing.

Surely goodness and kindness shall follow me
all the days of my life.
In the Lord's own house shall I dwell
for ever and ever.

Brian Pickett, *Songs for the Journey: The Psalms in Life and Liturgy*
(London: Darton, Longman & Todd, 2002), pp. 23–24, quoting Psalm
22/23 from *The Psalms: An Inclusive Language Version Based on the
Grail Translation from the Hebrew*, rev. ed. (London: HarperCollins
Publishers, 1995), pp. 30–31; © 1963, 1986, 1993 By Ladies Of The
Grail (England). Used by permission of GIA Publications, Inc., and
HarperCollins Publishers, exclusive agents. All rights reserved.

"Out of the deep"

"The peace of God passeth all understanding." Many, having it, feel as if they had
it not: but many, alas! wanting it, feel (like the Pharisees) as if they certainly had
it. Which is better: to kindle a fire of one's own, and compass oneself about with
sparks, and have to walk in *that* light; or to walk in darkness, and have no light,
only trusting (i.e. unweariedly trying to trust) in the name of the Lord, and "staying yourself" as you may "on our God"?

Let me beseech you, dear Sir, to go on trying this; and in a short time you will
see and know what a Rock you have been indeed standing on. Those who have
gone on trying in earnest to love and to cling to Him, in spite of all discourage-

ment, inward and outward, in spite of low spirits, and the bitter sense of useless-ness and unworthiness, they of all others may be said to walk by Faith, not by Sight. How can they fail to receive the blessing of Faith?

My dear Sir, excuse my running on in this way; sometimes the merest truism put in the homeliest way may help, where a higher sort of teaching had failed or might fail. But I trust that you will have more and more of that inward comfort and teaching which makes the soul happily independent of human suggestions, however well meant.

May the Almighty Guardian of our souls bring us all to himself, when and how he knoweth best.

Pray, my dear Sir, for
Your faithful and affectionate Servant in Christ,

John Keble

> John Keble, from "Letter 97, 'To an Aged Clergyman under Spiritual Depression,'" in *Letters of Spiritual Counsel and Guidance* (1870; London: Fount Paperbacks, 1995), pp. 120–21.

Boundless is thy love for me,
Boundless then my trust shall be.

> Robert Bridges (1844–1930)

Love II

Immortal Heat, O let thy greater flame
    Attract the lesser to it: let those fires,
Which shall consume the world, first make it tame;
And kindle in our hearts such true desires,
As may consume our lusts, and make thee way.
    Then shall our hearts pant thee; then shall our brain
    All her invention on thine Altar lay,
And there in hymns send back thy fire again:
Our eyes shall see thee, which before saw dust;
    Dust blown by wit, till that they both were blind:
    Thou shalt recover all thy goods in kind,
Who wert disseizèd by usurping lust:

All knees shall bow to thee; all wits shall rise,
And praise him who did make and mend our eyes.

George Herbert, from *The Church,* text as in *George Herbert and
Henry Vaughan,* Oxford Poets Series, ed. Louis L. Martz (Oxford and
New York: Oxford University Press, 1986), pp. 46–47.

What did I really see?

Many of us have made our world so familiar that we do not see it any more. It is
an interesting question to ask yourself at night: what did I really see this day? You
could be surprised at what you did not see. Maybe your eyes were unconditioned
reflexes operating automatically all day without any real mindfulness or recognition; while you looked out from yourself, you never gazed or really attended to
anything.... The human eye is always selecting what it wants to see and also evad-
ing what it does not want to see. The crucial question then is, what criteria do we
use to decide what we like to see and to avoid seeing what we do not want to see?
Many limited and negative lives issue directly from this narrowness of vision.

John O'Donohue, *Anam Cara* (London: Bantam Books, 1999), p. 87.

Prayer

O God, we do not always know why we are here.
We are often unsure of our purpose on earth.
Sometimes we hope to catch a glimpse of who you are
through the eyes of your startling vision,
which images *us* as your caring, compassionate people.

Rosemary C. Mitchell, in *Birthings and Blessings: Liberating Worship
Services for the Inclusive Church,* by Rosemary Catalano Mitchell and
Gail Anderson Ricciuti (New York: Crossroad Publishing Company,
1991), p. 105. Used by permission.

All human eyes have longing in them.

Ernesto Cardenal

FIFTH SUNDAY IN LENT

Ezekiel 37:1–14	Romans 8:6–11
Psalm 130	John 11:1–45

Resurrection

How do people resurrect? In a future moment outside history and with trumpets and angels coming from heaven? Or in the tension of the present, but "not yet among us", reign of God?

Latin American art and poetry are full of images of resurrection. The popular painters from Nicaragua depict the resurrection of the body with the familiar faces of people killed during the revolution leaving their graves. They are wearing jeans and shirts, smiling at each other, and giving us the impression of a community resurrecting from death. The fact is that Jesus's resurrection was also a community event: women and men witnessed how he came back from death, walked among them and continued the dialogue which existed before his crucifixion. Every death changes the life of the survivors because some humanity is removed from them. So it is legitimate to think that, starting with Jesus's resurrection, a whole community of people who suffered his loss when he was crucified came back to life again. Their eyes were opened in the sense that death took on another meaning; the resurrection became the paradigm showing us the durability and indestructibility of life and justice.

> Marcella Althaus-Reid, from "Doing the Theology of Memory:
> Counting Crosses and Resurrections," in *Life Out of Death: The
> Feminine Spirit in El Salvador,* by women in conversation with
> Marigold Best and Pamela Hussey (London: Catholic Institute for
> International Relations, 1996), pp. 194–95.

We want God's voice to be clear but it is not. . . . We want it to be clear as day, but it is deep as night. It is deep and clear, but with a dark clarity like an x-ray. It reaches our bones.

> Ernesto Cardenal

Lazarus

I don't intend it to happen.
It just sneaks up on me
and before I know it
there's been a kind of death,
part of me wrapped in a shroud
and buried in a tomb
while the rest of me stands by
wondering why the light has gone out.
Then you, my Friend, all knowing,
seek me out and knock
at the edge of my heart,
calling me to come forth.
I argue that I can't.
Death is death and I'm too far gone
for story book miracles.
But you keep on calling,
"Come forth! Come forth!"
and the darkness is pierced
by a shaft of light
as the stone begins to move.

My Friend,
I don't know how you do it
but the tomb has become
as bright as day, as bright as love,
and life has returned.

Look at me!
I'm running out,
dropping bandages all over the place.

Joy Cowley, *Psalms Down Under* (Wellington, New Zealand: Catholic Supplies [N.Z.] Ltd., 1996), p. 19. Used by permission.

A hard act to follow

Martha is a hard example to follow. She makes a very strong statement of faith at a time of great loss in her life. Death is the last complete mystery to us. Shelves of books on religion and philosophy have been written about the human fear of death. It is a great paradox to engage the idea in Martha's story that loss and faith are intertwined. Times of great grief and loss in our lives make us ask the hard questions of God. Why? Why this loss and this unbearable pain?

Perhaps it is the geography of Martha's story that gives us a hint of how Martha arrived at her strong faith statement. For Martha does not stay home this time, busy as a hostess for the funeral guests. She leaves and goes out to meet Jesus on the road, to confront him with the reality of her brother's death. Her first step to faith is the literal first step out of the house of grief and loss.

Renewal of faith beyond grief or loss is not a matter of simple words about God's will. A loving God does not will death and loss. Faith in new life comes out of and beyond a struggle of questions, anguish, and confrontation. Do we believe in life after death? Do we have faith in the renewal of joy in our lives in spite of depression and despair?

Martha's faith was not a simple one. She came to it out of her seeking. Our faith today, in a world filled with human trauma, cannot be a simple one either. In prayer and worship, we bring our suffering, our losses, our confusions, and our sense of overwhelming responsibility to God.

Mary Zimmer, from "Martha: Faith beyond Grief," in *Sister Images:*
Guided Meditations from Stories of Biblical Women (Nashville:
Abingdon Press, 1993), pp. 77–78. Used by permission.

One can rely on a friend. As a friend one is a person for other people to rely on. A friend remains a friend, even in disaster, even in guilt.

Jürgen Moltmann

I live each day to kill death

I am no longer afraid of death;
I know well
its dark and cold corridors
leading to life.

I am rather afraid of that life
which does not come out of death
which cramps our hands
and retards our march.

I am afraid of my fear
and even more of the fear of others,
who do not know where they are going,
who continue clinging
to what they consider to be life
which we know to be death!

I live each day to kill death;
I die each day to beget life,
and in this dying unto death,
I die a thousand times and
am reborn another thousand
through that love
from my People
which nourishes hope!

> Julia Esquivel, from *Women in a Changing World* (Geneva: World
> Council of Churches, January 1988). © WCC. Used by permission.

Life in fragments?

The important thing today is that we should be able to discern from the fragment of our life how the whole was arranged and planned, and what material it consists of. For really, there are some fragments that are only worth throwing into the dustbin (even a decent "hell" is too good for them), and others whose importance lasts for centuries, because their completion can only be a matter for God, and so they are fragments that must be fragments—I'm thinking, e.g., of the *Art of Fugue.* If our life is but the remotest reflection of such a fragment, if we accumulate, at least for a short time, a wealth of themes and weld them into a harmony in which the great counterpoint is maintained from start to finish, so that at last, when it breaks off abruptly, we can sing no more than the chorale, "I come before thy throne", we will not bemoan the fragmentariness of our life, but rather rejoice in it.

> Dietrich Bonhoeffer, *Letters and Papers from Prison: The Enlarged
> Edition,* trans. R. Fuller, F. Clarke, J. Bowden, and others (London:
> SCM Press, 1971), p. 219.

Seeking water, seeking shelter*

Seeking water, seeking shelter,
  gasps the thirsty, weary deer.
So my soul, in days of trouble
  longs for God's refreshment here.
In this stressful course of life
in its loneliness and strife,
"When", say I, "will God deliver?
Is his mercy gone for ever?"

No! he is my soul's true fortress.
  Though I hear those voices wild,
"Where's your God? Why has he left you?"
  he will not forget his child.
Come then, be my Advocate;
come, your servant vindicate:
then no more in fruitless sorrow
will I face a barren morrow.

Send your light and truth to lead me,
  then the path shall I discern
to my Father's house, where welcome
  greets the prodigal's return.
Then new songs shall fill my days,
every moment full of praise
with the faithful who surround him,
with the blest ones who have found him!

So, my soul, why such disquiet?
  Why such mourning, why such fear?
Day already breaks on darkness;
God has sought you; God is near.
Hope in God, and you shall live,
all delight he waits to give,

*Tune: GENEVA.

peace and power and every blessing
you shall know, this faith possessing.

Sixth Sunday in Lent

(Palm Sunday or Passion Sunday)

Isaiah 50:4–9a   Philippians 2:5–11
Psalm 118:1–2, 19–29   Matthew 21:1–11

Twenty centuries past

Twenty centuries past, what city has not heard of your coming?
From Beijing to Berlin, from Jerusalem to Johannesburg, from New York to
    New Delhi
surely the word has spread that you've come in peace, not violence
to enrich, renew, transform our lives, and bring us to shalom?

Blessed is he who comes in the name of the Lord. Hosanna in the highest.

Twenty centuries past, what city has not heard of your church?
From Catholic, Orthodox, or Reformed, Anglican, Evangelical, or
    Pentecostal
surely the message of acceptance, healing, confidence
in your royal advent, has been passed on through faithful living?

Blessed is he who comes in the name of the Lord. Hosanna in the highest.

Twenty centuries past, what city has not rejected you?
From penthouse to tenement, from factory to leisure centre, from theme
    park to concert hall,
surely the news is that this life is for taking, not giving
and what stands in the way of this lifestyle must now be removed?

Blessed is he who comes in the name of the Lord. Hosanna in the highest.

Twenty centuries past, what city does Christ seek to enter?
From leafy suburb to shanty town, from housing estate to west end flat,
    from salon to slum,
surely the sign of the church free from pride, united in deed,

must be the welcome Christ longs for as he enters your city?

Blessed is he who comes in the name of the Lord.

John Young, in *Kneelers: Prayers from Three Nations: Prayer Handbook Advent 2001–2002*, ed. Norman Hart (London: United Reformed Church, 2001), p. 47. © United Reformed Church 2001. Used by permission.

Where does the procession lead?

For you the procession represents a spiritual truth, namely, the glory of our heavenly fatherland; and the Passion shows the way that leads thereto. For if, as you take part in our procession today, the thought of the joy that is to be is in your mind, and the surpassing exultation there will be when we are caught up in the clouds to meet Christ in the air; if you desire with your whole heart to see that Day when Christ the Lord, the Head with all his members, shall be received into the heavenly Jerusalem, bearing the palm of victory and with angelic powers and the peoples of both Testaments crying on every side "Blessed is he that cometh!" instead of common crowds; if, I say, you consider during the procession whither you must hasten, then in the Passion learn the way that you must take! For this present tribulation is itself the way of life, the way of glory, the way to the heavenly habitation, the way of the Kingdom concerning which the thief cried from the cross, "Remember me, Lord, when thou comest into thy Kingdom!" He saw him going into his kingdom, and asked him, when he got there, to be mindful of himself. And he, the thief, arrived there too; and you can see how short a road it was, for on that very day he was accounted worthy to be with the Lord in Paradise. Thus the procession's glory makes the travail of the Passion bearable; for when one loves, nothing is difficult.

Bernard of Clairvaux, from a sermon for Palm Sunday, in *Saint Bernard on the Christian Year*, trans. and ed. a Religious of C.S.M.V. (London: A. R. Mowbray, 1954), pp. 74–75.

The humility of Christ is not the moderation of keeping one's exact place in the scale of being, but rather that of absolute dependence on God and absolute trust in him, with the consequent ability to move mountains. The secret of the meekness and gentleness of Christ lies in his relation to God.

H. Richard Niebuhr

Crowd behaviour

This is the problem of Palm Sunday. It is the very behaviour of the crowd that is worrying. Jesus moves from a position of having gained little recognition to one in which he is being crowned as "the people's king". Holy Week begins here because it is obvious that those who set him up will do him down. That is how crowds work. Any politician, celebrity, or sports star will testify that crowds, bound together in adulation, can quickly turn nasty, especially if you do not meet their expectations.

> Martyn Percy, "Sensing the Crowds," in Rowan Williams, W. H. Vanstone, Sylvia Sands, Martyn Percy, and Jim Cotter, *Darkness Yielding: Angles on Christmas, Holy Week, and Easter* (Sheffield: Cairns Publications, 2001), p. 76.

Dominator values?

Jesus' actions embody his words. . . . Consistent with all he has said and done, Jesus enters Jerusalem farcically, on a donkey. The church later read portentous meaning into this act on the strength of Zech. 9:9. But Mark and Luke make no reference to Zechariah, and may reflect something closer to Jesus' intent: lampooning the Davidic kingship by paradoxical reversal. The human being who has no place to lay his head is the same "king" who owns nothing and must borrow—not even a horse—an ass! It is conceivable that Zech. 9:9 is already farcical, and that Jesus took his inspiration from it. If he entered Jerusalem by the Horse Gate—it was on the east side, the direction from which Jesus was coming—the irony would be all the greater.

. . . We must reckon with the possibility that one impulse in the development of Christology was the attempt to insert Jesus back into the hierarchical world of domination by attaching to him honorific titles refulgent with power—the whole operation concealed behind a veil of obsequious devotion (itself a telltale sign of dominator values).

> Walter Wink, *Engaging the Powers: Discernment and Resistance in a World of Domination* (Minneapolis: Fortress Press, 1992), pp. 112–13.

Trust

The politics of the Holy Land are intractable. After centuries of hostility, it isn't surprising. The basic need is trust. Once there is a basis of trust, there is hope; once there is hope, the talking can be constructive.

God has placed us in a world where different aspirations, however deeply felt, can collide. The lesson we learn from Jerusalem on that first Palm Sunday is that the proud war-horse the Jews were expecting their Messiah to ride turned out to be the humblest of creatures, a donkey. Pride does not inspire trust; humility does. Do I trust the person who is nothing but "I can do this and that and the other, look at me"? Wouldn't I rather incline to trust the person who says: "That's a good idea of yours. Maybe you're right. Tell me more."?

Maxwell Craig, from "Palm Sunday," in *Lent and Easter Readings from Iona,* ed. Neil Paynter (Glasgow: Wild Goose Publications, 2001), pp. 48–49.

Prayer in Jerusalem

Jesus our brother,
as we dare to follow
in the steps you trod,
be our companion on the way.
May our eyes see
not only the stones that saw you
but the people who walk with you now;
may our feet tread
not only the path of your pain
but the streets of a living city;
may our prayers embrace
not only the memory of your presence
but the flesh and blood who jostle us today.
Bless us, with them, and make us long
to do justice, to love mercy,
and to walk humbly with our God.
Amen.

Janet Morley, *Companions of God: Praying for Peace in the Holy Land* (London: Christian Aid, 1994), p. 2. © Christian Aid and Janet Morley. Used by permission.

HOLY THURSDAY

Exodus 12:1–4 (5–10), 11–14	1 Corinthians 11:23–26
Psalm 116:1–2, 12–19	John 13:1–17, 31b–35

Christians are those who remember the story of Jesus within the community of the church, in and for their own time and in their own lives.

Nicola Slee

The Lord's passover

A community is only a community when the majority of its members is making the transition from "the community for myself" to "myself for the community", when each person's heart is opening to all the others, without any exception. This is the movement from egoism to love, from death to resurrection; it is the Easter, the passover of the Lord. It is also the passing from a land of slavery to a promised land, the land of interior freedom.

A community isn't just a place where people live under the same roof; that is a lodging house or an hotel. Nor is a community a work-team. Even less is it a nest of vipers! It is a place where everyone—or, let's be realistic, the majority!—is emerging from the shadows of egocentricity to the light of a real love. . . .

Love is neither sentimental nor a passing emotion. It is an attraction to others which gradually becomes commitment, the recognition of a covenant, of a mutual belonging. It is listening to others, being concerned for them and feeling empathy with them. It means answering their call and their deepest needs. It means feeling and suffering with them—weeping when they weep, rejoicing when they rejoice. . . . And if love means moving towards each other, it also and above all means moving together in the same direction, hoping and wishing for the same things. Love means sharing the same vision and the same ideal. So it means wanting others to fulfil themselves, according to God's plan and in service to other people. It means wanting them to be faithful to their own calling, free to love in all the dimensions of their being.

Jean Vanier, *Community and Growth* (London: Darton, Longman & Todd, 1979), pp. 10–11.

The meaning of Maundy Thursday

The Last Supper is not a simple, primitive fellowship meal; as far back as we can go in the tradition about Jesus, it is seen as 'intending' meaning, the event that finally sets Jesus and his followers apart from the continuities of Israel and makes the beginnings of a new definition of God's people. Maundy Thursday *means* Good Friday and Easter, the sealing of the new and everlasting covenant. In the costly gift of his chosen and beloved to the risk of rejection and death, God uncovers the scope of his commitment to him: he creates *faith.* And he creates a community of faith called, exactly as Israel is called, to show his nature in their life by following out the logic of Torah itself. Every act must speak of God, but not in such a way as to suggest a satisfying of divine demands, an *adequacy* of response to God's creative act. What we do now is to be a sign, above all, of a gift given for the deepening of solidarity—or, in Paul's language, ethics is about 'the building up of the body of Christ'. If our acts with one another speak of mutual gift and given-ness, they are signs of the radical self-gift which initiates the Church.

Rowan Williams, *On Christian Theology* (Oxford: Blackwell, 2000),
pp. 203–4.

If bread could talk, it would remind us of every mother who has offered her breast to her child, saying, "Take; eat; this is my body given for you. . . ."

Nathan Mitchell

Come to this table

Come to this table
   to meet the living God,
      love indescribable and beyond our imagining
      yet closer than our own breathing.

Come to this table
   to meet the risen Christ
      flesh of our flesh, bone of our bone,
      God-with-us, embodied in our living.

Come to this table
   to meet the life-giving Spirit,

interpreting our search for truth and justice,
breathing into us renewing power.

Come to find, to meet, to hold
the living, loving God
made new for us in bread and wine.

Jan Berry, in *Bread of Tomorrow: Praying with the World's Poor,* ed.
Janet Morley (London: SPCK/Christian Aid, 1992), pp. 93–94. © Jan
Berry. Used by permission.

Holding the cup

Before we drink the cup, we must hold it! . . .

One thing I learned [from my family] . . . drinking wine is more than just drinking. You have to know what you are drinking, and you have to be able to talk about it. Similarly, just living life is not enough. We must know what we are living. A life that is not reflected upon isn't worth living. It belongs to the essence of being human that we contemplate our life, think about it, discuss it, evaluate it, and form opinions about it. Half of living is reflecting on what is being lived. Is it worth it? Is it good? Is it bad? Is it old? Is it new? What is it all about? The greatest joy as well as the greatest pain of living come not only from what we live but even more from how we think and feel about what we are living. Poverty and wealth, success and failure, beauty and ugliness aren't just the facts of life. They are realities that are lived very differently by different people, depending on the way they are placed in the larger scheme of things. . . . Reflection is essential for growth, development, and change. It is the unique power of the human person.

Holding the cup means looking critically at what we are living. This requires great courage, because when we start looking, we might be terrified by what we see. Questions may arise that we don't know how to answer. Doubts may come up about things we thought we were sure about. Fear may emerge from unexpected places. We are tempted to say: 'Let's just live life. All this thinking about it only makes things harder.' Still, we intuitively know that without looking at life critically we lose our vision and our direction. When we drink the cup without holding it first, we may simply get drunk and wander around aimlessly.

Holding the cup of life is a hard discipline.

Henri J. M. Nouwen, *Can You Drink the Cup?* (Notre Dame, Ind.: Ave
Maria Press, 1996), pp. 26–27.

In the bread we eat the power that cannot be eaten,
In the wine we drink the fire that cannot be drunk.

Ephrem the Syrian (c. 306–373)

Mother Teresa

No revolution will come in time
    to alter this man's life
    except the one
    surprise of being loved.

It is too late to talk of Civil Rights,
    neo-Marxism,
    psychiatry
    or any kind of sex.

He has only twelve hours to live.
    Forget about
    a cure for cancer, smoking, leprosy
    or osteo-arthritis.

Over this dead loss to society
    you pour your precious ointment.
    wash the feet
    that will not walk tomorrow.

Mother Teresa, Mary Magdalene,
    your love is dangerous, your levity
    would contradict
    our local gravity.

But if love cannot do it, then I see
    no future for this dying man or me.
    So blow the world to glory,
    crack the clock. Let love be dangerous.

Sydney Carter, *The Two-Way Clock: Poems* (London: Stainer & Bell, 2000), pp. 82–83. © 1974 Stainer & Bell Ltd. Used by permission.

Good Friday

Isaiah 52:13–53:12

Hebrews 4:14–16; 5:7–9

Psalm 22

John 18:1–19:42

The cost of love

The theory that love is umbilically linked to sacrifice, demonstrated on the cross of Jesus Christ, makes lovely poetry, spills tears—but to be tied to it, however reluctantly, tests and tears. You soon learn the absolute emptiness of those who are prepared to give what has cost them nothing. Real love is expensive. So it should be; it demands a part of you. That is its cost.

Peter Owen Jones, *Small Boat, Big Sea* (Oxford: Lion Publishing, 2000), pp. 5–6.

No relation of mine?

This one who calls himself the Son of Man . . . it always rang a little hollow, you know. He was so faultless; I was pretty sure he was no relation of mine. The angels heralding his birth; the kings kneeling before the babe; the crowd and the glory; it all sucked him up into an unreachable heaven. The claim that he'd become one of us seemed unfathomable to me.

The closest I could come to understanding it was an old rich kid's game called "slumming." Sure, he set his crown down for a while—but when you can pick it up again, it's really not the same, is it?

But he finally convinced me. He showed his union card. It was at the very last, but he finally came down to stand with me in a way that told me he truly was irrevocably, nakedly human—and you can't take this away; I won't let you. I hold it in my hands like a gem I never thought I'd see.

jesus* unleashed the Accuser in his heart. He, too, had it hiding within him. It took all the power of Hell and Earth to pry it loose, but it finally came out.

The lowest bedrock shared by all of us; the very function of being turned into

---

*The author suffered from cystic fibrosis as well as diabetes. He uses lower-case j for the name of Jesus to indicate that he is not claiming Jesus' own authority in speaking about him.

flesh; the question that bends our spines in either spoken or unspoken ways; it was really there. jesus wasn't slumming. He truly became one of us.

The most graceful words in the New Testament are these:

My God, my God,
Why have you forsaken me?

> I have his confession on tape. You can hear it if you like.
> And now I know two things.
> This kin I have, he screamed his throat bloody raw at God . . .
>
> *And he survived.*

Not only did he survive, he was rescued, lifted up, brought out of the tomb!

There is no silence that can overtake me, no truth that can slay me; no wrath that can separate me from the love of God. I can come to God with anything—*anything*—and speak as freely as he. There is no prosecutor taking notes in heaven. There is only a loving God who wants to love truly and honestly, no holds barred. God wants no lie between us; no fakery. Somehow, that makes me want to scream a little less.

Bill Williams, with Martha Williams, Naked before God: The Return of
a Broken Disciple (Harrisburg, Pa.: Morehouse Publishing, 1998).

The liturgy of the world

The liturgy that Christ enacted on the cross represents the culmination of precisely *this* liturgy, the "liturgy of the world." This is the liturgy which reveals, ultimately, God's plan for human history, which shows the world not as some "evil, godless realm," but as a holy space permeated and filled by grace, as a "neighborhood" where God may be known and named. In the world's depths, at the center of each person, God's grace glows, burns, illumines, hallows, pleads, reproves, invites, emboldens, subverts and enlivens.

Nathan Mitchell, ed., in Assembly 22, no. 5 (November 1996): p. 735.

Noon has darkened*

I am at an impasse, and you, O God, have brought me here. From my earliest days, I heard of you. From my earliest days, I believed in you. I shared in the life of your

---

*Written after the sudden death of the author's son at the age of twenty-five.

people: in their prayers, in their work, in their songs, in their listening for your speech and in their watching for your presence. For me your yoke was easy. On me your presence smiled.

Noon has darkened. As fast as she could say, 'He's dead,' the light dimmed. And where are you in this darkness? I learned to spy you in the light. Here in this darkness I cannot find you. If I had never looked for you, or looked but never found, I would not feel this pain of your absence. Or is it not your absence in which I dwell but your elusive troubling presence?

Will my eyes adjust to this darkness? Will I find you in the dark—not in the streaks of light which remain, but in the darkness? Has anyone ever found you there? Did they love what they saw? Did they see love? And are there songs for singing when the light has gone dim? The songs I learned were all of praise and thanksgiving and repentance. Or in the dark, is it best to wait in silence?

> Nicholas Wolterstorff, in *Lament for a Son* (Grand Rapids:
> Wm. B. Eerdmans, 1987), p. 69.

The power of God's reign is not exhibitionistic. It is self-effacing, self-concealing. That power, like the leaven buried inside the mass of dough, is a fermentative power in the depth of humanity, in the womb of God's creation. It is the power of compassion. It is the power of the cross.

> Choan-Seng Song

"Behold the Man!"

I cannot go for more than a month without getting out of the studio, away from my own art, to look at the work of the best of my peers. So, on a sunny afternoon when most Southern Californians are headed for the beach, I am walking into a Los Angeles gallery, thinking about the usual subjects—love (some call it sex), death, rock and roll, and (my personal bias) God.

. . .'Behold the Man!'—this ancient exclamation flashes across my interior 'screen' when I enter the last room of the contemporary exhibition and am brought up short by a couch crowded with Jesus ragdolls. It is actually a soft blue, moiré-covered love seat centred on an elegant, floral-patterned area rug. Five large ragdolls are sitting or sprawling on the sofa; one headless doll (is it incomplete or mutilated?) lies on the rug. They wear traditional robes that look homespun and tiny, brown leather sandals on their delicate, wax-modelled feet. Each Jesus has a waxy face with a distinct expression, ranging from peaceful and saintly to a Charles Manson-like madness. . . . The title of Kim Dingle's work is 'My Struggles with Jesus'.

. . . Dingle's sculpture, not unlike a television talk-show host, asks of Jesus: 'Were you white, black, or brown?' (Incarnation is specific, concrete and very human.) 'Were you holy, cool, or crazed?' (Incarnation is monumentally extraordinary and unreasonable.) 'Were you rich or poor? Powerful or broken? Or both?' Since I believe that Christians ought to be more at home with complexity instead of less, my goal here is not to give answers so much as to circle around and hint at revelations that *enhance* rather than define the incarnation.

> Lynn Aldrich, from "Through Sculpture: What's the Matter with
> Matter?" in *Beholding the Glory: Incarnation through the Arts,* ed.
> Jeremy Begbie (London: Darton, Longman & Todd; Grand Rapids:
> Baker Book House Company, 2000), pp. 98–100. Used by permission.

Jesus will continue to be condemned to death so long as we do not establish the human and historical conditions that will allow justice to flower and right to flourish. And without justice and right, the kingdom of God will not be established.

> Leonardo Boff

To choose life

The more you grow into love, into the message of Jesus—to say it in such traditional, defenseless terms—the more vulnerable you make yourself. You simply become more open to attack when you have become conspicuous or when 'that of God' lights up in you. When you spread your life around rather than hoarding it, then the great light becomes visible within you. To be sure, you enter into loneliness, often you lose friends, a standard of living, a job, or a secure career, but at the same time you are changed. And the cross, this sign of isolation, of shame, of abandonment becomes, in this process, the tree of life, which you no longer like to be without at all. The dead wood of martyrdom begins to turn green. And you know at once where you belong. . . .

We *are* the tree of life.

> Dorothee Soelle, *Theology for Sceptics,* trans. Joyce L. Irwin (London:
> Mowbray; Minneapolis: Fortress Press, 1995), p. 104.

On this day

And on this day Christ died.
It was for love and was his only pride:
it was the rock he struck and travelled to,
on this day he did what he meant to do.
It was the wrath and whisper of the dove:
the pure and original spring of love.

Peter Levi, from "Good Friday Sermon 1973," in *Collected Poems 1955–1975* (London: Anvil Press Poetry, 1984), p. 206.
Used by permission.

EASTER

Acts 10:34–43
Psalm 118:1–2, 14–24

Colossians 3:1–4
John 20:1–18

A birthday

My heart is like a singing bird
    Whose nest is in a watered shoot;
My heart is like an apple tree
    Whose boughs are bent with thickset fruit;
My heart is like a rainbow shell
    That paddles in a halcyon sea;
My heart is gladder than all these
    Because my love is come to me.

Raise me a dais of silk and down;
    hang it with vair* and purple dyes;
Carve it in doves and pomegranates,
    And peacocks with a hundred eyes;
Work it in gold and silver grapes,
    In leaves and silver fleurs-de-lys;
Because the birthday of my life
    Is come, my love is come to me.

Christina Rossetti, from *Poems* (London: Macmillan, 1875).

When her name is called

There is some significance in what convinced this woman that Jesus stood before her. She does not recognize his voice in his question. What she recognizes is his voice calling her name. When her name is called by the risen Christ, she knows the new truth of the resurrection. . . .

*Probably 'variegated' (in heraldry blue and white).

Dear God,

We confess our confusion and busyness, which cause us to mistake your presence in our lives. Or we cannot feel your presence at all. Be with us in our searches. Grant us patience and steadfastness to listen for the calling of our names and to follow the purposes you have for us. Amen.

Mary Zimmer, from "Mary Magdalene: Called to Proclaim," in *Sister Images: Guided Meditations from the Stories of Biblical Women* (Nashville: Abingdon Press, 1993), pp. 84–85. Used by permission.

As we have died with him, and have been buried and raised to live with him, so we bear him within us, both in body and in spirit, in everything we do.

Leo the Great (fifth century)

On Peter's address to Cornelius

Peter hasn't even finished telling the story when already 'the Holy Spirit fell on all who heard the word.' This is the maximum moment of being disconcerted. That a holy story should be told to a group of the impure as something confrontational, something to make them feel bad about themselves so that they might purify themselves, maybe even going so far as to seek circumcision, is perfectly comprehensible. Yet, as you watch the story being told you notice that, rather than being confronted and downcast, the listeners all find themselves overwhelmed from within with a sense of delight, seeing the story as good news for themselves. That is seriously weird.

Peter then notoriously concludes, '"Can anyone forbid water for baptizing these people who have received the Holy Spirit just as we have?" And he commanded them to be baptized in the name of Jesus Christ.' In a very short space of time in Luke's storytelling we have gone from something rather like 'You are no part of our narrative' through 'You can be part of our narrative, but only on our terms' to 'Heavens, we are part of the same narrative, which isn't the one either of us quite thought it was and it isn't on the terms set by either of us.'

James Alison, *On Being Liked* (London: Darton, Longman & Todd, 2003), pp. ix, x.

Resurrection is always a mystery, always a miracle, but often we do not recognise resurrection when it comes to us. When all that separates and injures and destroys is overcome by that which unites, heals and creates in the ordinary routine of our daily lives, resurrection has taken place.

From *Birthed from the Womb of God: A Lectionary for Women,* comp. Dorothy Harvey (Wellington, New Zealand: Presbyterian Church of New Zealand, 1987), p. 28.

The prospect of death

This pattern in nature, that there is new life only where there is participation in death as well, is surprisingly duplicated, or reappears, in the spiritual existence of human beings. Neoorthodox theology drew a sharp distinction between the realm of nature and the personal realm of spirit. We, however, no longer do this, and especially on this point, for it is impossible to become fully human unless one is willing to face the prospect of death. No person or value can be defended unless one is ready to suffer and if necessary to die for that person or value—whether we speak of one's family or the integrity of another person or of freedom and justice in the community. None of these values of life can be effectively furthered without courage, the readiness to risk oneself for that in which one believes or for those to whom one is loyal—and this means facing the prospect of death. Hence courage is the basis of any virtue, the courage to stand where we must stand. In this sense, there is no real life unless it confronts and absorbs, takes in and makes a part of itself, death. As in nature, so in human existence life arises out of the prospect of death. . . .

For this reason the biblical God is the Lord of life but also the Lord over death; God is the giver of both to God's mortal creatures. Life and death in God's world are thus not completely antithetical, and the value of life depends in part on the presence of death in the good creation—and on our faith and our courage in facing the certainty of death.

Langdon Gilkey, *Blue Twilight: Nature, Creationism, and American Religion* (Minneapolis: Fortress Press, 2001), p. 171.

The Church is the first fruit of God's longing. Its life together, therefore, does not depend on excluding people and groups, but on a witness to the constantly inclusive activity of a God whose concern extends to a sparrow that falls on the ground.

Peter Selby

Sun dancing

Alexander Carmichael reported that: 'The people say the sun dances on this day in joy for a risen Saviour. Old Barbara Macphie at Dreimsdale saw this once, but only once in her long life. And the good woman, of high natural intelligence, described in poetic language and with religious fervour what she saw or believed she saw from the summit of Benmore.' . . . Had she gone looking for it, had she wanted it to happen, had she been intent above all on impressing others with something manifested to her alone, . . . she would doubtless told of recurrences. The singularity of her sighting makes an extraordinary movement of the sun on Easter morning all the more credible. The interpretation of that movement is, of course, another matter. But it has been pointed out that Barbara Macphie's experience . . . may have been touched by the same mystical perception as something recorded by Patrick in his *Confessio*. The saint was troubled in a dream by Satan, who 'fell over me like a huge rock, and none of my members [had] any prevailing power. . . . And amidst these things I saw the sun rise into the heaven, and while I was calling "Elia, Elia" with all my powers, look, the splendour of His sun fell down over me, and immediately shook off from me all oppressiveness, and I believe I was come to the aid of by Christ my Lord.' In both cases, it has been argued, the sun is not a metaphor or an image of Christ, but a medium through which Christ shines.

Geoffrey Moorhouse, *Sun Dancing: A Medieval Vision* (London:
Weidenfeld & Nicolson, 1997), pp. 207–8.

When I consider the past, and present, and future state of this body, in this world, I am able to conceive, able to express the worst that can befall it in nature, and the worst that can be inflicted upon it by man, or fortune; but the least degree of glory that God hath prepared for that body in heaven, I am not able to express, not able to conceive.

John Donne

Second Sunday of Easter

Acts 2:14a, 22–32   1 Peter 1:3–9
Psalm 16   John 20:19–31

Peace be with you

"Peace be with you," says the priest to the children of the church, for peace is multiplied in Jesus our Lord, who is our peace. "Peace be with you," for death is come to naught, and corruption destroyed through a Son of our race who suffered for our sake and quickened us all. . . . "Peace be with you," because you have been united—the People and the Peoples—and the barrier has been broken down by Jesus who destroyed all enmity. "Peace be with you," for new life is reserved for you by him who became a first-born unto all creatures in life incorruptible. "Peace be with you," because you have been summoned to the Kingdom aloft by him who entered first to prepare a place for us all.

. . . This is the peace in which there is no treachery and no hatred; but it is all light in light, and perfect love. Blessed is he that gives the Peace with love to his brother, for it is he that shall receive perfect peace in the midst of his mind. Peace is the name of Christ, who makes all to be at peace, for it is he that has made peace between earthly and heavenly beings. Blessed is he that makes his heart peaceful at the hour of the Mysteries, for all his debts and hateful deeds shall be forgiven him.

Narsai (fifth century), from the *Liturgical Homilies,* in *Texts and
Studies: Contributions to Biblical and Patristic Literature,* vol. 3,
ed. J. Armitage Robinson (Cambridge:
Cambridge University Press, 1909), pp. 8–9.

Sounding together

If it is typical of western modernity to see people as self-determining, isolated agents, sovereign over their carefully bounded 'space', the same is true of much thinking about the goal of the incarnation, which all too often is seen as the rescue of solitary individuals for heaven. But the true human goal of the incarnation is the creation of a new people, a community sustained by the Spirit, bound with that love which binds the incarnate Son to the Father (John 17:22). . . .

132

During a recent visit to South Africa, a number of times I sang the national anthem, 'Nkosi Sikelel iAfrika'. Wherever I sang it, it evoked in me an extraordinary sense of togetherness, even though I hardly knew the hymn and often hardly knew the people with whom I was singing. Part of the reason for that, no doubt, was that I knew this song had bound thousands together during the fierce decades of *apartheid*. Part of it was the overwhelming welcome I received at most of the assemblies where I sang it. But a large part of it also was its four-part harmony, in which no vocal line predominates over the others (unlike the British national anthem, for example). Sing this in South Africa and, in keeping with a vast range of African music, it will be in harmony. (Unlike the Western European tradition, singing in harmony does not need to be taught.) Your voice and all the others fill the same heard 'space'. It is a space not of a hundred voices each with their mutually exclusive and bounded 'place', but a space of overlapping sounds, an uncrowded, expansive space without 'edges' where distinct voices mutually establish each other. . . . Why is it that freedom and reconciliation have so often been celebrated in this kind of singing? Because, I suggest, people are experiencing a kind of concord which embodies the kind of freedom in relation to others—even our enemies—which the trinitarian gospel makes possible.

> Jeremy Begbie, "Through Music: Sound Mix," in *Beholding the Glory:*
> *Incarnation through the Arts,* ed. Jeremy Begbie (London: Darton,
> Longman & Todd; Grand Rapids: Baker Book House Company,
> 2000), pp. 151–52. Used by permission.

Invitation

Come, then, people of every nation, receive forgiveness for the sins that defile you. I am your forgiveness. I am the Passover that brings salvation. I am the lamb who was immolated for you. I am your ransom, your life, your resurrection, your light, I am your salvation and your king. I will lead you to the heights of heaven. I will show you the eternal Father. With my right hand I will raise you up.

> Melito of Sardis (second century), from an Easter homily, in *A Word*
> *in Season III: Easter,* ed. Friends of Henry Ashworth (Riverdale, Md.:
> Exordium Books, 1983), p. 5.

We are baffled

Christ is Risen
He is risen indeed!

We are baffled by the very Easter claim we voice.
Your new life fits none of our categories.
We wonder and stew and argue,
and add clarifying adjectives like "spiritual" and "physical."
But we remain baffled, seeking clarity and explanation,
we who are prosperous, and full and safe and tenured.
We are baffled and want explanations.

But there are those not baffled, but stunned by the news,
stunned while at minimum wage jobs;
stunned while the body wastes in cancer;
stunned while the fabric of life rots away in fatigue and despair;
stunned while unprosperous and unfull
and unsafe and untenured . . .
Waiting only for you in your Easter outfit,
waiting for you to say, "Fear not, it is I."
Deliver us from our bafflement and our many explanations.
Push us over into stunned need and show yourself to us lively.
Easter in us honesty;
Easter in us fear;
Easter in us joy,
and let us be Eastered. Amen.

> Walter Brueggemann, *Awed to Heaven, Rooted in Earth: Prayers of
> Walter Brueggemann* (Minneapolis: Fortress Press, 2003), p. 162.
> © 2003 Augsburg Fortress. Used by permission.

There lives more faith in honest doubt,
Believe me, than in half the creeds.

> Alfred Tennyson

Beyond Easter

I could go on—about people working in peacemaking, industrial relations, the health service, race relations, among young people. I could go on about local ecumenical projects and communities, the considerable numbers of people crossing denominations to study everything from the Bible to pastoral care and contemplative spirituality . . . but you know what I am saying. The place of the gospel is never abstract or academic, nor is it theoretical and dogmatic. It is always the place of engagement with the world. It is the place where the Word becomes flesh, where you can see the marks in the side.

Kathy Galloway, in *Lent & Easter Readings from Iona,* ed. Neil Paynter
(Glasgow: Wild Goose Publications, 2001), p. 128.

Sharing Jesus' faith

[One] reason why we should be cautious of explaining the disciples' response to Jesus' death principally in terms of their post-mortem encounters is the observation that these happenings do not seem to have been the basis for, nor indeed the substance of, Jesus' abiding presence within the community of faith which continued to form around him. In certain respects, this is obvious: while the resurrection appearances were clearly self-authenticating for those who experienced them, they were not readily transferable and, in consequence, could only offer indirect access to Jesus for those who were not privileged in this way. The portrayal of Thomas in the Gospel of John, chapter 20, as the one who believes no more than he can empirically verify, makes this point precisely as readers are encouraged to discover the 'risen' Jesus not through bodily encounter but through faith (John 20.24–29; cf. Mark 16.9–13; Luke 24.10–12). . . . Jesus' continuing presence after his death was principally discerned and communicated through characteristic resources, practices and perceptions. Central here was the vocation to share Jesus' faith—to participate in his spirituality, to embrace his vision of the Kingdom and to engage in his pattern of ministry.

Ian Wallis, *Holy Saturday Faith: Rediscovering the Legacy of Jesus*
(London: SPCK, 2000), p. 2.

Easter is not a part of the old accustomed divine order, or of the ordered world in which we live, but it is an absolutely new, unexpected act of the living God, which interrupts and runs counter to the uniform rise and fall of the world's rhythm. Here we have the beginning of something new.

Martin Niemoller

THIRD SUNDAY OF EASTER

Acts 2:14a, 36–41　　　　　　　1 Peter 1:17–23

Psalm 116:1–4, 12–19　　　　　Luke 24:13–35

Healing fire

My mother died at about six o'clock on the 30th of November. My father and I were called to the hospital. We sat for a while with her poor, wasted, jaundiced body.

We returned home. There was a profound silence and emptiness. I could see her standing at the bench and I could hear her voice—never to be again. We sat, not speaking, each with our own thoughts. We shed some quiet tears. My father spoke, "I think I will light a fire." He went out for some wood and I heard him chopping kindling. He set the fire. As the flames rose up the paper and wood, he turned to me and smiled. A knowing passed between us. I smiled. Lighting a fire had been a good thing to do. The fire was somehow comforting and cheering. The night was mild. The fire was not necessary for heating, but fire warmed our aching hearts.

John Hunt, *We Spirited People: A Personal, Enriching and Uniquely*
New Zealand Guide in Celtic Spirituality (Christchurch, New Zealand:
The Caxton Press, 1998), p. 44.

Liturgy is rehearsal of the whole story of Jesus' ministry, passion, death, resurrection; liturgy is doing something together in the light of the gospel.

John J. Vincent

The insistent presence—our hesitant response

The sun sets on the world, darkness presses,
Friend, today you seem obscured to us.

The darkness of hatred between people
Of different nations and languages;

The darkness of vengeance between castes,
classes, races and communities;

Darkness in exploiting the poor and illiterate,
Darkness in humiliating women and young girls;

Darkness in which Dalits accept their fate;
The darkness of religious pride:
'Truth is ours, the rest are false.'

An unending story this, and a death-blow to life;
Don't you see it now? Tell me, friend,
Who on earth would give his life for others?

. . . Lord of life, draw near to us,
Break through to us this day. Amen.

> Translation of a Kannada lyric, from "Liturgy: To Recognise the Risen
> One," in *Worship in an Indian Context: Eight Inter-Cultural Liturgies,*
> ed. Eric J. Lott (Bangalore: United Theological College, 1986),
> pp. 81–82. Used by permission.

Our faith in the God of revelation cannot be lived and understood abstractly, in some atemporal fashion. It can only be lived through the warp and woof of the events that make up history.

> Jean-Marc Ela

From encounter to relationship

I have many memories of encounters with people who made my heart burn but whom I did not invite into my home. Sometimes it happens on a long plane trip, sometimes in a train, sometimes at a party. . . .

Interesting, stimulating, and inspiring as all these strangers may be, when I do not invite them into my home, nothing truly happens. I might have a few new ideas, but my life remains basically the same. Without an invitation, which is the expression of the desire for a lasting relationship, the good news that we have heard cannot bear lasting fruit. It remains 'news' among the many types of news that bombard us every day.

It is one of the characteristics of our contemporary society that encounters, good as they may be, don't become deep relationships. Thus our life is filled with good advice, helpful ideas, wonderful perspectives, but they are simply added to the many other ideas and perspectives and so leave us 'uncommitted.' In a society with such an informational overload, even the most significant encounters can be reduced to 'something interesting' among many other interesting things.

Only with an invitation to 'come and stay with me' can an interesting encounter develop into a transforming relationship.

Henri J. M. Nouwen, *With Burning Hearts: A Meditation on the Eucharistic Life* (London: Geoffrey Chapman; Maryknoll, N.Y.: Orbis Books, 1994), pp. 55, 56–57.

Feet and hands

Feet and hands: These are the symbols I offer as we think about journeying together.

FEET—to stand for the moving-on that our faith demands of us,
HANDS—to stand for the togetherness, the companionship, the support most of us need, and may legitimately seek, as we set out in response to the promptings of the Spirit.

Feet and hands were involved in . . . [the] journey . . . of Cleopas and his companion on the road from Jerusalem to Emmaus. We don't know for sure who the companion was, but as they shared a house, it may be fair to assume that they were partners. Their identity doesn't matter greatly. The point is that here were two people who, in grief and disillusionment, shared a journey that was transformed by the drawing near and companionship of a third traveller—the one they finally recognized as Jesus himself. Thinking everything they'd hoped for was over, they'd been going back home . . . back to resume life where they'd left it off—much as Peter sadly reckoned he might as well go back to his fishing. But something happened to change the pace and direction of their feet, and the lift of their hands: one imagines that where, on the way to Emmaus, their feet had been slow and dragging and their hands supporting each other in shared agony, the return journey (verse 33: They got up *at once* and went *back* to Jerusalem) was marked by running feet and hands held out in shared joy. For between the agony and the joy were the hands of one who took bread, blessed, broke and gave—and, in that familiar action, told them everything they longed to know.

Kate Compston, from "On the Journey Together," in *Silence in Heaven: A Book of Women's Preaching,* ed. Susan Durber and Heather Walton (London: SCM Press, 1994), pp. 21–22. © Kate Compston 1994. Text amended by author.

Risen One, journeying with us, be present

Risen One, journeying with us,
Be present with grace as we meet in fellowship.

It is you who gave to us the world and our life,
Our freedom and our relationships.

It is you who taught us truth by being in our inner core,
Even when we lost touch with you.

You became human, lived as man with us
And gave newness of life for humankind.

It is you who underwent death and so defeated it;
Over death you brought life.

Now you break the bread and pour wine
That our inner eye may be opened,
That we may be united with you.

A Tamil lyric from "Liturgy: To Recognise the Risen One," in *Worship in an Indian Context: Eight Inter-Cultural Liturgies,* ed. Eric J. Lott (Bangalore: United Theological College, 1986), p. 83.
Used by permission.

Fourth Sunday of Easter

Acts 2:42–47	1 Peter 2:19–25
Psalm 23	John 10:1–10

Prayer of approach

Lord Jesus
in those days of wonder after Easter,
you called Mary and Peter by their names,
and they recognised you;
and we too draw near to hear our names
spoken in love
and to know you again.

You broke bread with your followers
on the road to Emmaus,
and in the blessing, they recognised you;
and we too come to share your blessing
and your broken life,
and to know you again.

You spoke peace to your disciples,
showed them the marks on your hands,
sent them out to bear witness to your risen life;
and we too come seeking peace,
seeking to bear witness
and to be sent out renewed.

Come among us now,
that we may recognise you
in each other,
and together know your healing and hope.

Kathy Galloway, in *Praying for the Dawn: A Resource Book for the Ministry of Healing,* ed. Ruth Burgess and Kathy Galloway (Glasgow: Wild Goose Publications, 2000), p. 138. © 2000 Kathy Galloway. Used by permission of Wild Goose Publications, Glasgow G2 3DH Scotland.

I think the Psalms are like a mirror, in which one can see oneself and the movements of one's heart.

Athanasius (296?–373)

Better than the Joneses

In some of the Psalms the spirit of hatred which strikes us in the face is like the heat from a furnace mouth. In others the same spirit ceases to be frightful only by becoming (to a modern mind) almost comic in naivety. . . .

. . . Worst of all in 'The Lord is my shepherd' (23), after the green pasture, the waters of comfort, the sure confidence in the valley of the shadow, we suddenly run across (5) 'Thou shalt prepare a table for me *against them that trouble me*'— or, as Dr. Moffatt translates it, 'Thou art my host, spreading a feast for me *while my enemies have to look on*.' The poet's enjoyment of his present prosperity would not be complete unless those horrid Joneses (who used to look down their noses at him) were watching it all and hating it. This may not be so diabolical as the [other] passages I have quoted; but the pettiness and vulgarity of it, especially in such surroundings, are hard to endure.

C. S. Lewis, *Reflections on the Psalms* (London: Geoffrey Bles, 1958),
pp. 20, 21.

The intimacy of the table

The table is one of the most intimate places in our lives. It is there that we give ourselves to each other. When we say: 'Take some more, let me serve you another plate, let me pour you another glass, don't be shy, enjoy it', we say a lot more than our words express. We invite our friends to become part of our lives. We want them to be nurtured by the same food and drink that nurtures us. We desire communion. That is why a refusal to eat and drink what a host offers is so offensive. It feels like a rejection of an invitation to intimacy.

Strange as it may sound, the table is the place where we want to become food for each other. Every breakfast, lunch or dinner can become a time of growing communion with each other.

Henri J. M. Nouwen, *Bread for the Journey* (London: Darton,
Longman & Todd, 1996), p. 58.

Christianity and socialism

If we are to move from death to life, from slavery to liberation, from acquisitiveness to holiness, we need to work both at the level of personal and corporate spiritual discipline, and at the level of political restructuring. And this must raise the question of the future of socialism. The struggle for alternatives to capitalism will occupy Christians and all people of moral concern during the twenty-first century. Socialism, as a political movement, is quite modern. In its origins in the 1830s, it was seen as the opposite of individualism. At the heart of the socialist vision was social or common ownership of the necessities of life. Common ownership and democratic control of the means of production was originally far more central than state control or nationalisation which developed later. Socialists have always recognised that there are many forms of social ownership, of which co-operative ownership is one.

> Kenneth Leech, *The Sky Is Red: Discerning the Signs of the Times*
> (London: Darton, Longman & Todd, 1997), p. 153.

I want to repeat to you what I said once before: the shepherd does not want security while they give no security to the flock.

> Oscar Romero

So . . .

So I ask you to share my prayer, that 'the mountain be cast into the depths of the sea', the fear be lifted from all our hearts and that we may develop the daring, viscerally moved, shepherdly heart of love along with the creative projects such a heart will enflame as we follow our Lord outside the camp.

> James Alison, *On Being Liked* (London: Darton, Longman & Todd,
> 2003), p. 130.

Fifth Sunday of Easter

Acts 7:55–60   1 Peter 2:2–10
Psalm 31:1–5, 15–16   John 14:1–14

Love makes the whole difference between an execution and a martyrdom.

Evelyn Underhill

Trust in the real God

We do not need a lecture on psychology to tell us that courage is not the virtue of those 'who do not know what fear is'. I do not believe that there are such people. Jesus was in an agony of fear in the garden and those hours come to us all. Courage is possessed by the person who estimates the fear-causing situation, but summons all his [or her] resources and meets it. Courage comes by doing courageous things when we want to run away, and let us remember that a little child going upstairs to bed in the dark, and imagining all sorts of bogeys and horrors, often shows as much courage as a soldier whose impulsive dash during some peak of mental excitement wins him a medal for bravery.

So let us, fifty times a day if need be, set before us a picture of *the real God*, utterly loving, whatever we have done, infinitely strong, resourceful and purposeful, finding this way for us when that way is closed for whatever reason, who will not allow us to be lost and defeated if we trust him, and who is generous beyond all thoughts of generosity. Let us commit ourselves to him every morning, for the real God is to be trusted, and whatever happens to us—called, as it may be by others, failure, catastrophe or defeat—we shall know that eternal love still bears us on its bosom, and that we shall find our way home without regret.

Leslie Weatherhead, *Prescription for Anxiety* (London: Hodder & Stoughton, 1956), p. 51.

Coming and going

Lord Jesus
we are glad that you came

143

from God
but are sad at your going.
In all our anxieties
be for us
our way, our truth and our life.

Help us
to hold tight and follow
your way;
in faith and doubt
take us
with you, and with God

Teach us
from scripture and the present
your truth;
in word and deed
keep us
with you, and with God

Show us
in good times and bad
your life;
in joy and sorrow
hold us
with you, and with God

Lord Jesus
we are glad that you came
from God
give us faith that in your going,
we may see and know
the Father
loving us through you.

Tony Burnham, in *Say One for Me: Prayer Handbook 1990,* ed.
Graham Cook (London: United Reformed Church, 1990), May 13. ©
Tony Burnham 1990. Used by permission.

It is not the religions themselves that are true, and save anyone, but God. God saves men and women within the Christian way, the Muslim way, the Jewish way, the Buddhist way.

John Hick

The call

Come, my Way, my Truth, my Life:
Such a Way, as gives us breath:
Such a Truth, as ends all strife:
Such a Life, as killeth death.

Come, my Light, my Feast, my Strength:
Such a Light, as shows a feast:
Such a Feast, as mends in length:
Such a Strength, as makes his guest.

Come, my Joy, my Love, my Heart:
Such a Joy, as none can move:
Such a Love, as none can part:
Such a Heart, as joys in love.

George Herbert, from *The Church,* text as in *George Herbert and
Henry Vaughan,* ed. Louis L. Martz (Oxford and New York: Oxford
University Press, 1986), pp. 141–42.

The meaning of belonging

Human communities—all human communities—define themselves by the boundaries they draw (that is what 'define' means), by knowing who does not belong, and being aware of what is distinct from themselves. The word 'family' makes no sense unless it makes clear that there are those who do not belong. Name what group you like, and you will in the naming be calling attention to what is not part of it. All groups do it: the clubs, the communities we know, the ethnic groupings we belong to, all of them presuppose people who do not belong, and in the process draw attention to them. In describing the identity of any group we belong to we have an ironic interest in making sure that those who do not belong stay 'out there', and thereby contribute to our own sense that we are together 'in here'.

So we achieve a sense of belonging generally at someone else's expense. In the process of becoming members of something we create at the same time a multitude of others against whom, in some sense, we shall need to defend our interests. The loyalties and solidarities human beings make for themselves bring out some of the fiercest conflicts.

> Peter Selby, *BeLonging: Challenge to a Tribal Church* (London: SPCK, 1991), p. 2.

In Jesus' name

A Christian prays in Jesus' name in the sense that he is in union with Jesus. Thus, the theme of asking "in my name" in [John] xiv 13–14 continues and develops the indwelling motif of 10–11: because the Christian is in union with Jesus and Jesus is in union with the Father, there can be no doubt that the Christian's requests will be granted. This context of union with Jesus also suggests that the requests of the Christian are now no longer thought of as requests concerning the petty things of life—they are requests of such a nature that when they are granted the Father is glorified in the Son (13). They are requests pertinent to the Christian life and to the continuation of the work by which Jesus glorified the Father during his ministry (xvii 4).

> Raymond E. Brown, *The Gospel according to John XIII–XXI*, The Anchor Bible (New York: Doubleday & Co., Inc., 1966; London: Geoffrey Chapman, 1971), p. 636.

'I am the Way'

Thou art the Way.
Hadst Thou been nothing but the goal,
    I cannot say
If Thou hadst ever met my soul.

    I cannot see—
I, child of process—if there lies
    An end for me,
Full of repose, full of replies.

I'll not reproach
The road that winds, my feet that err.
    Access, Approach
Art Thou, Time, Way, and Wayfarer.

Alice Meynell, from *Poems of Alice Meynell* (London: Burns, Oates & Washbourne, 1923).

SIXTH SUNDAY OF EASTER

Acts 17:22–31	1 Peter 3:13–22
Psalm 66:8–20	John 14:15–21

Waiting for the Spirit

Our whole lives are therefore lives lived in the expectation of the unexpected, we live, as Christians, in this condition of waiting, open to every possibility of demand; but we will as often as not be unprepared when it comes, for we never know when that Spirit will surprise us. We wait for the Spirit, therefore, but he always comes, for the Spirit is already in our waiting. Which is why the whole reality of the resurrection is found in both at once: in the waiting and in the coming, for the waiting is in the coming and the coming is in the waiting.

Denys Turner, *Faith Seeking* (London: SCM Press, 2002), p. 115.

Christian love is not the world's last word about itself—it is God's last word about himself, and so about the world.

Hans Urs von Balthasar

God moves on

The world has in fact begun to crack. The moment of truth for humanity seems to have arrived. We seem destined for destruction at our own hands. But behold, miracle of miracles, out of the cracks a light shines. The venomous snake has not crushed the light. The light burns. It gives warmth. It gives hope. And as the dreamer timidly advances towards the light, he discovers that there are many, many others who are also moving toward it from different directions—from behind iron curtains, from across human barriers, from behind the walls of our own frightened souls. Yes, we all need that light, for that light is the only hope— we, the poor and the rich, the oppressed and the oppressors, the theists and the atheists, Christians, Muslims, Jews, Buddhists, and Hindus. We all must get to that light, for it is the light of love and life, the light of hope and future. The movement of persons toward that light must have constituted a formidable power, for the snake, the demon, begins to loosen its grip on the globe. Its power is broken. Its threat is removed.

And so God moves on. God moves from the Tower of Babel to Pentecost, from Israel to Babylon. God moves in Europe, in Africa, in the Americas, in Asia. As God moves, God suffers with the people, sheds tears with them, hopes with them, and creates the communion of love here and there. . . . Until the time when the communion of love is firmly established in the world of strife and conflict, of pain and suffering, God moves on in compassion. We have no alternative but to move on with God toward that vision of a community of compassion and communion of love.

> Choan-Seng Song, *The Compassionate God: An Exercise in the Theology of Transposition* (London: SCM Press, 1982), p. 260.

God in the midst*

God is unique and one—
Maker, Sustainer, Lord!
Patterns of life were spun
by his creative Word.
    Of his intention, love and care
    we are with growing trust aware.

Love came to earth in Christ,
our common life to share,
choosing to be the least,
willing a cross to bear.
    He died and rose, that we might live
    and all our love—responding—give.

The Holy Spirit moves
people to trace God's plan;
such inspiration proves
more than the mind can span.
    Each listening heart is led to find
    the will of God for humankind.

*Suggested tune: LITTLE CORNARD.

God shall forever reign,
Ruler of time and space;
here, in the midst of life,
seen in the human face.
We give expression to our creed
by love in thought and word and deed.

Fred Kaan, from *The Only Earth We Know: Hymn Texts* (Carol
Stream, Ill.: Hope Publishing Company; London: Stainer & Bell,
1999), p. 10. © 1968 Hope Publishing Company, Carol Stream, IL
60188 for USA and Canada; and Stainer & Bell Ltd. for all other
territories. All rights reserved. Used by permission.

Heirs, not servants

Jesus shows us what we are meant to be. He shows us that we are created for a life of intimate relationship with God, and that that relationship makes us what we truly are. We know Jesus to be the Son of God because he is obedient to God, not because he has power. We know that, because he was willing to be obedient and to allow himself to be defined in relation to God, not on his own terms, he opens up a whole new kind of power, resurrection power. Resurrection power brings life out of death, creates community, opens up relationship, allows us to step into a place that we have not made or earned, but simply accepted, in gratitude. It is the place of God's children, standing by Jesus and knowing ourselves to be heirs, not servants.

The paradox that we see in Jesus is that it is *only* through service, through obedience, through accepting servant status that we come to be children, not slaves. Trying to get there under our own steam, relying always on our own powers, is going to keep us in slavery.

Jane Williams, *Perfect Freedom* (Norwich: Canterbury Press, 2001),
pp. 32–33.

The by-products of affliction

From afflicted people I learned a very valuable lesson, about which there is a conspiracy of silence. Many problems just have no answer, so it's no use trying to invent one. You can only learn to live with the problems or transcend them. It's no use saying they will go away and that there is a happy ending in this world for everyone—for this is not true—though you can try for it. If you are visiting an afflicted person, over-hopeful chatter gets you off the hook, if your visit isn't too long, but you can tell by the expression on people's faces that they know you're playing the game to help yourself, not to help them.

It's also no use pretending that God isn't in it or involved. If He isn't, then He is only present in buttercups, and simply divine with daisies, and who wants that sort of twaddle—not a person in pain. And it's no good saying that suffering sanctifies you and pain redeems you. Sometimes it does, sometimes it doesn't. You need some energy even for sanctification, and suffering or intense pain strips you, so that you don't have much energy left. You need every bit you've got just to hold on.

But there is something more. I have met some afflicted people who were not especially saintly or particularly pious. They certainly did not ask God to forgive them. Many felt it was *their* job to forgive *Him*. But they knew that the centre of the world was not in the world, and in their affliction and in their pain they managed to fix their attention on God and keep it there.

Lionel Blue, *Bright Blue: Rabbi Lionel Blue's Thoughts for the Day*
(London: British Broadcasting Corporation, 1985), p. 61.
© Lionel Blue. Used by permission.

Preach faith until you have it.

Peter Böhler (c. 1712–1775)

Tell me why!

God, explain to me
the cruelty of your world!
Make sense of those
who make no sense!
Tell me why the innocent die
and evil people live
to kill again!
Tell me why the faithful
are shunned,
and the self-righteous
point their fingers!

Tell me why the wounded
are wounded,
and sorrow falls
on the shoulder of sorrow!
Tell me why the abused
are abused,
and the victims
victimized!
Tell me why the rains
come to the drowning,
and aftershocks
follow earthquakes.
O God, is this any way
to run a world?
O Merciful One, let us rest
between tragedies!
Speak to us
for we are your people.
Speak to us of hope
for the hopeless
and love for the unloved
and homes for the homeless
and dignity for the dying
and respect for the disdained.

ASCENSION

Acts 1:1–11   Ephesians 1:15–23

Psalm 47   Luke 24:44–53

Leading captivity captive

Now the mystery of Christ's death is fulfilled, victory is won, and the cross, the sign of triumph, is raised on high. He who gives us the noble gifts of life and a kingdom has ascended into heaven, *leading captivity captive.* Therefore the same command is repeated. Once more the gates of heaven must open for him. Our guardian angels, who have now become his escorts, order them to be flung wide so that he may enter and regain his former glory. But he is not recognized in the soiled garments of our life, in clothes reddened by the winepress of human sin. Again the escorting angels are asked: *Who is this King of glory?* The answer is no longer, *The strong one, mighty in battle* but, *The Lord of hosts,* he who has gained power over the whole universe, who has recapitulated all things in himself, who is above all things, who has restored all creation to its former state: *He is the King of glory.*

> Augustine of Hippo, from a homily on the First Letter of John (*Tract. 4.4–6*), in *A Word in Season: Monastic Lectionary for the Divine Office, III: Easter,* ed. Friends of Henry Ashworth (Riverdale, Md.: Exordium Books, 1983), pp. 173–74.

Perspective

Ascension means a
God-like view of things,
Rising above our usual
Limitations.
Rise, then, and know
The glory of a life
Set free from fear.

> Ann Lewin, from *Flashes of Brightness* (Peterborough: Foundery Press, 2001), p. 20. © 2001 Trustees for Methodist Church Purposes. Used by permission.

The future of God in human hands

Most forms of Christianity believe that God is not God without humanity since God took humanity upon himself and became human in Jesus Christ. This humanity of God is interpreted and lived in many different ways, with a variety of implications for human responsibility. A systematic analysis of all these ways is impossible here; I want to highlight that sort of interpretation of incarnation that loads human beings with awesome responsibility, which, for God's sake, should not be refused. The first step is to remember that the incarnation of God in Jesus is not to be regarded merely as a single secluded event, a special privileging of one man over against all others, but rather as the pivotal revelation, realized in one person, of the relation God intends and seeks to have with all humanity. Incarnation means that God chooses to be intimately related to humanity, through flesh and blood, in historic community. God's oneness with humanity is not merely a triumphant transformation of humanity, empowering and raising it by divine indwelling to a level beyond itself. That might be read as closer to the abolition of humanity than the affirmation of it. Instead, God is united with human being by becoming as vulnerable to human beings as human beings in general are.

This is one reason why the actual story of Jesus seems to me to be so important. There God is one with human beings not ideally but actually, by being in the hands of human beings, at their disposal, from the cradle to the cross. One of the central but most overlooked ways in which God shares human vulnerability and is in human hands is that Jesus was and is talked about, interpreted in an endless variety of ways. That is to say, others decide who he is and what he counts for. There is no way by which we can avoid responsibility in this process of interpreting Jesus, which will last, so some Christians say, until he is revealed in the coming glory. Meantime, he is there to be talked about and, if you wish, to be laughed at—or with.

Haddon Willmer, ed., in *20/20 Visions: The Futures of Christianity in Britain* (London: SPCK, 1992), pp. 147–48.

The early church's belief in the Ascension can be read as its refusal to allow its Lord to be localized or spatially restricted. The Ascension in its simplest terms means that Jesus is mobile. He is not a baal, but the Lord of all history.

Harvey Cox

To distance oneself [from the biblical text] means to be new to the text (to be a stranger, a first-time visitor to the text), to be amazed by everything, especially by those details that repeated readings have made seem so logical and natural. It is necessary to take up the Bible as a new book, a book that has never been heard or read before.

Elsa Tamez

Who is this king of glory?

By offering himself to God the Father as the firstfruits of all who are dead and buried, [Christ] gave us a way of entry into heaven and was himself the first human being the inhabitants of heaven ever saw. The angels in heaven, knowing nothing of the sacred and profound mystery of the incarnation, were astonished at his coming and almost thrown into confusion by an event so strange and unheard of. *Who is this coming from Edom?* they asked; that is, from the earth. But the Spirit did not leave the heavenly throng ignorant of the wonderful wisdom of God the Father. Commanding them to open the gates of heaven in honor of the King and Master of the universe, he cried out: *Lift up your gates, you princes, and be lifted up you everlasting doors, that the king of glory may come in.*

Cyril of Alexandria, *Commentary on St. John's Gospel,* Book 9, in
Christ Our Light: Patristic Readings on Gospel Themes, I:
Advent–Pentecost, trans. and ed. Friends of Henry Ashworth
(Riverdale, Md.: Exordium Books, 1981), p. 241.

Swing low, sweet chariot

Swing low, sweet chariot,
so that Christ may take the reins.
Swing low, sweet chariot,
lift him up to where he reigns,
above the rulers of the world.

Swing low, sweet Spirit,
sweep earth and ocean with your wind.
Swing low, sweet Spirit,
blow your gifts along our streets,
and litter our land with all your signs.

Swing low, sweet Spirit,
take Christ's people in your power.
Swing low, sweet Spirit,
pour Christ's own ways into their homes,
and do not be absent from their work.

Swinging Spirit, sweetening wind,
blow low across our darkening world,
pick people up and lift them high,
until they can see that all is yours,
that in your light,
the cities smile,
the deserts bloom,
the oceans live,
and earth itself
is once again your ball.

Graham Cook (ed.), from 'Swing low, sweet chariot,' in *Say One for Me: Prayer Handbook 1990* (London: United Reformed Church, 1990), Easter 6. © Graham Cook 1990. Used by permission.

The hope, the risk, and the wonder

Christians understand that the glory of human existence is that human beings have the freedom and power to develop in the image of God. God took a risk in creation. Love is always threatened by the misery caused by the misuse of our human powers in selfishness, stupidity and ignorance. Whatever our religious faith, and whatever our own perceptions of the reality of God, we need to come together to address pressing human questions, making our contribution from what resources for human being we have perceived and are seeking to develop.

Our humane mission now—as Christians and as faithful believers in God—is not primarily to convert but to share; not to conflict but to collaborate. We are not called to write off our neighbours but to seek to understand and to contribute some shareable insights into our mission, our hopes and our enjoyments. Where that will get us, God only knows.

The assurance of faith includes the promise that in the end we shall know as we are known. Thus it will prove to be the case that personal human beings—and our like anywhere else in any universe of universes—are not molecular accidents evolved by chance. Our source and resource is not an energy that exploded out of nothing on the way to collapsing into nothing. The mystery is far greater than that. Hence the hope, the risk and the wonder of going on.

David Jenkins, *The Calling of a Cuckoo: Not Quite an Autobiography* (London and New York: Continuum, 2002), p. 175.

Lines from a hymn

On the day of Your ascension may we be lifted up;
with the new bread may we be His remembrance.

Ephrem the Syrian, from *Ephrem the Syrian: Hymns,* trans. and intro. Kathleen E. McVey; from The Classics of Western Spirituality (New York: Paulist Press, 1989), p. 94. © 1989 by Kathleen E. McVey, Paulist Press, Inc., New York/Mahwah, N.J. Used with permission of Paulist Press. *www.paulistpress.com*

Ascension

Why do you stand looking up at the sky?—Acts 1:11

It wasn't just wind chasing
thin, gunmetal clouds
across a loud sky;
it wasn't the feeling that one might ascend
on that excited air,
rising like a trumpet note,

and it wasn't just my sister's water breaking,
her crying out,
the downward draw of blood and bone . . .

It was all of that,
mud and new grass
pushing up through melting snow,
the lilac in bud by my front door
bent low
by last week's ice storm.

Now the new mother, that leaky vessel,
begins to nurse her child,
beginning the long good-bye.

SEVENTH SUNDAY OF EASTER

Acts 1:6–14   1 Peter 4:12–14; 5:6–11

Psalm 68:1–10, 32–35   John 17:1–11

The Shaker vision

In the Shaker vision everything is gift—not just those realities of our lives which arrest our attention, but all the literally countless realities from the smallest to the greatest. Ultimately we realize all is the Gift of the all-giving God Who is Love.

. . . For Believers the ultimate Gift is God-in-Christ giving Himself to us all so that we can become anointed with the Divine Nature and so live the Christlife. It is a gift to fill our need, felt in our urge to transcend the limits of natural existence and death. To accept the gift is to acknowledge we are not absolute in ourselves—in a Shaker phrase, to dethrone ourselves as our own lead, and accept the Divine Lead. Taking the Christ Gift means an active embrace of a new kind of life to rise out of mortal life and into the Resurrection. This involves the essential Christian commitment to *metanoia* expressed in the mystery of the Cross: dying to (the false sense of) self and rising into unity with the Eternal Christ, thus becoming a single new kind of human being. Shakers speak of this as *crossing one's own nature,* taking up the cross against that life which leads only to death, and following Christ into the regeneration of Eternal Life.

Robley Edward Whitson, ed., *The Shakers: Two Centuries of Spiritual
Reflection* (Ramsey, N.J.: Paulist Press, 1983), pp. 258–59.

Prayer of a martyr

Thank you, Christ, for this. Take care of me, because it is for you that I am suffering. Lord, protect your servants: stay with them to the end, and then they will be able to glorify your name for all eternity.

Euplus (d. c. 304)

The here and there Jesus

Are you here or there, Jesus?
I had heard you were here:
   challenging my narrow mindedness,
bleeding and in pain,
   embracing vulnerability.

They told me you'd gone, but where to:
   obscured by clouds,
shining with glory,
or encompassing the cosmos?
Are you here or there Jesus?

The sun rises and I look for you;
   from east to west I search.
The day ends and I need you still,
   in light and dark alike.
Are you here or there Jesus?

In trying to be faithful,
   perhaps I've boxed you in to here and now
   and confined you to one body.
I'm afraid you'll go away.
If you're there are you still here, Jesus?

Your glory is hard to understand
   with its other-worldly mystery
   and cosmic far-away feel.
Yet you offer me this glory too
   as a sign of down-to-earth holiness.

Could you be here *and* there, Jesus?
I know you embrace my humanity
but perhaps a bit of your mountain top glory
   would make me shine with joy.
Perhaps you can be the here *and* there Jesus.

Janet Lees, in *Edged with Fire: Prayer Handbook 1994,* ed. Kate
Compston (London: United Reformed Church, 1994), Week 20. ©
Janet Lees 1994. Used by permission.

The way of suffering

If God, too, is one who suffers, then suffering is not simply something bad to which one can surrender or stand up in resistance. It becomes instead a reality that has something to do with the far-near God and that fits into God's incomprehensible love. The way of suffering that is not just tolerated but freely accepted, the way of the passion, becomes therefore part of the disciple's way of life.

Suffering does not necessarily separate us from God. It may actually put us in touch with the mystery of reality. To follow Christ means to take part in his life. According to Paul's Letter to the Colossians, it is the believers' task to 'complete what is lacking in Christ's afflictions' (1:24). In Christianity suffering is not explained, for example, on the basis of Satan's power or the sin of humans; it is viewed positively for the sake of Christ. At times it is even transfigured, as the place of encounter with God where we make a gift (sacrifice) and God invites us to her/himself by bearing the suffering with us.

> Dorothee Soelle, *The Silent Cry: Mysticism and Resistance,* trans.
> Barbara and Martin Rumscheidt (Minneapolis: Fortress Press, 2001),
> p. 138.

Still another energy derived from suffering is the manner in which letting pain be pain links us with others. All social movements and organization were born of pain.

> Matthew Fox

Spiritual discipline

The spiritual life is a gift. It is the gift of the Holy Spirit, who lifts us up into the kingdom of God's love. But to say that being lifted up into the kingdom of love is a divine gift does not mean that we wait passively until the gift is offered to us. Jesus tells us to set our hearts on the kingdom. Setting our hearts on something involves not only serious aspiration but also strong determination. A spiritual life requires human effort. The forces that keep pulling us back into a worry-filled life are far from easy to overcome. Here we touch the question of the other side of discipleship. The practice of a spiritual discipline makes us more sensitive to the small, gentle voice of God. The prophet Elijah did not encounter God in the mighty wind or in the earthquake or in the fire, but in the small voice. . . .

Through a spiritual discipline we prevent the world from filling our lives to such an extent that there is no place left to listen. A spiritual discipline sets us free to pray or, to say it better, allows the Spirit of God to pray in us.

Henri J. M. Nouwen, from *Circles of Love,* ed. John Garvey
(London: Darton, Longman & Todd, 1990), p. 41.

Who is like you?

Who is like you, my Lord Jesus Christ,
my sweet love?
You are boundless in might and majesty,
and yet you care for the humble.
Who can compare with you in power, Lord?
Yet you choose the weak of the world.
Who can be as gracious as you are?
You laid the foundations of heaven and earth,
and their thrones and powers worship you,
and yet you seek your pleasure with human beings.

Gertrude the Great, from *Exercitia Spiritualia Septem,* in *The Heart of
Love: Prayers of German Women Mystics,* trans. Brian Pickett
(Slough: St. Paul Publications, 1991), p. 77. © Brian Pickett.
Used by permission.

PENTECOST

Acts 2:1–21   1 Corinthians 12:3b–13

Psalm 104:24–34, 35b   John 7:37–39

The gift of the Holy Spirit

It is clear in the New Testament that the Spirit is a gift, not a reward. The descent of the Spirit upon Jesus at his baptism in the Jordan, often depicted as a dove with wings outspread sailing downward toward him, comes before his initiatory period of testing in the wilderness, not after. In most initiation sequences, one would expect the order to be reversed; after testing and trial, one is confirmed with a new cloak of blessing. But the empowerment of the Spirit is not earned, it is freely given. And so with the early church at Pentecost. It was not their courage or clarity that evoked the blessing of the Spirit, for they were vulnerable and confused. The Spirit is a gift, not a possession. The Spirit inspires and gives the breath of life to the church, but the church does not encompass, contain, or own the Holy Spirit. The path of the Spirit certainly does not lead us only from church to church. For those of us who are Christians, we understand it to be the Holy Spirit that drives us beyond the comforts and certainties of what we know to the very boundaries where Christians and Hindus and Muslims meet.

> Diana L. Eck, *Encountering God: A Spiritual Journey from Bozeman to Banaras* (Boston: Beacon Press, 1993), p. 134.

The Holy Spirit is the source of community and the Spirit's work is more related to the building of community than to the edification of the isolated individual.

> Jim Wallis

Litany

    O Rain from heaven,

        Temper us, we beseech Thee!

    O Gate of heaven,

        Open us, we beseech Thee!

O Cave of the heart,
    Illumine us, we beseech Thee!
O Waters of salvation,
    Prove us, we beseech Thee!
O Hidden Garden,
    Enfold us, we beseech Thee!
O Beauty of the deep,
    Sound us, we beseech Thee!
O Guardian of the Dance,
    Choose us, we beseech Thee!
O Desire of the Eternal Hills,
    Enchant us, we beseech Thee!

Meinrad Craighead, *The Litany of the Great River* (New York: Paulist Press, 1991). © Meinrad Craighead 1991. Used by permission.

The mystery of knowledge

A limpid sound arises amidst the silence; a trail of pure colour drifts through the glass; a light glows for a moment in the depths of the eyes I love. . . .

Three things, tiny, fugitive: a song, a sunbeam, a glance . . .

So, at first, I thought they had entered into me in order to remain there and be lost in me.

On the contrary: they took possession of me, and bore me away.

For if this plaint of the air, this tinting of the light, this communication of a soul were so tenuous and so fleeting, it was only that they might penetrate the more deeply into my being, might pierce through to that final depth where all the human faculties are so closely bound together as to become a single point. Through the sharp tips of the three arrows which had pierced me the world itself invaded my being and had drawn me back into itself.

We imagine that in our sense-perceptions external reality humbly presents itself to us in order to serve us, to help in the building up of our integrity. But this is merely the surface of the mystery of knowledge; the deeper truth is that when the world reveals itself to us it draws us into itself: it causes us to flow outwards into something belonging to it everywhere present in it and more perfect than it.

Pierre Teilhard de Chardin, *Hymn of the Universe* (London: Collins, 1965; New York: Harper & Brothers, 1965), pp. 79–80.

To make things new that never were

We name you wind, power, force, and then,
    imaginatively, "Third Person."
We name you and you blow . . .
    blow hard,
    blow cold,
    blow hot,
    blow strong,
    blow gentle,
    blow new . . .
Blowing the world out of nothing to abundance,
blowing the church out of despair to new life,
blowing little David from shepherd boy to messiah,
blowing to make things new that never were.
    So blow this day, wind,
        blow here and there, power,
        blow even us, force,
Rush us beyond ourselves,
Rush us beyond our hopes,
Rush us beyond our fears, until we enact your newness in the world.
    Come, come spirit. Amen.

Walter Brueggemann, *Awed to Heaven, Rooted in Earth: Prayers of
Walter Brueggemann* (Minneapolis: Fortress Press, 2003), p. 167.
© 2003 Augsburg Fortress. Used by permission.

The background of resurrection is always impossibility. And with impossibility staring us in the face, the prelude to resurrection is invariably doubt, confusion, strife, and the cynical smile which is our defence against them. Resurrection is always the defiance of the absurd.

Harry Williams

Exuberant Spirit of God

Exuberant Spirit of God,
bursting with brightness of flame
into the coldness of our lives

to warm us with a passion for justice and beauty
we praise you.

Exuberant Spirit of God,
sweeping us out of the dusty corners of our apathy
to breathe vitality into our struggles for change,
we praise you.

Exuberant Spirit of God,
speaking words that leap over barriers of mistrust
to convey messages of truth and new understanding,
we praise you.

Exuberant Spirit of God,
flame
   wind
     speech,
burn, breathe, speak in us;
fill your world with justice and with joy.

Jan Berry, in *Bread of Tomorrow: Praying with the World's Poor,* ed.
Janet Morley (London: SPCK/Christian Aid, 1992), p. 145.
© Jan Berry. Used by permission.

The Holy Spirit is a very political bird—one which doesn't stop for border guards. The authoritative lines are crossed. Indeed in Pentecost those lines are blown right off the spiritual map.

Bill Wylie Kellerman

TRINITY SUNDAY

Genesis 1:1–2:4a   2 Corinthians 13:11–13

Psalm 8   Matthew 28:16–20

'Behold, it was very good'

Constable is, and sought to be, a painter of creation. He is the painter of Genesis 1. If we wanted an epigraph for his work it would be: 'and God saw all that God had made and behold it was very good.' . . .

Art is a school of attention and, as Simone Weil put it, prayer consists in attention. All great art helps us to see, attend to, sense, the depth, mystery and glory of God's creation. This is especially true of the great landscape painters of the beginning of the nineteenth century. In the light of their work let us pose the question, 'Why a world?' Why this material sensual place, this interweaving of quarks and gluons, which we inhabit? Why blood, bone, semen and faeces? Why senses?

. . . The senses are what allow us to explore the world we are given, but I want to go further and suggest that God chooses this form of reality, and endows us with senses, to celebrate and to explore the mystery and the magic of God's own creation. Not just that we celebrate and explore it, but that God celebrates and explores us.

T. J. Gorringe, *The Education of Desire: Towards a Theology of the Senses* (London: SCM Press, 2001), pp. 1–4.

The dance of love

> The dance of love is in our bones,
> it gives life purpose, shape and form,
> it challenges our vast concerns
> and questions each deceptive norm.
>
> This cosmic dance inflames each star
> and gives the supernova light,
> it fashions ethics and informs
> each human thought, each human right.

This dance, the universal force,
that brings all living art to be,
will never cease or lose its power,
this ground of loving certainty.

When it comes to the crunch

A friend of mine won a competition to write a short play for radio. It had to be three minutes long, witty and wry, and use sound effects. He chose to write on the first three chapters of Genesis, and his play featured two lowly 'angels' who were back-room boys. They were in God's workshop and their task was to 'dub' sound on to creation. The story tells us that God created fish, birds, animals, seas, rivers—but not a thing about the sounds they make.

The two angels set about their task grumbling, 'It's all right for 'im upstairs to say "Let there be birds," but who's gotta put the soundtrack on a flock of bleedin' seagulls—muggins 'ere. And it must be different from the parrot, the sparrow, and the cormorant. . . .' As they talk about their work . . . attention focuses on a box in the corner of the sound workshop. 'What's that box for?' asks the junior, apprentice angel. 'Ah, you don't want to touch that,' replies the senior angel. 'That box is full of sounds you don't want to hear—a child crying, a mother dying, the sound of war, screams, the rattle of death. Once you open the box, you'll release the noises of chaos, and you'll never get them back in.'

When the senior angel leaves for a coffee break, the apprentice goes to the box and inspects it more closely. It looks such a nice box. How can one small box contain so many sounds? He prises open the lid and lifts it slightly. He hears no scream, nor the sound of war, only the crunch of teeth into a delicious, crisp, green apple.

Incarnation

Medicine has said, "The body is a machine,
cells organised by genes and nutrition.
It often needs repair."
The Church has said, "The body is a sin,
frail, a burden to the spiritual life.
It must be subjugated."
Philosophers have said, "The body
is the servant of mental processes.
We think therefore we are."
The market place has said, "The body
is big business, to be measured in dollars.
We sell it beauty and youth."
The body says, "Listen to me!
I am the supreme gift of the divine.
I am the miracle of love made by love.
I am celebration! I am dance!
I am the pleasure of God!"

> Joy Cowley, *Psalms for the Road* (Wellington, New Zealand: Catholic
> Supplies [N.Z.] Ltd., 2002), p. 99. Used by permission.

When "science" meets "religion"

Let me say that a close and aware rereading of these chapters [Genesis 1 and 2]
shows that the critique of biblical tradition on ecological grounds, that it has
ignored the value and integrity of nature, is well-taken indeed. Incidentally, I
repeated the . . . critique of this inheritance at an ecological conference some
years ago on the same platform with Carl Sagan. After my talk, he shook my
hand warmly and said—he was a very charming man—"I'm so glad to hear
someone from religion criticizing religion!" I thanked him and said I would be
equally glad to hear someone from science criticizing science. He said
"Humph!" and walked away.

> Langdon Gilkey, *Blue Twilight: Nature, Creationism, and American
> Religion* (Minneapolis: Fortress Press, 2001), p. 69.

Genesis 1

Break into our darkness,
formless God,
with the light
of your presence.

Split the cosmic silence
and speak in the void
of our shapeless lives.

Plant seeds of love
in barren hearts;
nourish us with your
life-giving Spirit.

Mould us, so we become
the image of yourself,
and every face
of our universe
displays the stamp
of your creative love.

Then help us rest
in you and see
that LIFE is good.

Carol Dixon, from *Worship Live* no. 26 (London: Stainer & Bell, Summer 2003), p. 11. © Carol Dixon. Used by permission.

Personality as relationship

'In God we live, and move and have our being.' In Christian understanding, there are three persons in one God, so united that each one shares totally with the other two. The Divine Persons are essentially relations, as distinct from being Persons who relate. We are made in the image of God. Essentially, we too are, insofar as we are in relationship with the rest of creation. Our personality is not something we possess and with which we then relate to other people and things: personality is something we discover through our relationships and is itself a relationship. . . .

When studying theology, I found the Doctrine of the Trinity the most difficult, boring and irrelevant to everyday life. Now it seems to me the most exciting and relevant. All doctrines are imperfect expressions of something intuited, they are examples of faith seeking understanding. When the understanding tries to operate without the intuition, its formulations become sterile.

Gerard W. Hughes, *God, Where Are You?* (London: Darton,
Longman & Todd, 1997), p. 257.

Nothing can be itself without being in communion with everything else, nor can anything truly be the other without first acquiring a capacity for interior presence to itself.

Thomas Berry

Reverence for creation

I was trained as a biologist, and I can appreciate the challenge and the technical mastery involved in isolating, understanding, and manipulating genes. I can think of fascinating things I'd like to do as a genetic engineer. But I only have to stand still for a minute and watch the outcome of thirty million years' worth of hummingbird evolution transubstantiated before my eyes into nest and egg to get knocked down to size. I have held in my hand the germ of a plant engineered to grow, yield its crop, and then murder its own embryos, and there I glimpsed the malevolence that can lie in the heart of a profiteering enterprise. There once was a time when Thoreau wrote, 'I have great faith in seed. Convince me that you have a seed there, and I am prepared to expect wonders.'

By the power vested in everything living, let us keep to that faith. I'm a scientist who thinks it wise to enter the doors of creation not with a lion-tamer's whip and chair, but with the reverence humankind has traditionally summoned for entering places of worship: a temple, a mosque, or a cathedral. A sacred grove, as ancient as time.

Barbara Kingsolver, *Small Wonder* (London: Faber & Faber, 2002).

'Almighty Mother'?

'Inclusive language' does not have to mean replacing 'Almighty Father with (an equally problematic) 'Almighty Mother'. I have found that to discover how and why the feminine has been omitted from our way of addressing God is to discover also what else has been left out. To release ourselves from the habit of always using certain predictable (and perhaps scarcely noticed) formulae for the beginning of a prayer, may free the imagination to explore the unimaginable ways in which God reaches us.

Janet Morley, *All Desires Known* (London: SPCK, 1992), p. xi.

PROPER 4

Ordinary Time 9

Sunday between May 29 and June 4 inclusive (if after Trinity Sunday)

Genesis 6:9–22; 7:24; 8:14–19   Romans 1:16–17; 3:22b–28 (29–31)

Psalm 46   Matthew 7:21–29

No more sinking sand
(After reading Matthew 7:24–29/September 30, 1993)

God of heaven and lord of earth,
Tamer of heaven, lover of earth,
    sovereign over the waters that surge,
    provider for birds, beasts, and fish,
    chooser of Israel and commander of all humanity.
Your vistas remind us
    of how close and small we keep our horizons,
    how much we blink at your power, and wince from your justice,
    how much we waver in the face of your commanding mercy.
You, you, you only, you, God of heaven and lord of earth.
Comes the rain upon our parade,
    and the floods upon our nations,
    and the winds upon our personal configurations,
Comes your shattering and your reconfiguring
    in ways we doubt or we fear.
    We discover yet again, how sandy we are,
    with the quaking of our foundations
        and our fantasized firmaments.
    We are filled with trembling and nightmares that disturb.
And then you-rock-solid-stable-reliable-sure
    You rock against our sand,
    You rock of ages,

You rock that is higher than us treading water,
You rock of compassion—
be compassionate even for us, our loved ones
and all our needy neighbors,
You rock of abidingness for our sick,
and for those long loved, lingering memories,
dead and in your care,
You rock of justice for the nations,
fed up with our hate,
exhausted by the greed of our several tribes,
You rock of communion in our loneliness,
rock of graciousness in our many modes of gracelessness.
Come be present even here and there, and there and there,
Move us from our sandy certitudes to your grace-filled risk,
Move us to become more rock-like
in compassion and abidingness and justice,
Move us to be more like you in our neighborliness
and in our self-regard.
Yes, yes, yes—move us that we may finally
stand on the solid rock, no more sinking sand.
God of heaven. Lord of earth,
hear our resolve, heal our unresolve,
that we may finish in sure trust and in glad obedience.
We already know what to do by our careful pondering
of you. Amen.

Walter Brueggemann, *Awed to Heaven, Rooted in Earth: Prayers of
Walter Brueggemann,* ed. Edwin Searcy (Minneapolis: Augsburg
Fortress, 2003), pp. 16–17. © 2003 Augsburg Fortress.
Used by permission.

It's fundamental to my belief in God that he or she discloses him- or herself to all people in all cultures at all times, because all human beings are capable of having an apprehension of God.

Richard Harries

A question of authority

The Christian movement, as far back as we can trace it, is a *missionary* movement: that is, it works on the assumption that it has something to say that is communicable beyond its present boundaries and is humanly attractive or compelling across those boundaries. . . .

In giving to the outcast, the powerless, the freedom to take part in renewing the world and setting aside the existing tyranny of faceless powers and human betrayals, God brings life out of emptiness, reality out of nothing: Jesus Christ, as the bodily presence of that summons, the concrete medium for that gift to be given, is the presence in our world of the absolute creative resource of God, God's capacity to make the difference between something and nothing.

Rowan Williams, *On Christian Theology* (Oxford: Blackwell, 2000),
pp. 230, 231.

The house on the rock

You know, I have this feeling
that the wise man who built on the rock,
had previously built a house on the sand.
He'd learned that sand meant wasted effort
and solid rock was the way to go.
How much wiser that man was
than the one who built on the rock
simply because he didn't know
the sand was there.
Mind you, for people like me,
that wisdom is hard won.
I built several houses on the sand
before the message got home.
Maybe that's why I value rock so much.
At times, I've heard people say
that they don't know why God
allows the pain of sin in this world.
Well, if I substitute *sand* for *sin*,

I think I have something close
to an answer.

Joy Cowley, *Psalms for the Road* (Wellington, New Zealand:
Catholic Supplies [N.Z.] Ltd., 2002), p. 31. Used by permission.

The Ark

I called the community l'Arche after Noah's ark which saved humanity from the flood. The community of l'Arche wants to provide a refuge for people with mental handicaps, who can so quickly be drowned in the waters of our competitive society.... Here we touch on the paradox of l'Arche.... People with mental handicaps, so limited physically and intellectually, are often more gifted than others when it comes to the things of the heart and to relationships. In a mysterious way they can lead us to the home of our hearts. Their intellectual handicaps are counterbalanced by a special openness and trust in others. Certain social conventions and ideas about what is important mean nothing to them. They live closer to what really matters. In our competitive societies, which put so much emphasis on power and strength, they have great difficulty in finding their place; they are losers in every competition. But in their thirst and their gift for friendship and for communion, the weaker people in society can touch and transform the strong, if the strong are only prepared to listen to them. In our fragmented, often broken societies, in our towns made of steel and glass and loneliness, people with disabilities can act as a kind of cement that binds people together. This is their role in society. They have a special part to play in the healing of hearts and in destroying the barriers which separate people from one another and prevent them from living happily and humanly.

Jean Vanier, *Our Journey Home: Rediscovering a Common Humanity
Beyond Our Differences,* trans. Maggie Parham (London:
Hodder & Stoughton, 1997), pp. ix, x–xi.

The job

Enter the first applicant.

'You understand that this is a simple test we are giving you before we offer you the job you have applied for?'
'Yes.'

'Well, what is two plus two?'
'Four.'

Enter the second applicant.

'Are you ready for the test?'
'Yes.'
'Well, what is two plus two?'
'Whatever the boss says it is.'

The second applicant got the job.

Which comes first, orthodoxy or truth?

Anthony de Mello, S.J., *The Song of the Bird* (Anand, India: Gujarat
Sahitya Prakash, 1982), pp. 95–96.

One can believe in God with a very complete set of arguments, yet not have any faith that makes a difference in living.

Georgia Harkness

Proper 5

Ordinary Time 10

Sunday between June 5 and 11 inclusive (if after Trinity Sunday)

| Genesis 12:1–9 | Romans 4:13–25 |
| Psalm 33:1–12 | Matthew 9:9–13, 18–26 |

Touch

Touch is one of the most immediate and direct of the senses. The language of touch is a language in itself. Touch is also subtle and distinctive and holds within itself great refinement of memory. A concert pianist came to visit a friend. He asked her if she would like him to play something for her. He said, 'At the moment I have a lovely piece from Schubert in my hands.'

John O'Donohue, *Anam Cara* (London: Bantam Books, 1999), p. 101.

Born-again sinner

Why is it that religion makes some people so judgemental, so miserable, so legalistic, so fanatical, so bigoted, so violent? Why is it that so many wars around the world are fuelled by religion? And why is it that some people are better human beings *before* they become religious? Are these not reasons to shun religion? Well my answer would be 'yes' if by religion is meant the kind of religion which is evident in our scripture [Matthew 9] today. No religion is better than bad religion. . . .

Jesus was not interested in making people religious, but leading them to a loving relationship with himself, and therefore with God. He offered forgiveness and healing to sin-sick souls as the basis of new life, opening up a path of discipleship, compassion and mystical union with God. This means that once I let go my own self-righteous stance and admit myself a sinful, violent, self-centred individual, then open my life to the forgiveness and healing of Christ, a

178

new principle of life is implanted. This is called being 'born again' of the Spirit of God.

Brother Ramon, S.S.F., *The Way of Love: Following Christ through Lent to Easter* (London: Marshall Pickering, 1994), pp. 107–8.

Travel suddenly opens the windows of the soul to the reality of God in other people.

Eric James

Sin that drains our life-blood

Christianity has much to say about how the incompleteness of death may be overcome, but for the moment let us confine ourselves to the image of sin as a haemorrhage. It is of course a strong image, but justified, I believe—most worryingly, perhaps, not so much with regard to conspicuous wickedness, as in any sort of situation where a particular fault, not necessarily itself immoral, starts to eat away at the soul: to drain us of our life-blood, and so eventually destroy our whole personality.

Let me give three brief examples from people I have known, all academics, all distinguished clerics, and all now dead. I think of one who became so obsessed with frustrated ambition that it poisoned every relationship into which he entered, and indeed eventually led to his own death. I think of another whose failure to face his own homosexuality precluded him from an effective ministry because that very failure caused difficulties in his treatment of women. Or I think of a third, whose desperate insecurity led to endless public parading of his achievements; considerable though they were, the net result was that his character was seen by others as simply that of a vain and foolish man.

Three examples chosen at random. Would that such phenomena were rare, but they are not. It can happen even to those who, as in these three cases, are consciously seeking to follow the Christian gospel. So let me end by setting this question squarely before you: Is there a 'haemorrhage' in your own life that needs to be faced, or one which you can help a friend to face? If so, face it sooner rather than later; for only that way can the healing touch of Christ's garment, as in the story, stop the draining of your blood, the draining of your resources for goodness, and bring you back to a full life, restore you to health. There is then a miracle, a miracle that can also be ours.

David Brown, *The Word to Set You Free: Living Faith and Biblical Criticism* (London: SPCK, 1995), pp. 126–27.

It is as though a strong wind had begun to blow, opening eyes and loosening tongues, shifting stances, enabling arms to reach out to new embraces and hands to take up other tools, impelling feet to take other steps, raising the voice so its song and its lament might be heard. Woman begins to take her place as agent of history.

Ivone Gebara

Shame is not the end of the story

It's this whole mess of blame and guilt and separation and bad judgment and fear and loathing and the voices that haunt us from the past saying . . . you don't fit . . . you're not wanted . . . get lost . . . that the Bible calls sin. Sin is living out of our fears. Sin is not being free. It's the seepage of our whole sense of ourselves. It's feeling like the woman with the haemorrhage of blood. I imagine that she might have felt something like this:

> Shame, or not shame.
> I never know.
> I know that all the messages of flesh
> and blood scream at me, 'shame, you should feel shame,
> you are not clean, you do not measure up
> to what the standard is.'
> This seepage, slippage, flow and flood,
> this blood that comes and comes
> but will not come in proper places
> but shames and blames and bleeds
> upon the rags of pride and shame
> and stains and taints and taunts
> and shames and haunts the wretchedness
> of those who claim, or would absorb it.
> This blood, that I cannot contain
> that rises, swells, torments, distends,
> that weakens, wastes, defeats, unsexes,
> undermines and unacceptably lays low,
> this shame, this means that never finds an end,
> this blood, this flood, this torrent never spent,
> this shame, this shame, this shame.

But shame is not the end of the story. Or it needn't be. Like the woman, perhaps there is something else, some instinct, some deep desire or belief, even some despair, that says, ever so quietly . . . 'this isn't true. *This is not true.* THIS IS NOT THE WAY IT'S MEANT TO BE. THIS IS A LIE.' That small voice haunts us, drives us, to take a risk, to reach out, to touch the hem of a cloak, to claim back our humanity, our belonging, our life, to put an end to fear. That small voice is the voice of God!

Kathy Galloway, "Shame," in *Silence in Heaven: A Book of Women's Preaching*, ed. Susan Durber and Heather Walton (London: SCM Press, 1994), pp. 28–29. © Kathy Galloway 1994. Used by permission.

Prayer for life's journey

O Lord our God,

let *the shelter of your wings* give us hope.

Protect us and uphold us.

You will be the Support that upholds us

from childhood till the hair on our heads is grey.

When you are our strength we are strong,

but when our strength is our own we are weak.

In you our good abides for ever,

and when we turn away from it we turn to evil.

Let us come home at last to you, O Lord,

for fear that we be lost.

For in you our good abides and it has no blemish, since it is yourself.

Nor do we fear that there is no home to which we can return.

We fell from it;

but our home is your eternity

and it does not fall because we are away.

Augustine of Hippo (354–430), from *Confessions*, book 4.16, trans. R. S. Pine-Coffin (Harmondsworth, Middlesex: Penguin Books Ltd., 1961), pp. 89–90. (Line arrangement by compilers.)

PROPER 6

Ordinary Time 11

*Sunday between June 12 and 18
inclusive (if after Trinity Sunday)*

Genesis 18:1–15 (21:1–7)   Romans 5:1–8
Psalm 116:1–2, 12–19   Matthew 9:35–10:8 (9–23)

Suffering God

God does not explain why there is suffering—God suffers alongside us. God does
not explain why there is sorrow—God became the sorrowful one. God does not
explain why there is humiliation—God practises self-emptying love. We are no
longer alone in our vast loneliness. God is with us. We are no longer in solitude,
but rather in solidarity. The arguments from reason are silenced. It is the heart
that speaks. It tells of a God who does not ask questions but who acts, who does
not offer explanations but lives out an answer.

Leonardo Boff, *The Path to Hope*
(Maryknoll, N.Y.: Orbis Books, 1993).

Prayer

O One Who Laughs
at the incongruity
of life
and human nature,
name us not Mara,
which means Bitterness,
but name every one of us
Laughter,
for we laugh
at the incongruity
of our frail, fallible, gullible selves

formed in the image of You.
Laugh us to light-hearted life
in the Spirit
so that we are able to face
and endure
times of sacrifice
and doubt.
Sustain us in the tradition
which our matriarchs have established.
May we live by their vision
and move with their strength,
now and forever.
Amen.

Miriam Therese Winter, *WomanWisdom: A Feminist Lectionary and Psalter. Women of the Hebrew Scriptures: Part One* (New York: Crossroad, 1991), p. 28. © Medical Mission Sisters. Used by permission.

We're all lovable

As Paul put it, 'While we were still weak, . . . Christ died for irreverent folk . . . God confirms his love for us, because while we were still sinners Christ died for us' (Romans 5:6, 8). The point Paul is making (unlike some of his successors) is not that we are grotesquely sinful, but that God is astonishingly and unfailingly generous.

Jesus embodied God's good news not only in the words he said, but in the way he lived his life. He ate with ordinary, irreligious, 'unworthy' people, and he included among his followers the kind of people a religious teacher wasn't supposed to associate with—such as women and tax collectors. He stood up for these 'sinful' people against the religious authorities of the day, and finally, he even died to preserve the integrity of his good news. . . .

Paul was saying that, in Jesus, we discover something fundamentally important about God: God's love takes us up precisely when we are least deserving of it, when we are least lovable. God expresses his love specifically for those who don't deserve it.

God's love can do more than this—and does. The good news is that it will never do less. When you are least lovable, God says, 'I love you.' When you are least worthy, God says, 'You are forgiven.' Take yourself down to your lowest, most unattractive, most undeserving state—and there is God's love for you, as alive as ever.

William Countryman, *The Truth about Love: Re-Introducing the Good News* (London: Triangle, 1993), pp. 2–3.

It is the heart that is not yet sure of its God that is afraid to laugh in his presence.

George MacDonald

Meeting a leper on the way

God's word to [St] Francis was: Take the bitter for the sweet. He does not say that the bitter will become sweet, although it sometimes does. What is being recommended here is that we act out of God's values even though they are not yet ours on the level of our feelings. Let the bitterness of a thing, God says, stand as a cipher for sweetness; do not be put off by feelings of distaste, which are like a litmus test revealing what is still unredeemed in us. This is not an exhortation to become a doormat to the world, but a hint that our reactions have something to tell us about ourselves. The bitterness is a merciful revelation, telling us that we are still angry, proud, resentful, revengeful and so on. God is not saying that if it hurts, it must be good for us, but that to kiss our leper is to open our hearts. When we do this, we are most God-like, bringing joy to ourselves and those around us.

By accepting this reversal of our values, we surrender ourselves to the unknown. The Gospel is full of advice to do just this: Lose your life in order to save it, take up your cross and follow me, leave your family and discover your neighbour, set out on a journey with no provisions. Choose the bitter, God advises Francis, choose freely what must be. Instead of being constrained and imprisoned by circumstances, begin to discover freedom even within situations which you do not like and cannot change. Godly living is a learned skill, and like all skills is perfected by practice. If we wait until we feel like it, we shall never enter our leprosarium, never meet our leper, never come to that particular awareness of the sacred which can only be found by embracing reality. God is in what is—including the leper within. So we come full circle: the leper is us, and the leper is Christ.

Sister Frances Teresa, O.S.C., *Living the Incarnation: Praying with Francis and Clare of Assisi* (London: Darton, Longman & Todd, 1993), pp. 28–29.

Commissioning and blessing

Be bold in the claiming of the gospel for the whole creation.

Be brave in the lifting up of the life of God in every place.

Be firm in carrying the holy name of Jesus Christ into the palaces of worldly power.

Be gentle in the understanding of ourselves and one another.

And may the songs of the Creator sound with love in all the earth,

the tenderness of Christ Jesus cover the wounds of the people

and the truth in the Holy Spirit rise free in every age.

Amen.

> Dorothy McRae-McMahon, *Prayers for Life's Particular Moments*
> (London: SPCK, 2001), p. 95.

'Cure the sick'

David

David is in his late thirties, married with two young children. He lives in a dormitory town thirty miles from the city where he works. He works for a large computer company which has been 'downsizing' and his job is far from secure. Although he is well paid, he has a large mortgage and he works long hours on top of the drive to work. In addition, he works to constant deadlines and often has to bring work home at weekends. He is constantly tired and irritable, his family time is very limited, and his relationship with his wife, who is at home all day, is becoming difficult as communication becomes less. He knows that his way of life is damaging to his health, but feels caught in a trap of financial obligations and does not know who to talk to. If he talks to colleagues, they might think he cannot cope and his job will be at risk. But he doesn't know if he can tell his wife about the warning signals he has been getting about his health.

Questions

1. What kind of changes in his environment would be good news for David, and would contribute to his wholeness and to his hope for the future?
2. How do you think David feels about his life? How does his story make you feel?
3. Where do you see positive change and signs of hope in our society that will lead towards healing and justice for everyone?
4. What are you able to do in your own community to bring about healing? How

can you challenge the suffering and injustice that you see happening? Where are you able to share in the healing ministry in your own community?

Kathy Galloway, in *Praying for the Dawn: A Resource Book for the Ministry of Healing*, ed. Ruth Burgess and Kathy Galloway (Glasgow: Wild Goose Publications, 2000), p. 116. © 2000 Kathy Galloway. Used by permission of Wild Goose Publications, Glasgow G2 3DH Scotland.

Happy are they who know that discipleship simply means the life which springs from grace, and that grace simply means discipleship.

Dietrich Bonhoeffer

PROPER 7

Ordinary Time 12

*Sunday between June 19 and 25
inclusive (if after Trinity Sunday)*

Genesis 21:8–21
Psalm 86:1–10, 16–17

Romans 6:1b–11
Matthew 10:24–39

Deserts of the mind

Hagar's desert was a literal one. Today, ours are often deserts of the mind or heart. I drove into one on the interstate the day I left a job, after learning of the real reason the environment there had become intolerable. Why had my name been used in a lie? What possible motivation could other professionals have had to stoop so low? One had once been betrayed by male ministers. Was she, like Sarah perhaps, just passing it on? The repercussions lasted for months. Like Hagar, the only choice was to sit in the desert and wait for God. . . .

Hagar's story is for those desert times in our lives. They are the times when we have been enslaved or betrayed, when we feel expendable because the power structures of our lives seem oblivious to our gifts. Most of all, Hagar's story is for the times when we have been rejected or abandoned and need more than anything to hear God's voice. Because in those times God's presence is required to open our eyes, so that we can see the well that contains the water of consolation, mercy, and assurance.

Mary Zimmer, from "Hagar: God's Comfort and Protection," in *Sister
Images: Guided Meditations on the Stories of Biblical Women*
(Nashville: Abingdon Press, 1993), pp. 102, 105. Used by permission.

O God, help me! Lord, how You afflict your lovers!

Teresa of Avila

Life-giving conflict

[My] aim . . . is to describe some of the healthy, life-giving conflicts in which we are involved as moral and spiritual beings; or, in short, the conflicts in which we are involved in our relationship with God. If anybody made clear the necessity of such conflict, Jesus did. It was at the centre of his teaching, summed up in the warning "I came not to send peace but a sword," or "Whoever will save his life will lose it and whoever loses his life will save it." In everything he said he made clear that there is no such thing as an easy, comfortable, placid relationship with God. If we think that there is and that we have attained to it, that merely shows that we are asleep or dead or, perhaps more accurately, simply as yet unborn. We haven't begun to be disciples of Jesus unless we know something, a very little, of the joy— with which he endured the cross.

H. A. Williams, *Tensions* (London: Mitchell Beazley, 1976), p. 14.

Losing life and finding it

Stability means that I must not run away from where my battles are being fought, that I have to stand still where the real issues have to be faced. Obedience compels me to re-enact in my own life that submission of Christ himself, even though it may lead to suffering and to death. And *conversatio,* openness means that I must be ready to pick myself up, and start all over again in a pattern of growth which will not end until the day of my final dying. And all the time the journey is based on that Gospel paradox of losing life and finding it. . . . The goal of my changing life is not self-fulfilment, even though so much of the personal growth movement popular today seems to suggest that that is so. . . . My goal is Christ. And I shall attain that goal only by continuing struggle.

Esther de Waal, *Seeking God: The Way of St. Benedict*
(London: Fount, 1984), p. 78.

Via negativa

To reach satisfaction in all
    desire its possession in nothing.
To come to possess all
    desire the possession of nothing.
To arrive at being all

desire to be nothing.
To come to the knowledge of all
  desire the knowledge of nothing.
To come to the pleasure you have not
  you must go by a way in which you enjoy not.
To come to the knowledge you have not
  you must go by a way in which you know not.
To come to the possession you have not
  you must go by a way in which you possess not.
To come to be what you are not
  you must go by a way in which you are not.
When you turn toward something
  you cease to cast yourself upon the all.
For to go from all to the all
  you must deny yourself of all in all.
And when you come to the possession of the all
  you must possess it without wanting anything.
Because if you desire to have something in all
  your treasure in God is not purely your all.

> John of the Cross, *The Ascent of Mount Carmel,* bk. 1, ch. 13.11, in
> *John of the Cross: Selected Writings,* edited with an introduction by
> Kieran Kavanaugh, O.C.D., from The Classics of Western Spirituality,
> © 1987 by the Washington Province of Discalced Carmelite Friars,
> Inc. (Mahwah, N.J.: Paulist Press, 1987), pp. 78–79. Used with
> permission of Paulist Press. *www.paulistpress.com*

By taking up the cross, I received strength against many things which I had thought impossible to deny; but many tears did I shed, and bitterness of soul did I experience, before I came thither.

Mary Penington (c. 1625–1682)

A startling sculpture

I am confronted and oddly refreshed by the startling sculpture of a Las Vegas–based artist, the Reverend Ethan Acres. Like the city of extravagance he calls home, Acres is a current phenomenon of excess in the contemporary art world.

He earned a Master of Fine Arts Degree at the University of Nevada and also has a degree from a Bible college as a minister of the gospel. He gives Sunday services in a camper turned tacky chapel parked beside the gallery where his works are being exhibited. . . .

Entering the gallery, I am immediately engaged with a large camel, knitted out of woolly yarn, standing in a desert landscape made from glued together matchsticks, and looking like the image on a pack of cigarettes. He (I know this because it has a pink yarn penis) is unravelling to a single long thread which stretches across the wall and passes through the eye of a protruding, oversized needle. I visually follow the thread down to the floor where it ends in an abject pile of tangled brown and pink yarn. I am deeply moved. Here is physicality translated to another state yet retaining its full identity, a body pushed through a process of painful passage where everything is changed, but nothing is lost.

. . . When I read the title of the work, 'Camel Passing Through the Eye of a Needle', I feel the tears behind my eyes. Staring at the silly, lumpy pile of yarn that looks like stringy guts, I think I am witnessing a miracle. Jesus said: 'It is easier for a camel to go through the eye of a needle than for someone who is rich to enter the kingdom of God' (Luke 18:25). I had always dwelt on the hopelessness of this situation, overlooking his simple next statement, 'What is impossible for mortals is possible for God' (v. 26). (Including the incarnation!) Ethan Acres reveals, in his 'pathetic' materials, the unnerving possibility of real transformation—the entire camel does make it through the tiny eye, but is radically and humbly altered on the other side. Simple, common material seems laden with eternal significance.

Lynn Aldrich, 'Through Sculpture: What's the Matter with Matter?' in
Beholding the Glory: Incarnation through the Arts, ed. Jeremy Begbie
(London: Darton, Longman & Todd; Grand Rapids: Baker Book
House Company, 2000), pp. 111–12. Used by permission.

I call it an illusion for Christians to seek peace, as though the gospel wanted to make life comfortable for them. The contrary is true. 'I have not come to bring peace on earth, but a sword.' As long as the fight is going on, we have peace only in the fight. Our peace is not a well-being: it is a participation in Christ, in God in the flesh against all other things in the flesh.

Christoph Friedrich Blumhardt

PROPER 8

Ordinary Time 13

Sunday between June 26 and July 2 inclusive

| Genesis 22:1–14 | Romans 6:12–23 |
| Psalm 13 | Matthew 10:40–42 |

A mother's perspective

Sarah is old, old and very tired. Her mind wanders, sometimes she laughs and sometimes she weeps and those who love her do not know why. Her mind wanders across all her long life and she struggles to make it into a story: the story of her life, the story of Sarah.

It is hard to make sense of it sometimes. There are gaps, gaps in the story that make it impossible to understand. She does not know what happened between Abraham and Isaac in the land of Moriah. She does not speak to Abraham anymore, and she knows that Isaac will never tell her. Now he is grown he will toss his head and speak of women with contempt. He will take him a wife from a distant people, a woman he has never met and into whose eyes he has not looked deep, to see if they share a laughter which will sustain them even in the desert.

Abraham came back from the land of Moriah smug, contented, smooth and sleek. Isaac came back from the land of Moriah like a wild animal, bound but not tamed. For months afterwards he would wake in the night screaming and his mother, in the women's tent, would hear her boy child sobbing and could not go to him, comfort him, hold him. There was a look in his eyes still, evasive, distant, the look of a man who uses pride to cover betrayal.

Sara Maitland, "Sacrifice," in *Angel and Me: Short Stories for Holy Week* (London: Mowbray, 1995), p. 30.

Lament Psalm

O God, even my friends
bring me books
with ten steps

to overcome grief
as though healing
comes in paperback,
and filling my time
with one-two-threes
will bring peace
to my soul
and energy to my body.

Why don't they try
to understand?
The worst of all
are those who say
I must accept his death
as though his death
is acceptable.
No!
His death is unacceptable!
And I will not be comforted!

In my suffering
I am told I must
grieve correctly.
O merciful God!
What are they doing?
Aren't we supposed
to go to you
with our tears?
Isn't it in your word
that we will be
comforted?

I come to you, Holy One,
for I know
my salvation
is not in 'coping,'
but is in hope,

hope that comes
only from you.

O God, in your time
the scales will fall
from my heart
and I will see again,
and seeing, I will fall
to my knees
in thanksgiving
to you, O Gracious One,
only to you.

Ann Weems, *Psalms of Lament* (Louisville, Ky.: Westminster John Knox Press, 1995), pp. 22–23. © 1995 Ann Barr Weems. Used by permission of Westminster John Knox Press. Do not duplicate without written permission from Westminster John Knox Press, 100 Witherspoon Street, Louisville, KY 40202.

Accepting hospitality

There is a knock at the door and I have to respond; as I lay four extra places for supper I know that soon four people will be sitting round the table sharing the meal. If I am actually afraid and defensive (or aggressive, which is much the same), anxious and insecure about the impression that I shall be making, I may offer a glass of sherry or a bowl of soup but any real hospitality of the heart will be lacking; I shall merely have fulfilled the social expectation. I cannot become a good host until I am at home in my own house, so rooted in my centre . . . that I no longer need to impose my terms on others but can instead afford to offer them a welcome that gives them the chance to be completely themselves.

Esther de Waal, *Seeking God: The Way of St. Benedict* (London: Collins Fount Paperbacks, 1984), p. 120.

We cannot possibly let ourselves get frozen into regarding everyone we do not know as an absolute stranger.

Albert Schweitzer

'. . . He is at home here . . .'
(for Robin)

It is a long way
from Yarrow Valley to the Jordan
Valley.
Miles, language, climate, politics, time,
create vast distances between them.
But you leap these at a bound,
(having made friendship, vision,
humour and respect
your giant's boots)
and land
on common ground.

Kathy Galloway, *Love Burning Deep: Poems and Lyrics* (London: SPCK, 1993), p. 55. © Kathy Galloway. Used by permission.

Parties and gifts

Jesus . . . evidently gave a lot of thought to eating, and attached great significance to it, especially to parties. How a person thinks about parties, he appears to say, tells you a great deal about how that person thinks about the kingdom—which is one word for it; another word for it is the resurrection. . . .

Parties, Jesus implies, are not transactions: they are gifts. You don't qualify to be invited. You can't be too busy to receive a gift. You don't look a gift horse in the mouth; but neither do you resent its expense. Gratitude for a gift consists first in receiving it well, not first in thoughts of returning the gift. But parties are gifts of food and drink; and when we humans offer one another food and drink we offer one another the gift of life.

Denys Turner, *Faith Seeking* (London: SCM Press, 2002), pp. 116–17.

Love seeks only one thing: the good of the one loved. It leaves all the other secondary effects to take care of themselves. Love, therefore, is its own reward.

Thomas Merton

PROPER 9

Ordinary Time 14

Sunday between July 3 and 9 inclusive

Genesis 24:34–38, 42–49, 58–67   Romans 7:15–25a

Psalm 45:10–17   Matthew 11:16–19, 25–30

Prayer of Rebecca

Blessed are You,
Matriarch of the Universe,
for creating me
and re-creating me
more and more in Your image
as I enter daily
more deeply
into the meaning
and the mystery
of Your unconditional love.
I who am
daughter of earth
daughter of word
daughter of fire and Spirit,
lift my heart and the whole of my being
in prayer and praise to You.
Blessed are You,
Shekinah-Shaddai.
Blessed are You forever.
Amen.

Miriam Therese Winter, *WomanWisdom: A Feminist Lectionary and Psalter* (New York: Crossroad, 1991), p. 55. © Medical Mission Sisters. Used by permission.

Children's play ends with the universal resurrection of the dead. Adults' play ends with universal burial. Whereas the resurrection is the paradigm of the world of children, the world of adults creates the cross.

Rubem Alves

Out of the mouths ...

[John was] a Down's syndrome child of exceptional energy who needed little sleep. His father never joined us in the evening, for it took him a long time to get John off to sleep. I persuaded him to let me take over one evening, so that he could join the others at a café. I tried every trick I knew to quieten John, but he kept on jumping around in the bed and pulling out the sheets. I started to tell him a story, making it up as I went along. On the previous day we had all been up in the mountains at Gavarnie and John had ridden a donkey. We started the story from there. John's donkey had wings and took off over the mountains, racing the eagles. I thought I heard John say something, but doubted my ears. We were just coming to land in a beautiful palace courtyard high in the mountains, having left the eagles far behind, when I heard him speak again. This time it was unmistakable: 'Silly bugger,' he said! When his father returned, John was still wide awake and ready for more play.

Gerard W. Hughes, *God, Where Are You?* (London: Darton, Longman & Todd, 1997), p. 112.

Nurtured by rest

I remember when I was a boy, if my father saw me sitting reading a book he would say, "Can't you find something to do?"

As an adult, I have found it very hard to rest. Other than on holiday, if I sit down with a novel, I feel guilty.

There are always things to be done, people to see. I have had every waking hour filled with doing something useful. I have taken pride in my efficient use of time. When for any reason I have got held up, such as at traffic lights, I have felt irritated.

Someone told me, "At a red traffic light, remember 'R' is for rest. You have been given a little rest."

John Hunt, *We Spirited People: A Personal, Enriching and Uniquely New Zealand Guide in Celtic Spirituality* (Christchurch, New Zealand: The Caxton Press, 1998), p. 96.

Come, then. Let us also, while we have time, drink of the well of vision where Isaac walks, and where he goes out to reflect. Notice how many things happen at the waters to invite you, too, to come daily to the waters of the Word of God, and be present at his springs like Rebecca.

Origen (c. 185–c. 254)

Look at the children

One of the first stories about children is found in Matthew—the wayward children [11:16–19]. . . .

In light of the status of children and how little esteemed their opinions and behaviors were, Jesus' description of this generation of Jews—or us—is hardly flattering. These believers reject both the call to repentance and the austerity of John's message and Jesus' call to feasting with the bridegroom and the extensive mercy of God. They 'squat in the town squares,' thoughtlessly ignoring the prophets and the word of God, playing games with religion. These believers are not just children; they are unaware, and unresponsive to any message that God sends to them. Are we believers in this generation any better? God's wisdom is often ignored by the children of this world.

Then, at the other end of this same chapter [11:25–30], Jesus must have startled his listeners and disciples again. . . .

What a switch! The wisdom of God belongs to children, merest children, before it belongs to adults, wise in religion and the ways of society and culture. Jesus gives thanks that this is the way God is revealed in the world through him, his own child. Revelation is not first to the learned and clever but to the ones who don't count, the ones ignored in the street, the ones who are only useful as menial servants and slaves, as property. Remember, the Aramaic word for child and slave/servant is the same.

Megan McKenna, *Not Counting Women and Children: Neglected Stories from the Bible* (Tunbridge Wells: Burns & Oates; Maryknoll, N.Y.: Orbis Books, 1994), pp. 70–71.

O Lord, Jesus Christ, who art as the shadow of a great rock in a weary land, who beholdest thy weak creatures weary of labour, weary of pleasure, weary of hope deferred, weary of self; in thine abundant compassion, and fellow feeling with us, and unutterable tenderness, bring us, we pray thee, unto thy rest. Amen.

Christina Rossetti (1830–1894)

PROPER 10

Ordinary Time 15
Sunday between July 10 and 16 inclusive

Genesis 25:19–34   Romans 8:1–11
Psalm 119:105–112   Matthew 13:1–9, 18–23

Barley Field

Rows of perfect plants
dark green
stretch out
to meet the pristine blue
of summer sky,
a nursery picture
almost beautiful
in its uniformity.

No sound is heard
no hum of bees
no call, no song of birds
no added colour from the butterfly
but round the field
a damaged food chain
reaches to the arctic.

Dorcas Symms, from *Six Poems* (Edinburgh: School of Poets, 1997).
© Dorcas Symms 1997. Used by permission.

To grow is to emerge gradually from a land where our vision is limited, where we are seeking and governed by egotistical pleasure, by our sympathies and antipathies, to a land of unlimited horizons and universal love, where we will be open to every person and desire their happiness.

Jean Vanier

Birth to the barren

The notion of 'barrenness' of course refers to a biological problem of having no children. It is clear, however, that the motif also is treated metaphorically, . . . to refer to a loss of a future and therefore to hopelessness. . . . Conversely, 'birth' then comes to be taken metaphorically as the opening of a future and the generation of an alternative by the miraculous power of God. The notion of barrenness may be taken as a condition of despair in our society. Thus, for example, 'eunuchs' of both genders have their manhood and womanhood taken away by the pressure and demand of the corporation, the academy, or the church. Indeed, it is clear that professors and pastors often have their energies and family lives taken from them just as effectively as corporate types. They have insufficient energy to bear or to beget, and who wants to birth new children for Babylon? Our history always begins with the barren, with Sarah, with Rebekah, with Rachel, with Hannah, and with Elizabeth. Among those, always as good as dead, the wondrous gift is given. The inability to bear is a curious thing, and we know that for all our science the reasons most often are historical, symbolic, and interpersonal. It is often news— good news, doxology—that brings the new future to effect and the new energy to birth.

> Walter Brueggemann, *The Prophetic Imagination* (Minneapolis:
> Fortress Press, 2001), p. 75 (omitting biblical references).

The spirit and the flesh

The hierarchy of body and soul, which linked [human beings] both to the gods above and to the animal world below in the benign and differentiated order of an eternal universe, concerned Paul not in the slightest. The universe itself was about to be transformed by the power of God. Paul spoke of the 'sting' of death [1 Corinthians 15:26, 55], of the stubborn war of the flesh, of the dark counter-Law of 'sin which dwells in my members' [Romans 7:23]. These were towering forces for him; but by giving them a palpable face, he could present them as so many 'enemies,' who had been definitively conquered by Jesus when he rose from the grave. Their defeat would soon be made manifest, when Jesus gave back to God the kingdom of a universe from which every force of evil had been banished [1 Corinthians 15:24–26]. Thus the human person, divided between *the spirit* and *the flesh*, was not primarily a being torn between body and soul. Rather, with Paul, we see human beings caught in a hurried instant, as they passed dramatically from a life lived *in the flesh*, tensed against the Law because subject to the tyranny of half-seen powers reared in rebellion to God, to a life of glorious freedom lived *in Christ, in the spirit*: 'The Spirit of Him who raised Jesus from the dead dwells in you, he will . . . give life to your mortal bodies also' [Romans 8:11].

Peter Brown, *The Body and Society: Men, Women and Sexual Renunciation in Early Christianity* (London: Faber & Faber, 1989; New York: Columbia University Press, 1988), pp. 48–49.

A prayer of confession

Death is
fear, lies, hate, envy, avarice, greed, lust, pride, destructiveness, violence,
    cruelty.

Save us from death.

Life is
love, truth, courage, laughter, giving, creativeness, tenderness, humility,
    kindness.

Give us life.

Forgive us.

When we choose death instead of life.

Light us.

To life—the life of Jesus.

May God forgive us all
May we forgive ourselves
And one another.

The St. Hilda Community, *The New Women Included: A Book of Services and Prayers* (London: SPCK, 1996), pp. 79–80.
Used by permission.

Parables

The parable is a prime genre of Scripture and certainly the central form of Jesus' teaching. Current scholarship sees the parable as an extended metaphor, that is, as a story of ordinary people and events which is the context for envisaging and understanding the strange and the extraordinary. In the parabolic tradition people are not asked to be 'religious' or taken out of this world; rather, the transcendent comes *to* ordinary reality and disrupts it. The parable sees 'religious' matters in 'secular' terms. Another way to put this is to speak of Jesus as the parable of God: here we see the distinctive way the transcendent touches the worldly— only in and through and under ordinary life.

If Jesus as the parable of God, as well as Jesus' parables, are taken as models of theological reflection, we have a form that insists on uniting language, belief, and life—the words in which we confess our faith, the process of coming to faith, and the life lived out of that faith. And at each of these levels we discover the necessarily parabolic or metaphoric character of our confession, for Christian language must always be ordinary, contemporary, and imagistic (as it is in the parables); Christian belief must always be a process of coming to belief—like a story— through the ordinary details of historical life (as it is in the parables, though in a highly compressed way); Christian life must always be the bold attempt to put the words and belief into practice (as one is called to do in the parables).

Sallie McFague, *Speaking in Parables: A Study in Metaphor and Theology* (London: SCM Press, 1975, 2002), pp. xiv–xv.

Holidays, relaxation, and the simple pleasures of life are as important for the mystic as they are for other people.

Martin Israel

Proper 11

Ordinary Time 16

Sunday between July 17 and 23 inclusive

Genesis 28:10–19a   Romans 8:12–25

Psalm 139:1–12, 23–24 Matthew 13:24–30, 36–43

The knower and the known are one. Simple people imagine that they should see God, as if he stood there and they here. This is not so. God and I, we are one in knowledge.

Meister Eckhart (1260?–1327)

God's home is here*

God's home is here with humankind,
for heaven broke out on earth
when Yesu, born a little child,
ennobled human birth.

With eyes of faith we see beyond
the cruelty, death and pain.
We see that Christ, once slain by sin,
is here alive again.

Alive again and with us all,
Christ leads to victory.
Through Christ we know that God is here,
in darkness, light we see.

So do not fear the tyrants' power
nor think that God might fail.

*Tune: St. Andrew.

God's home is here this very hour,
and goodness will prevail.

Tom Colvin, *Come, Let Us Walk This Road Together; 43 Songs from
Africa* (Carol Stream, Ill.: Hope Publishing Company, 1997), no. 29.
© 1997 Hope Publishing Company, Carol Stream, IL 60188.
All rights reserved. Used by permission.

Building the future

Ours is a period of rapid and profound change. The coming years will see the most unprecedented changes if the present trends of evolution and revolution continue. We shall see either the growing maturation of the human race in global fellowship or destruction on a scale hitherto unknown. The peoples of the world are groping toward a new age of greater justice, while the forces of injustice are also gathering strength.

The church harbors a germ of hope for humankind. This is due, first of all, to the universality and radicality of the gospel of Jesus Christ. The Scriptures can present a message that is capable of motivating believers to respond meaningfully to the challenge of persons and of the whole world system in crisis. In spite of its accommodation to the world powers, the Christian churches represent an enormous reservoir of good will that can be harnessed for justice and peace. Christians are at the centers of power and decision-making. They can influence the course of future human evolution. The task is an urgent one. Millions of lives depend on it. But it cannot be achieved without a deep transformation of all Christians, a process of death/resurrection: dying to an exploitive world in order to rise with the whole of humankind in justice, sharing, and personal fulfillment.

Tissa Balasuriya, *Planetary Theology* (Maryknoll, N.Y.: Orbis Books;
London: SCM Press, 1984), pp. 128–29.

All power for good is derived from God.

Cyprian (200?–258)

The struggle to hope

It is important to remember that 'hope is a piece of work, not a state of mind'. Much of our ministry in the future, as in the past, will consist in the nurturing and sustaining of hope in the midst of unutterable pain and anguish. It has been said that real ministry occurs when the skin of the soul is rubbed raw. Yet it is here, at the heart of pain and apparent emptiness, that the community of the resurrection often emerges. In the apostolic age, the most powerful element in evangelism seems to have been the quality and witness of the Church's own life as a community of the resurrection. The power of God, which created the Christian movement as a resurrection force, has to be experienced in the hope of a new order and a new humanity which stands beyond extermination. The truth about the risen Christ must be proclaimed and lived with confidence and humility. When confronted by the horror of death and destruction, of despair and desolation, we need to hold one another firm in the faith that, in the worlds of the Orthodox liturgy of Easter, 'Christ is risen from the dead, trampling down death by death, and upon those in the tombs bestowing life'.

Kenneth Leech, *The Sky Is Red: Discerning the Signs of the Times*
(London: Darton, Longman & Todd, 1997), p. 252.

Don't be weary, traveller

Don't be weary, traveller,
Come along home to Jesus,
Don't be weary, traveller,
Come along home to Jesus.

My head got wet with the midnight dew,
Come along home to Jesus,
Angels bear me witness too,
Come along home to Jesus.
CHORUS

Oh, where to go I did not know,
Come along home to Jesus,
Ever since He freed my soul,
Come along home to Jesus.
CHORUS

I looked at the world and the world looked new,
Come along home to Jesus,
Looked at my hands and they looked so too,

Come along home to Jesus.
CHORUS

Traditional African American spiritual

The drama of redemption

In some churches, especially those associated with early Celtic Christianity, nature was involved in the drama of redemption. In a commentary on the Anglo-Saxon poem 'The Dream of the Cross' Robert Murray contends that it goes beyond the theme of cosmic and creaturely compassion for the suffering servant but 'dares to entrust the expression of Christ's suffering to the voice of a dumb creature. The effect is that the Cross's pain stands for the pain of all creatures, with which St Paul saw all creation groaning (Romans 8:19–22).' The tree is united with Christ in his agony.

Sean McDonagh, Passion for the Earth: The Christian Vocation to
Promote Justice, Peace and the Integrity of Creation (London: Geoffrey
Chapman, 1994), p. 142.

All creation wept

They reviled us both together.
I was made wet all over with the blood
Which poured from his side, after he had
Sent forth his spirit. And I underwent
Full many a dire experience on that hill.
I saw the God of hosts stretched grimly out.
Darkness covered the Ruler's corpse with clouds,
His shining beauty; shadows passed across,
Black in the darkness. All creation wept,
Bewailed the King's death; Christ was on the cross.

Lines from 'The Dream of the Rood,' from A Choice of Anglo-Saxon
Verse, trans. Richard Hamer (London: Faber & Faber, 1970), pp.
163–64, used by permission of Faber and Faber.

Easter Monday

The Easter service brought tears to [Mr Smith's] eyes and he decided to turn over a new leaf. . . . He left Church in a gentle mood, which so startled Mrs Smith that she dropped a sauce boat, and became speechless when Smithie picked up the pieces and gave her a glass of his precious port. They had a lovely Easter dinner with wine and felt like a family again.

But the wine gave Mr Smith a hangover and next morning he had words with Mrs Smith about the bacon. Now she's upset and takes it out on Master Smith, who takes it out on their dog, Fluffy.

Mr Smith invokes heaven to testify to his innocence, stamps out, and blasphemes when he arrives at the pub too early. It's his first relapse into sin since his religious rebirth and Easter Monday marks his fall. Over his bitter he decides to chuck religion as it changes nothing.

Now I'd like to give him and you some advice. Be patient! It takes time for grace to do its work in you—a lifetime. And it's harder being fair to your family than to strangers, because there's more expectation. Liturgy, you see, deals in blacks and whites, but in daily life you have to distinguish between different shades of grey, which is much more difficult. So pick yourself up and don't give up when things go wrong. . . .

And one last tip. After any religious service, give the door a good look as you go out, and ask yourself how you're going to get your religion through it. If you can't, is it more real than *Dallas* or *Dynasty*? That's what makes Easter Monday so critical. Take care now!

Lionel Blue, *Blue Horizons* (London: Hodder & Stoughton, 1989),
pp. 83–85.

Proper 12

Ordinary Time 17
Sunday between July 24 and 30 inclusive

| Genesis 29:15–28 | Romans 8:26–39 |
| Psalm 105:1–11, 45b | Matthew 13:31–33, 44–52 |

Sisters

In Genesis 29 and 30, which describe the marriages of Rachel and Leah and the birth of their children, we see that the struggle between the two sisters continued every day. They shared a household, a kitchen, a family, a man, that man's love, that man's sexual favours. Think how threatening our siblings can be to us, how strong can be the desire to know ourselves the favourite child; think how much greater would be the desire to know oneself the favourite, or the more successful, wife.

Jewish law, which permitted Jewish men to have more than one wife, did insist on absolute fairness; the wives must receive equal food, clothing, love and sexual attention. This tended to discourage polygamy even before it was formally interdicted for Jews in European countries. A man could not marry two sisters, because of the rivalry that would ensue. Jacob struggled for one night only with the angel. Next day he was reconciled with his brother, but he carried the resulting limp for the rest of his life. Leah and Rachel had to struggle daily to maintain the equilibrium of their household, to remain full of strength and self-respect, able to love each other, their husband and their children, and they succeeded. This is a much more useful example to us of creative struggle with God and human beings than Jacob's dramatic night by the riverside. More of the struggles to maintain self-respect and love for others in our lives come as part of our continual everyday interactions with family and work partners through the years than as one-night stands with angels.

Rachel Montagu, from "In the Beginning," in *Hear Our Voice: Women Rabbis Tell Their Stories*, ed. Sybil Sheridan (London: SCM Press, 1994), pp. 43–44.

It is love which gives things their value.

Carlo Carretto

Passionate remembering

It is a fact of life that we can have two quite different accounts of the same event depending upon whether we were losers or winners. We are told that history has been written by the winners and this is certainly true from my experience. When working in Ireland I had to learn to shut up and do a lot more listening and relearn history in all its complex levels. In my school history lessons I was never introduced to Irish literature and culture, only English victories in that country. History may be written by the winners but the so-called losers carry their own version of the same story and it colours their outlook on life in general and relationships with the winners (in their story) in particular. I well remember being deeply moved when I listened to a Welsh clergyman praying for the healing of his nation with great passion: 'Lord, Forgive our people for not being willing to receive the Gospel from English people because they stole our language and robbed us of our land.' When I wanted to include his story in another book my editor wanted me to change the words to 'suppressed our language'. My response was to challenge him to ask a Welshman whether he felt robbed or suppressed!

Russ Parker, Healing Wounded History (London: Darton, Longman &
Todd, 2001), pp. 44–45.

Evolution in religion

We carry on a biblical tradition in the fullest sense not by reenacting rituals expressive of our biblical ancestors' experience of God's action in their lives, but by taking up the rites of our culture and time as our biblical ancestors did in their time. As we go through this process we may end up with—in fact, we stand a better chance of coming to—ritual expressions that relate in the deepest sense to those of our Jewish and Christian ancestors.

By following this route, we stand a chance of coming to know the Spirit of a chosen people—not separate but one with all people. So within our culture's rites we can clearly proclaim our belief in the holiness of our land, in the sacredness of our history, and in the fullness of our time with the grace of a living God. So too can we communicate a sense of hope while confronting our desperate condition, and we can be free to love in a way that is unconditional.

Gerard A. Pottebaum, The Rites of People, rev. ed. (Washington, D.C.,
The Pastoral Press, 1992), p. 66.

Buried treasure

The Kingdom of God is also said to be like a treasure that someone finds and hides in a field. Then, in his joy, he sells all he has and buys that field. If you are capable of touching that treasure, you know that nothing can be compared to it. It is the source of true joy, true peace, and true happiness. . . .

That treasure of happiness, the Kingdom of Heaven, may be called the ultimate dimension of reality. When you see only the waves, you might miss the water. But if you are mindful, you will be able to touch the water within the waves as well. Once you are capable of touching the water, you will not mind the coming and going of the waves. You are no longer concerned about the birth and the death of the wave. You are no longer afraid. You are no longer upset about the beginning or the end of the wave, or that the wave is higher or lower, more or less beautiful. You are capable of letting these ideas go because you have already touched the water.

Thich Nhat Hanh, *Living Buddha, Living Christ* (London: Rider, 1996;
New York: Riverhead Books, 1995), pp. 156–57.

A revelation of God's love

And in this he showed me something small, no bigger than a hazelnut, lying in the palm of my hand, as it seemed to me, and it was as round as a ball. I looked at it with the eye of my understanding and thought: What can this be? I was amazed that it could last, for I thought that because of its littleness it would suddenly have fallen into nothing. And I was answered in my understanding: It lasts and always will, because God loves it; and thus everything has being through the love of God.

In this little thing I saw three properties. The first is that God made it, the second is that God loves it, the third is that God preserves it. But what did I see in it? It is that God is the Creator and the protector and the lover.

Julian of Norwich, *Showings*, trans. Edmund Colledge, O.S.A., and
James Walsh, S.J. (Ramsey, N.J.: Paulist Press, 1978), p. 183.

A dynamic mystery and the day that will come . . .

The metaphoric mode of the parable is suggesting that God's domain has the astonishingly mysterious quality, within our familiar world, that for instance pertains to the transforming new life which comes from the death of the seed, deep in the soil. That God's domain permeates wholly and mysteriously our everyday life as the yeast does which becomes one with the bread it creates. That while we go about the ordinariness of our daily living miraculous things are happening 'in the fields' all around us; on which our prosperity, indeed our very survival, depends.

Ruth Etchells, *A Reading of the Parables of Jesus* (London: Darton, Longman & Todd, 1998), pp. 63, 169–70.

A song of celebration*

Sing, one and all, a song of celebration,
of love's renewal, and of hope restored,
as custom yields to ferment of creation,
and we, his Church, obey our living Lord.

Rejoice that still his Spirit is descending
with challenges that faith cannot refuse:
and ask no longer what is worth defending,
but how to make effective God's good news.

We need not now take refuge in tradition,
like those prepared to make a final stand,
but use it as a springboard of decision
to follow him whose Kingdom is at hand.

To follow him: to share his way of living;
to shape the future as, in him, we should;
to step across the frontiers of forgiving,
and bear the burdens of true brotherhood.

Creative Spirit, let your word be spoken!
Your stock of truth invigorates the mind;
your miracles of grace shall be our token
that God in Christ is saving humankind.

Fred Pratt Green, *Partners in Creation: The Hymn Texts of Fred Pratt Green,* comp. Bernard Braley (London: Stainer & Bell; Carol Stream, Ill.: Hope Publishing Company, 2003), No. 138, p. 149. © 1982 Hope Publishing Company, Carol Stream, IL 60188 for USA and Canada; © 1973 Stainer & Bell Ltd. for all other territories. All rights reserved. Used by permission.

*Tune: WRAXHILL, *Partners in Creation*, p. 200.

The Holy Spirit is not something that stands by itself, something that we can pray for and have as a thing in itself, it is born from Love and is of Love, all its treasures are of Love, and if we are to believe our Gospels it is received by Love and Love only.

Florence Allshorn

PROPER 13

Ordinary Time 18
Sunday between July 31 and August 6 inclusive

Genesis 32:22–31   Romans 9:1–5
Psalm 17:1–7, 15   Matthew 14:13–21

Wrestling with God

One of the finest aspects of the story [Jacob wrestling with the angel] in my view is that after Jacob had struggled all night he was in the end not happy to let go of the mysterious guest. He does not let him breathe freely. *Survivre n'est pas vivre.* Survival is not sufficient. Jacob wants more; with and in spite of his dislocated hip he wants more than to have just managed to get away. He wants God to be other than God now is. The demon, the one who suffocates people, the God who exacts satisfaction must be different still. What should 'wrestling' with God really mean, other than to press God so hard that God becomes God and lives out more than God's dark side?! . . .

We ask many times about the meaning of prayer. To wrestle with God in order that God might be God is an answer to this question.

> Dorothee Soelle, *Theology for Sceptics,* trans. Joyce L. Irwin (London: Mowbray; Minneapolis: Fortress Press, 1995), pp. 54–55.

Prudence will decide on the issues that are worth fighting for, as well as the means to be used in the struggle. Prudence tells us when it is necessary to bypass an issue or pursue it to the extent of polarization.

> Tissa Balasuriya

Holy places

A friend always prays on the seashore. There is a weight of powerful memory for him tied up in a particular seafront kiosk. Another friend has a 'safe place' she goes to in the woods when times are difficult. . . . A third person I know loves to walk the city streets, finding that the combination of company and aloneness that the street provides is perfect for prayer, while the people and buildings she passes evoke every conceivable human strength and weakness—every glory and every frailty.

Some of the most tragic of human conflicts are associated with the sense of memory caught up in place. The Holy Places in Israel are a clear case in point.

But our personal 'holy places' need not become the occasion of conflict—rather, they can be a solace and bring healing. Even if the memories associated with some places are difficult, they remain important and must be honoured.

Mark Barrett, O.S.B., *Crossing: Reclaiming the Landscape of Our Lives*
(London: Darton, Longman & Todd, 2001), pp. 92–93.

Silence took hold of me

Silence, I had always known, is helpful for prayer, and I used to try to keep silence in retreats, but keeping silence can be a noisy business and does not necessarily still the spirit. The island silence was of a different kind. I did not 'practise' silence; it took hold of me. Prayer became much less of an exercise and more of a repose. God is everywhere and God is mystery. I already knew that was true, but on the island there was the space and time to relish the truth, so be seized and permeated by it. Being alone on this tiny islet of the sea, I was forced to meditate on the tininess, insignificance and precariousness of my existence. Our own world is a speck in the vast universe, this island did not even merit a dot on most maps. These rocks were formed millions of years ago and here was I sitting on them, an ant-like creature, a very recent newcomer to life for all my fifty years, passing through life fleetingly on my way to death.

Gerard W. Hughes, *In Search of a Way: Two Journeys of Spiritual
Discovery* (London: Darton, Longman & Todd, 1986), p. 24.

As Jesus did

**Loving God,
help us to be Christ to all those
whose lives touch ours.**

May we see others
as Jesus did,
with eyes of compassion.

May we listen,
as Jesus did,
to the cries of broken hearts
and a broken world.

May we reach out to others,
as Jesus did,
with healing and hope.

May we serve others,
as Jesus did,
with no strings attached.

May we break bread with others,
as Jesus did,
that the hungry may be fed.

May we celebrate with others,
as Jesus did,
your abundant provision.

Loving God,
help us to be Christ to all those
whose lives touch ours.

John Slow, in *Kneelers: Prayers from Three Nations* (London: United
Reformed Church, 2001), p. 101. © United Reformed Church 2001.
Used by permission.

Christianity has taught us to care. Caring is the greatest thing, caring matters
most.

Friedrich von Hügel

Let your God love you

Be silent.
Be still. Alone,
Empty
Before your God

Say nothing.
Be silent.

Be still.
Let your God
Look upon you.
That is all.
God knows,
Understands,
Loves you with
An enormous love.
God only wants to
Look upon you
With Love.
Quiet.
Still.
Be.

Let your God—
Love you.

Edwina Gateley, from *There Was No Path but I Trod One*
(Trabuco Canyon, Calif.: Source Books, 1996). © Edwina Gateley.
Used by permission.

Proper 14

Ordinary Time 19
Sunday between August 7 and 13 inclusive

Genesis 37:1–4, 12–28　　　　　　Romans 10:5–15
Psalm 105:1–6, 16–22, 45b　　　　Matthew 14:22–33

Present moment

When I was a young monk in Vietnam, each village temple had a big bell, like those in Christian churches in Europe and America. Whenever the bell was invited to sound (in Buddhist circles, we never say 'hit' or 'strike' a bell), all the villagers would stop what they were doing and pause for a few moments to breathe in and out in mindfulness. At Plum Village [a Buddhist community], every time we hear the bell, we do the same. We go back to ourselves and enjoy our breathing. Breathing in, we say, silently, 'Listen, listen,' and breathing out, we say, 'This wonderful sound brings me back to my true home.'

Our true home is in the present moment. The miracle is not to walk on water. The miracle is to walk on the green earth in the present moment. Peace is all around us—in the world and in nature—and within us—in our bodies and our spirits. Once we learn to touch this peace, we will be healed and transformed. It is not a matter of faith; it is a matter of practice. We need only to bring our body and mind into the present moment, and we will touch what is refreshing, healing, and wondrous.

Thich Nhat Hanh, *Living Buddha, Living Christ* (London: Rider, 1996;
New York: Riverhead Books, 1995), pp. 23–24.

God's over-ruling providence

I saw that God in fact does everything, however little that thing may be. Indeed, nothing happens by luck or chance, but all is through the foresight and wisdom of God. If it seems chance or luck to us, it is because we are blind and short-sighted. Things which God's wise foreknowledge saw before creation, and which he so rightly and worthily and constantly brings to their proper end in due time, break upon us suddenly and take us by surprise. And because of this blindness and

216

lack of foresight we say they are chances and hazards. But they are not so to our Lord God. Hence it follows that we must admit that everything that is done is well done, for it is our Lord God who does it.

> Julian of Norwich, *Revelations of Divine Love,* trans. Clifton Wolters
> (Harmondsworth, Middlesex: Penguin Books, 1966), chap. 11, p. 80.

Reading the Bible

Beginning to read the Bible seriously is rather like visiting a vast art museum. We are bewildered at first by the profusion of images and tend to survey them all in a daze, pausing before only a few of the most famous or striking works. But if we begin to make regular visits we learn to contemplate just one object at a time and let it work on our imagination. In time a single painting or sculpture can come to show us many things about life. It can work many changes in our understanding and vision if we allow it to. In the same way one scriptural symbol can in time work changes in us at several levels through the power of the Spirit.

> Martin L. Smith, *The Word Is Very Near You: A Guide to Praying with
> Scripture* (Cambridge, Mass.: Cowley Publications, 1989), p. 64.

Every effort to make society sensitive to the importance of the family is a great service to humanity.

> John Paul II

Widening boundaries

On a flight from Dallas to New York I sat next to a Frenchwoman who lived in New York and represented a French company owned by Americans. She was definitely French but she was more than that—a member of a new breed for whom national boundaries were becoming meaningless. I felt a great affinity with her world without boundaries, but I wondered how she managed and ordered her allegiances. What sort of people do we need to become in order to survive and flourish in this new millennium? Have we the will to *imagine* a world that can construct boundaries and yet have the wisdom to transcend them, when necessary, in the service of a widening vision of community?

> Alan Jones, *Living the Truth* (Cambridge, Mass.: Cowley Publications,
> 2000), pp. 141–42.

Prayer is God, who works all things in humankind.

Gregory of Sinai (fourteenth century)

Prayer is . . .

Much of the strain of our earliest efforts to pray derives from our beginning not by praying as we are, but as we think we ought to. . . . So we recite the jingles of the humble as if we could smother our vanity with merely pious thoughts. We tell our Father—who in any case sees what we do in secret—that it is not my will that should be done and suppress the sinking feeling that he just might take us at our word. We pretend to be more humble, less bored, less bloody-minded and more in love with God than we really are. We pray not out of ourselves as we really are, but as we think we would pray if we were better than we are, as if the force of mere thought were able to change the reality and truth of ourselves.

Denys Turner, Faith Seeking (London: SCM Press, 2002), p. 99.

Affirmation of faith

We believe that what we see before us is never all that is possible,
that beyond our present is a future which could be new
with more than enough for all,
and compassion greater than our own.

We believe in a God
who comes to the fearful people
across waters of life which threaten to swamp us
and whose company is love
beyond our understanding.

We believe in a greater power for good
than anything within each of us and all of us,
which stands between us
and at the centre of the universe
in ways of mystery and grace.

Dorothy McRae-McMahon, In This Hour: Liturgies for Pausing
(London: SPCK, 2001), pp. 86–87. Used by permission.

The spiritual man or woman can afford to take desperate chances, and live dangerously in the interests of their ideals; being delivered from the many unreal fears and anxieties which commonly torment us, and knowing the unimportance of possessions and of so-called success.

Evelyn Underhill

Proper 15

Ordinary Time 20

Sunday between August 14 and 20 inclusive

Genesis 45:1–15   Romans 11:1–2a, 29–32
Psalm 133   Matthew 15:(10–20) 21–28

Descendants of Abraham

Hidden, eternal, unfathomable, all-merciful God,
beside you there is no other God.
You are great and worthy of all praise;
your power and grace sustain the universe.

God of all faithfulness without falsity, just and truthful,
You chose Abraham, your devout servant,
to be the father of many nations,
and you have spoken through the prophets.
Hallowed and praised be your name throughout the world.
May your will be done wherever people live.

Living and gracious God, hear our prayer;
our guilt has become great.
Forgive us children of Abraham our wars,
our enmities, our misdeeds towards one another.
Rescue us from all distress and give us peace.

Guardian of our destiny,
bless the leaders and rulers of the nations,
that they may not covet power and glory,
but act responsibly
for the welfare and peace of humankind.
Guide our religious communities and those set over them,
that they may not only proclaim the message of peace
but also show it in their lives.

And to all of us, and those who do not belong among us,
give your grace, mercy and all good things,
and lead us, God of the living,
on the right way to your eternal glory.

Hans Küng, Judaism, trans. John Bowden (London: SCM Press, 1992;
New York: The Continuum International Publishing Group, 1992),
pp. 581–82. Used by permission.

Consequences

With hindsight we can see the hand of God on Joseph's life and that his dreams also had a deeper, more prophetic edge to them than anyone realised at the time. However, this does not disguise his obvious relish at being his father's favourite and his boasting of his importance to his brothers, who despised him for it.

. . . It would be cheap and easy to say that surely it is OK because God was in all of [the consequences of this sibling rivalry], and used it to provide the Israelites with food and shelter when the future, colossal famine destroyed the surrounding area (Genesis 50:19–21). We must stay focused on the human story and realise that God's sovereignty in our affairs does not make wrong right, but can become the opportunity to right wrongs and bring healing.

Russ Parker, Healing Wounded History: Reconciling Peoples and
Healing Places (Darton, Longman & Todd, 2001), pp. 130–31.

Never push anyone

Never push anyone in the area of faith and love. Wait patiently for God's hour for each person. These things need time to mature and unfold in God's way, and we must not act independently to interfere with His plan. One of the worst mistakes people in some religious circles make is to go blundering with their human will into the inner growth of something God is doing through Jesus. In each one of us this inner growth took time, and no human being had any business meddling or interfering with it. It needed to be clarified and illumined by God's light and purified by His fire. Then, when we were inwardly ready, we could accept Christ's truth, God's love, and the peace of His Kingdom.

Eberhard Arnold, God's Revolution: Justice, Community, and the
Coming Kingdom, 2d ed. (Farmington, Pa., and Robertsbridge, East
Sussex: Plough Publishing House, 1997), pp. 116–17.

Despite our wicked divisions, there is a unity which is a fact.

Arthur Michael Ramsey

Individual experience

Some of our most ubiquitous experiences of family include our experience of close-ness and fusion with others; our alienation and separation from them; our sense of being inside and outside simultaneously (either of these being felt to be positive or negative), our experience of transition, and our repeated attempts to reconcile our lived reality with a utopian concept of family life. Depending upon the quality of these experiences in our lives we shall hear the gospel in a radically different way, and because *every one* of us is deeply affected by our experiences of family life, both the preacher and the hearer of the Good News engage with the gospel through the medium of the internal and external family experience of each of them. No one can claim to have better or more experiences of family life—the validity of each person's experience is the same. But the experience of each of us is different and it may be a hard struggle for the preacher and the hearer of the good news to identify with the experience and perception of the other. Expertise in family belongs to us all, but we may be worlds apart in the kind of family experience we have had.

Sue Walrond-Skinner, *The Fulcrum and the Fire: Wrestling with Family Life* (London: Darton, Longman & Todd, 1993), pp. 4–5.

Who are *we*?

In re-creating the *we*, Gandhi began at the household level or with the village of one thousand people; his vision was to extend the ethics, the care, and the com-mon sense of the household to the whole of humankind. He began with the sym-bols of the domestic, the immediate, the near at hand. In religion, this means that the locus of religious life is not to be sought afar, by leaving home and society to journey to the far shore, the horizon, the frontier. The proper arena for religious life is not the Himalayas or the hermitage—not out there, but right here in the interrelatedness and struggles of the household and the village, on the 'frontiers of encounter.' This is where the *we* must be reconstituted: in how one behaves as well as in what one believes.

Diana L. Eck, *Encountering God: A Spiritual Journey from Bozeman to Banaras* (Boston: Beacon Press, 1993), p. 206.

Getting needs met

At the end of the autobiographical book and movie, *Out of Africa,* Karen von Blixen has lost everything. She has immigrated to South Africa to join her new husband in a farming venture. She has suffered illness and infertility resulting from his infidelity. The harvested coffee crop, which was her last chance to save the farm, has been destroyed in a fire. But she has formed a mutual devotion with the Kikuyu, a native tribe whose members made her farm a possibility. Burdened by the threat that they may lose any chance of remaining on the land, she goes to petition the new governor at a reception being held in his honor. When she is introduced, Karen kneels at his feet to beg for land for the Kikuyu. The governor is mortified with embarrassment. He urges her to stand as the sedate British crowd is politely, but obviously appalled by her behavior. But she is desperate and continues to plead until the governor's wife gives her a nod. . . .

Dear God,

Forgive us when we are passive or timid about those on the outside of the church. Bless the quick-witted, assertive woman in each of us who trembles even as she dares. Open our spirits to your strength. Infuse us with the power of your love. Lead us to the ones who need the healing balm of a Christian community. Show us the door we are to knock on for their sake. Amen.

> Mary Zimmer, from "The Canaanite Woman: Getting Needs Met," in
> *Sister Images: Guided Meditations from the Stories of Biblical Women*
> (Nashville: Abingdon Press, 1993), pp. 139, 143. Used by permission.

PROPER 16

Ordinary Time 21
Sunday between August 21 and 27 inclusive

| Exodus 1:8–2:10 | Romans 12:1–8 |
| Psalm 124 | Matthew 16:13–20 |

Who are our pharaohs?

We live under powerful forces that run through our lives that tell us how we should live—and what we need to live. We live under a creed of power with phrases like: "growth at any price," "profit at any price," "competition at any price," "limited liability," "charity," "controls."

Our institutions exist for the life and health of the institution—where once they existed for the life and health of the people in them: the children, the sick, the elderly. We are living under Pharaoh's rule, under Caesar's ways, under the *Pax Romana*.

Who are our pharaohs? Any institution or any person who rules or controls our lives.

. . . Pharaoh stands at the barricaded door and demands that we sign death certificates. He has no idea what he is asking of us. For we know who we are. For we are the people who follow the life-bearing God. We are the people who follow one God.

Nancy Hastings Sehested, "Let Pharaoh Go," in *And Blessed Is She:
Sermons by Women*, ed. David Albert Farmer and Edwina Hunter
(Valley Forge, Pa.: Judson Press, 1994), pp. 215–16.

We are the story

At one time or another, each of us fills each of the roles in this story [Exodus 2:1–10]. We have been enslaved by someone else's fear. Each of us has been the maidservant because in every need or ministry, somebody has to wade into the muddy water to pick up the basket. And just as the maidservant isn't named, so we also may have missed out on any credit. We have some of the resources and the compassion of Pharaoh's daughter, or we wouldn't be in this life-style called *Christian*. We are often set to watch over someone or something as vulnerable as

224

a baby floating in a basket in a river. Then we, too, must step out, ask the question or make the proclamation that establishes a connection that defies enslavement and stakes a claim for freedom.

> Mary Zimmer, from "Miriam: Making Connections," in *Sister Images: Guided Meditations from the Stories of Biblical Women* (Nashville: Abingdon Press, 1993), p. 22. Used by permission.

The first confession of the Christian community before the world is the *deed*.

> Dietrich Bonhoeffer

What is redemption?

In prison Bonhoeffer spent a lot of time reading and thinking about the Bible, particularly the theme of redemption in the Old and New Testaments. In doing so he realized that Christians have tended to turn on its head the Old Testament stories of *God's saving actions in history*. We have made "redemption" mean something that occurs, in Bonhoeffer's words, "on the far side of the boundary drawn by death . . . *in a better world beyond the grave*."

Yet "isn't this a cardinal error, which separates Christ from the Old Testament," interpreting Christ along the lines of the redemption myths of the ancient pagan world of Egypt and Babylon? For in the Old Testament, the Israelites clearly understood redemption to refer to something here and now, a deliverance into this very time and place, not hereafter.

And isn't this really true of the central Christian story of redemption, as well? Isn't it true that the Christian follows Christ *into* the forsakenness of the world, rather than away from it? If so, then *"this world must not be prematurely written off."* It is the arena of our salvation. Christian redemption, Bonhoeffer says from prison, is not redemption "from cares, fears, and longing, from sin and death" but instead living "life on earth in a wholly new way."

> Wayne Whitson Floyd, *The Wisdom and Witness of Dietrich Bonhoeffer* (Minneapolis: Fortress Press, 2000), p. 33.

Shaped for discipleship

What a beginning for a chosen people!
The vocabulary of cruelty tells it all: task-masters; oppression;

forced labour; grinding down slaves; making life bitter; harsh demands;
ruthlessly using; 'if a child is a boy kill him . . . throw him into the Nile.'
Threats to powerful thrones have to be dealt with, controlled.

(Are we really hearing an ancient story? It sounds familiar!)

And out of this catalogue of oppression and injustice
a reluctant leader emerges—hidden in a rush basket,
floating in a reed bed, drawn out of the water,
chosen by God.

Perhaps true courage and tenacity, true hope and faith,
do not come through ease but through testing:
 forged in the crucible of oppression,
 shaped by grinding down,
 drawn from dangerous waters.

After all, even Rocks like Peter know fragility.
Millennia of rain and wind and ice can shatter solidity;
storms of self-doubt, stubbornness, denial, faith too fragile
for water-walking, shape apostles too.

They know that the vulnerable are raised,
that their strength is in their weakness,
that fragility and certainty together build the church
on the foundation of One whose garden of resurrection
blossomed from the rubbish heap of death.

Noel Davies, in *Kneelers: Prayers from Three Nations: Prayer
Handbook Advent 2001–2002*, ed. Norman Hart (London: United
Reformed Church, 2001), p. 107. © 2002 United Reformed Church.
Used by permission.

Is it not true?

Is it not true that God needs human hands to wield the instruments through which healing is done, and human eyes to look in compassion on the outcast, and a human presence to stand by the lonely, and human brain-power to make deserts fertile and feed the hungry? And human political skills to fight for a just and a humane social order? Is it not functionally true?

When people say, 'O God, do this, do that, do the other', by what agency do they imagine that this will be done? Bolts of lightning? Magical interference with the natural order? If God has supernatural agents and ministers of his grace they are opaque to human eyes. All we can say is that somewhere there is a human spirit and a human heart that is prepared to incarnate his will and purpose in a given place at a given time. I find that truth humbling and immensely dignifying, because it seems to me that this is a tremendous vote of confidence. It is a quite extraordinary act of faith—not our faith in God (our faith in God waxes and wanes this way and that)—but of God's faith in us, such that he is prepared to commit himself into treacherous hands like these; that he is prepared to make a cosmic wager, to take a chance that we will not let him down.

Now that is a one-sided truth, the notion of God's dependence upon us. But it is a truth that invests every human encounter with a quite remarkable significance. But it seems to me that the pay-off line is that, just as the Word had to become flesh under Pontius Pilate in order that the world might be saved, unless the Word becomes flesh in people like us the world will not know that it *has* been saved. It will not know the things that belong to its peace.

Colin Morris, "Encountering Others: The Politics of Belief," in
Encounters: Exploring Christian Faith, ed. Michael Mayne (London:
Darton, Longman & Todd, 1986), pp. 52–53. Used by permission.

"Who do you say that I am?"

At the heart of the gospels is a confessional crisis. It is portrayed in the synoptics as the precise narrative center of the story, a watershed moment on which all other action turns. Who is Jesus Christ? (And what is his Way in the world?) The crisis provokes the question and the question the crisis. Close at hand is the disorienting voice of Satan, spreading its confusion. Indeed, the voice is heard within the discipleship community itself. And for the first time, openly and plainly, the cross is discussed and enjoined.

All readers of the gospel pass through that confessional moment, personally, and are compelled to declare themselves for one way or the other. In every age and place the community of faith must also make that declaration in answer to the Living Lord.

Bill Wylie Kellermann, *Seasons of Faith and Conscience: Kairos,*
Confession, Liturgy (Maryknoll, N.Y.: Orbis Books, 1991), p. 35.

Come to us, creative Spirit

Come to us, creative Spirit,
in our Father's house,
every natural talent foster,
hidden skills arouse,
that within your earthly temple
wise and simple
may rejoice.

Poet, painter, music-maker,
all your treasures bring;
craftsman, actor, graceful dancer,
make your offering:
join your hands in celebration!
Let creation
shout and sing!

Word from God Eternal springing,
fill our minds, we pray,
and in all artistic vision
give integrity.
May the flame within us burning
kindle yearning
day by day.

In all places and for ever
glory be expressed
to the Son, with God the Father,
and the Spirit blest.
In our worship and our living
keep us striving
towards the best.

PROPER 17

Ordinary Time 22

Sunday between August 28 and September 3 inclusive

Exodus 3:1–15   Romans 12:9–21
Psalm 105:1–6, 23–26, 45c   Matthew 16:21–28

The gift of vulnerability

A wound, symbolically, is an opening, and an opening is a way to new possibilities. We are offered the gift of vulnerability—the walls are shattered, the defences are broken down. With new eyes we look more honestly at who and what we are. As we step beyond fear we accept the gift of authenticity, entering a path which cannot be actively sought but only accepted as gift. At this moment I am offered the gift of being who I am, and I can accept others with a new depth of understanding of who they are.

Mark Barrett, O.S.B., *Crossing: Reclaiming the Landscape of Our Lives*
(London: Darton, Longman & Todd, 2001), p. 66.

Encounter with God

It is in the desert, alone, that Moses encounters—or rather is encountered by—God. At the miracle of the burning bush Moses knows an overwhelming sense of the holiness of the place, such that he feels impelled to remove his shoes. And then God commands Moses to be the instrument by which he will save the people of Israel from the Egyptian oppression, Moses hesitates, asks for God's credentials, and hears God's mysterious revelation as 'I am who I am': beyond definition by any comparison or contrast, but One who simply is . . . who he is—not one understood in terms of other things, but the One in terms of whom everything else finds its meaning. The desert seems a fitting place for such a revelation: the desert, itself devoid of anything in terms of which comparison might be made, the desert whose barrenness matches, by contrast, the transcendent fulness of God.

Andrew Louth, *The Wilderness of God* (London: Darton,
Longman & Todd, 1991), p. 30.

Affirmation and intercession

Let us affirm our faith together:

**We believe that every place
is the sacred ground of your creation, O God.
You are always there before us.
You are always there beside us.
You will walk the way ahead of us.
Bless, we pray, the sacred ground of the world
where we live and work.**

We place this earth in the bowl
and we name our sacred ground before our God:

The people name the places where they live.

We remember other places around the world
which is also your sacred ground:

The people name the places.

Be revealed there, O God.
Show us the power of your justice, love and peace. Amen.

Dorothy McRae-McMahon, *Prayers for Life's Particular Moments*
(London: SPCK, 2001), p. 74. Used by permission.

You never know how much you really believe anything until its truth or falsehood
becomes a matter of life or death to you.

C. S. Lewis

Signed with the cross

From you, my crucified love, sweet Jesus,
let me receive the sign of your holy cross
in my heart as on my forehead,
that I may live for ever under your protection.
Give me the living faith of heavenly teaching
that I may run the way of your commandments

with a ready heart.
Through you may I live in such a way
that I may worthily become the temple of God
and the home of the Holy Spirit.

Gertrude the Great, *Exercitia Spiritualia Septem,* trans. Brian Pickett,
in *The Heart of Love: Prayers of the German Women Mystics*
(Slough: St. Paul Publications, 1991), p. 58. © Brian Pickett.
Used by permission.

Serving God in suffering

The question is not about bearing suffering, enduring the pain; it is about serving
God in it. In other words, it is about how life may be redeemed, and (as illumi-
nated for all time by the manner of the death of Christ on Calvary) good brought
out of evil and new life emerge from the old. Life is not about fairness or unfair-
ness. . . . It is about making certain choices: between one action and another,
between generous self-giving and selfish holding back; and it is also about what
we make of the harsh, unlooked-for blows that come to us all: sickness and pain,
grief and old age. . . . There are those who are able to use their sickness, their pain,
even their dying as a time for growth and a new-found trust in the God who holds
us in death as in life and will not let us go.

Michael Mayne, *A Year Lost and Found* (London: Darton,
Longman & Todd, 1987), pp. 70, 71.

Spiritual repercussions of the atom bomb

We are at the precise point where, if we are to restore complete equilibrium to the
state of psychic disarray which the atomic shock has induced in us, we must
sooner or later (sooner?) decide upon our attitude to a fundamental choice; the
point where our conflicts may begin again, and fiercely, but by other means and
on a different plane.

I spoke of the Spirit of the Earth. What are we to understand by that ambigu-
ous phrase?

Is it the Promethean or Faustian spirit: the spirit of autonomy and solitude;
Man with his own strength and for his own sake opposing a blind and hostile Universe; the rise of consciousness concluding in an act of possession?

Is it the Christian spirit, on the contrary: the spirit of service and of giving; Man struggling like Jacob to conquer and attain a supreme centre of consciousness which calls to him; the evolution of the earth ending in an act of union?

Spirit of force or spirit of love? Where shall we place true heroism, where look for true greatness, where recognise objective truth?

Pierre Teilhard de Chardin, *The Future of Man* (London: Collins, 1964; Fount Paperbacks, 1977), pp. 152–53.

Love begins as love for one or for a few. But once we have caught it, once it has taken possession of us, and has set up its own values in the heart of the self, there are no limits to those it can touch, to the relationships which it can transform.

John Austin Baker

PROPER 18

Ordinary Time 23
Sunday between September 4 and 10 inclusive

Exodus 12:1–14   Romans 13:8–14

Psalm 149   Matthew 18:15–20

Love is his meaning

I desired many times to know in what was our Lord's meaning. And fifteen years after and more, I was answered in spiritual understanding, and it was said: What, do you wish to know your Lord's meaning in this thing? Know it well, love was his meaning. Who reveals it to you? Love. What did he reveal to you? Love. Why does he reveal it to you? For love. Remain in this, and you will know more of the same. But you will never know different, without end.

So I was taught that love is our Lord's meaning. And I saw very certainly in this and in everything that before God made us he loved us, which love was never abated and never will be. And in this love he has done all his works, and in this love he has made all things profitable to us, and in this love our life is everlasting.

Julian of Norwich, *Showings (Long Text)*, chap. 86, trans. Edmund
Colledge, O.S.A., and James Walsh, S.J. (New York: Paulist Press;
London: SPCK, 1978), p. 342.

Violence attracts violence

No-one is born to be a slave. No-one seeks to suffer injustices, humiliations and restrictions. A human being condemned to a sub-human situation is like an animal—an ox or a donkey—wallowing in the mud.

Now the egoism of some privileged groups drives countless human beings into this sub-human condition, where they suffer restrictions, humiliations, injustices; without prospects, without hope, their condition is that of slaves.

This established violence, this violence No. 1, attracts violence No. 2, revolt, either of the oppressed themselves or of youth, firmly resolved to battle for a more just and human world.

. . . Let us have the honesty to admit, in the light of the past and, perhaps, here and there, in the light of some typical reactions, that violence No. 3—governmental repression, under the pretext of safeguarding public order, national security, the free world—is not a monopoly of the under-developed countries.

There is not a country in the world which is in no danger of falling into the throes of violence.

Helder Camara, *Spiral of Violence* (London: Sheed & Ward, 1971),
pp. 30, 36–37.

Prayer of confession

Gathering God, our vision for community is never as loving as yours.
We confess that there are people who we would rather not bring near to us
or to you.

Silent reflection

Forgive us when our love is not like your love.
If we really think others are not worthy to approach you
and that we are more worthy than they are:
**Forgive us, O God, and remind us that none of us is worthy,
that your love is a free gift to all of us.**

When we demand that people achieve our measure of good
or our perceptions of the right way to be with you:
**Forgive us, O God, and remind us that we are not God
and that there are many paths towards you.**

If we think we can put boundaries around your love
and hold you to ourselves within our own community of faith:
**Forgive us, O God, and remind us that we will never own you
and that you break free of all our limitations.**

We confess, before the bounty of your life,
that we often make you a small God in our own image.
**Forgive us, yet again, O God of Grace.
Amen.**

Words of assurance

The forgiveness of God surpasses all that we can ever know.
Even as God gathers the world into costly grace,
so we are included, and we are no longer strangers.
take your place in the love of God!
Amen!

Dorothy McRae-McMahon, *In This Hour: Liturgies for Pausing*
(London: SPCK, 2001), pp. 99–100. Used by permission.

The story of a church

[We were led] to reflect on the nature of community, and on what promotes (or hinders) the growth of community. We were clear about what community was *not*. We had noted from our own experience that a breakdown of community often occurred when problems needed to be solved—that the men in the group often tended to "take over" with a particular style of problem-solving, anxious to get "results" quickly and efficiently. Others noted that community was lost when others simply told them what to do, leaving no room for movement, for one's own style. It was abundantly clear that there would be no unity *or* renewal when one person, or a few, were "calling the shots".

We had learned that God delivers and frees us in order to connect us—to God, to ourselves, to each other, and to the earth on which we live. We saw that if this "connectedness" negates or denies the freedom or wholeness of any part of it, then it is *not* the community that God in Christ offers and enables, and that if we are connected to God's love through Christ, then nothing can undo or separate us from it.

We recognized that looking at the community of women and men is an issue of justice, and an issue of compassion. If any one group in the church retains or attains power and the cost is disempowerment, exclusion, or the demeaning of another, we are not being faithful to the gospel. If theology "looks the other way" on issues of justice or compassion, or chooses one to the exclusion of the other, then we are not being faithful.

Sandra Winter Park, "Towards the Community of Women and Men
in the Church: The Story of St. John's Presbyterian Church, Berkeley,
California," in *Beyond Unity-in-Tension: Unity, Renewal and the
Community of Women and Men*, ed. Thomas F. Best, Faith and Order
Paper no. 138 (Geneva: WCC Publications, 1998), p. 97.

Outrageous God

It's all a little outrageous. It may even seem that God is inclined to overdo these things. But at least the message is clear! Not *because* we're good; *before* we're good. Big gesture. Meant for us all. No exceptions. Christ died for *irreverent* people, for *sinners*—and, yes, for the relatively pious and good, too. But you don't have to maintain a perfect, unsmudged record for God to love you. That's already settled. God does love you.

So I can't be the only forgiven one. God has forgiven everyone else in the same way and at the same moment as me. That's a fundamental reality I have to live with. God's forgiveness isn't available to me as a separate, private arrangement. It's available to me only as part of this big package.

This reality has consequences. If I want to withhold forgiveness from my neighbor, I'm effectively withholding it from myself, too. If I am willing for God to forgive my neighbor, I'm allowing God to forgive me, too. It's all or nothing, everybody or nobody.

L. William Countryman, *Forgiven and Forgiving* (Harrisburg, Pa.:
Morehouse Publishing, 1998), p. 42.

What does it mean to treat someone like a Gentile or a tax collector? Or, more precisely, how did Jesus treat Gentiles and collectors? According to Matthew, Jesus had a reputation for fraternizing with both.

Carol M. Bechtel

He came singing love*

He came singing *love* and he lived singing *love;*
he died, singing *love.* He arose in silence.
For the *love* to go on we must make it our song;
you and I be the singers.

He came singing *faith* and he lived singing *faith;*
he died, singing *faith.* He arose in silence.
For the *faith* to go on we must make it our song;
you and I be the singers.

*Tune SINGING LOVE, *Reading the Signature*, p. 8.

He came singing *hope* and he lived singing *hope;*
he died, singing *hope*. He arose in silence.
For the *hope* to go on we must make it our song;
you and I be the singers.

He came singing *peace* and he lived singing *peace;*
he died, singing *peace*. He arose in silence.
For the *peace* to go on we must make it our song;
you and I be the singers.

Colin Gibson, *Reading the Signature: New Hymns and Songs* (Carol
Stream, Ill.: Hope Publishing Company, 1994), p. 8. © 1994 Hope
Publishing Company, Carol Stream, IL 60188. All rights reserved.
Used by permission.

The greatest gift

God wants us to become clearer in discernment, but he also wants us to become
more loving, more understanding, and more merciful. Church discipline must
exist, but we must remember Jesus' words, "He who judges will be judged" and
"With the same measure you use, you will be measured." Love is the greatest gift.

J. Heinrich Arnold, *Discipleship* (Farmington, Pa., and Robertsbridge,
East Sussex: Plough Publishing House, 1994), p. 40.

PROPER 19

Ordinary Time 24
Sunday between September 11 and 17 inclusive

Exodus 14:19–31   Romans 14:1–12
Psalm 114   Matthew 18:21–35

The exodus, with its picture of a God who takes the side of the oppressed and powerless, has been a beacon of hope for many in despair.

Robert Allen Warrior

Not once, but seventy-seven times

If I forgive, and my brother continues to offend another seventy-six times, then my forgiveness does not seem to be helping him! But in trying to forgive, we become more aware of the many-layered nature of our consciousness. Having forgiven once, we find further layers of consciousness within us which have not yet forgiven; not just seven layers, but seventy-seven, and as we reach deeper layers, we have to learn to forgive the one offence again and again. So our offender has helped us to understand the nature of faith and of Jesus's teaching.

Gerard W. Hughes, *God of Compassion* (London: CAFOD and
Hodder & Stoughton, 1998), p. 88.

If you want to rest here below, and hereafter, in all circumstances say, Who am I? and do not judge anybody.

Joseph of Panephysis (fourth century)

The nature of love

A boy who came from a Christian home had offended his parents during Advent with a rather spectacular offence. He was asked to say sorry, but refused. And the more his parents gently asked, the more stubborn about it all he became. Christmas came nearer and nearer and as far as the boy was concerned he didn't care if his presents and rejoicings on Christmas Day were sacrificed, he was not going to say sorry. Eventually the great day arrived, and far from there being no gifts there were bigger and better ones than usual. His parents reckoned that the more wilful he had become the more the display of their love was required. Immediate collapse of wilfulness; tears of repentance flowed.

In most liturgies, after the confession the priest stands up and solemnly pronounces the absolution. It usually begins: Almighty God, who forgives all those who truly repent, etc. I find it hard to say, for although I believe that God loves us to be repentant, his absolution and forgiveness do not depend on it.

Michael Ball, *The Foolish Risks of God* (London and New York:
Mowbray, 2002), p. 32.

On a hard journey

Leader: O God who travels with us in the shadows,
        you know who we are.
        We long for life which is full and free.
        We long to know the truth
        and we want to leave behind us
        all the things which hold us back.

        (silent reflection)

        We want to move forward in faith
        but the way seems so dangerous
        and we stand in helpless fear
        before the hiddenness in our past
        and in our future.

        (silent reflection)

Leader: Stand beside us, gentle Christ.
People: **Walk before us, brave Jesus.**
        Call us on into life, Holy Spirit.
        Amen.

Dorothy McRae-McMahon, from 'Liturgy for a Hard Journey,' in
Echoes of Our Journey: Liturgies of the People (Melbourne: The Joint
Board of Christian Education, 1993), p. 75. © Dorothy McRae-
McMahon. Used by permission.

The way of forgiveness*

When the story is told
of enemy atrocities
and our own abuses of human rights

how shall we forgive?
how shall we learn to live?

In the aftermath of war
in the exaltation of success
and the bitterness of defeat

how shall we forgive?
how shall we learn to live?

When lives are spent,
cities derelict, the land destroyed
and the cost is reckoned

how shall we forgive?
how shall we learn to live?

When we are confronted with terror
and evil done in the name of justice;
when we are torn by anger and shame

how shall we forgive?
how shall we learn to live?

> Jan Berry, in *Celebrating Women: The New Edition,* ed. Hannah Ward,
> Jennifer Wild, and Janet Morley (London: SPCK; Harrisburg, Pa.:
> Morehouse Publishing, 1995), p. 79. © Jan Berry. Used by permission.

Forgive as you are forgiven

We cannot forgive others before we are forgiven and reconciled, but when we are within the forgiven and forgiving family of God, then we are to forgive as we have been forgiven. If this principle does not have free play among us, then we have seriously to question whether we have truly received the divine forgiveness that melts the heart. It is not that God withholds his forgiveness, but that we erect bar-

---

*Written at the time of the first Gulf War.

riers, close doors, harden our hearts, so that we are not capable of receiving, and therefore of offering to others, true forgiveness. . . .

It is clear that we cannot deal with God in one compartment of our lives, and with our fellows in another. A marriage can only grow as mutual forgiveness is shared. A friendship can only mature if differences and divergent views and temperaments are acknowledged, appreciated and allowed for. Otherwise estrangement takes place, turning to alienation, with a loss of spontaneity and peace. If we do not forgive, then we cannot be forgiven. If we are not compassionate, then we shall lose the spirit of compassion. If we are covetous, materialistic and legalistic in our relationships, then our souls will shrivel, and we shall lose the dimension of eternity.

Brother Ramon, S.S.F., *The Way of Love: Following Christ through Lent
to Easter* (London: Marshall Pickering, 1994), pp. 43–44.

God whose holy name
defies our definition,
but whose will is known
in freeing the oppressed:
make us to be one
with all who cry for justice;
that we who speak your praise
may struggle for your truth,
through Jesus Christ. Amen.

Janet Morley, *All Desires Known* (London: SPCK, 1992), p. 4.
Used by permission.

Proper 20

Ordinary Time 25
Sunday between September 18 and 24 inclusive

Exodus 16:2–15	Philippians 1:21–30
Psalm 105:1–6, 37–45	Matthew 20:1–16

Why work?

The habit of thinking about work as something one does to make money is so ingrained in us that we can scarcely imagine what a revolutionary change it would be to think about it instead in terms of the work done. It would mean taking the attitude of mind we reserve for our unpaid work—our hobbies, our leisure interests, the things we make and do for pleasure . . . and making *that* the standard of all our judgments about things and people. We should ask of an enterprise, not "will it pay?" but, "is it good?" . . . of goods, not "can we induce people to buy them?" but "are they useful things well made?" of employment, not "how much a week?" but "will it exercise my faculties to the utmost?" And shareholders in—let us say—brewing companies, would astonish the directorate by arising at shareholders' meetings and demanding to know, not merely where the profits go or what dividends are to be paid, not even merely whether the workers' wages are sufficient and the conditions of labour satisfactory, but loudly, and with a proper sense of personal responsibility: What goes into the beer?

Dorothy L. Sayers, *Why Work?* (London: Methuen & Co., Ltd., 1942), pp. 9–10.

The desert is a threat, a warning, a spur to activity, between the garden of Eden and the city of God.

Andrew Louth

Grumbling in the wilderness

Most people's wilderness is inside them, not outside. . . . Perhaps I've been robbed,

242

robbed of my easy certainties, my unthinking convictions, that this is black and that is white, and Uncle George was a saint, and what they told me to believe is true and the opposite false, and my parents are wonderful people, and God's in his heaven and all's right with the world, and science is the answer to everything, and St Paul was a nice man, and there's nothing like fresh air or reading the Bible for curing depression—fantasies, like children's bricks, out of which I thought I should build my life, and which now have melted into air, into thin air, leaving me with nothing. Out of what bricks, then, I ask in despair, am I to build? Is it to go on always like now, just—tomorrow and tomorrow and tomorrow—a slow procession of dusty greyish events with a lot of forced laughter, committee laughter, cocktail laughter and streaks of downright pain?

H. A. Williams, *The True Wilderness: A Selection of Addresses*
(London: Constable, 1965; Fount Paperbacks, 1979), pp. 28–30.

God's generosity

God is a generous giver, but we can only see and enjoy God's generosity when we love God with all of our hearts, minds and strength. As long as we say: 'I will love you, God, but first show me your generosity', we will remain distant from God and unable to experience what God truly wants to give us, which is life and life in abundance.

Henri J. M. Nouwen, *Bread for the Journey* (London: Darton,
Longman & Todd, 1996), p. 145.

One day at a time

The way through the wilderness imposes on Israel a life full of difficulties and miseries. The most basic human needs—food and drink—are barely ensured. But whenever Israel suffers thirst, water is given (Exodus 15:25; 17:5–6); whenever there seems to be no food, sustenance is provided (Exodus 16:35). There is a remarkable detail in the story of the manna. God commands Moses to tell the people to gather only one day's portion each morning and two days' portion on the day preceding the Sabbath. As usual, the Israelites do not keep this commandment; they gather more, keep it overnight and in the morning it is worm-eaten and foul. This is characteristic of the way in which Yahweh helps his people in the wilderness—from day to day. Israel is not permitted to live in security lest she forget that she is utterly dependent on her God. She receives daily bread, and a daily portion only, from the hand of God. God's help does not miraculously change the wilderness into a paradise; the desert situation cannot be forgotten, not even for one day.

Ulrich W. Mauser, Christ in the Wilderness, Studies in Biblical
Theology no. 39 (London: SCM Press, 1963), p. 22.

Earning our way?

Christ 'does' nothing in his Passion. It is all done *to* him. But in its happening it achieves the salvation of the world, past, present and future, and that salvation is totally inclusive. Waiting, hoping, in that market-place, whatever the reason, and whatever they did as they waited, was a work. We do not know why or what causes people not to be 'earners' in the way we think they should be and we have no right to judge. 'Waiting, being passive, is a great work.'

The main realization is, of course, that working for God, worshipping God is its own reward. We need no more, whether it is here or after death. The Kingdom of God is already come. So there is no need to envy the pennies of the latecomers. We are only thankful that they have joined the working band. They who started on their joyful labours early cannot laud [*sic*] it over those who started late. Extravagant generosity shown by the landowner should be the happiness of the early birds as well as the late ones. He knows more about the hearts and souls of all the labourers than we do.

Michael Ball, The Foolish Risks of God (London and New York:
Mowbray, 2002), p. 75.

In the days

> In the days
> when there is
> no paid work
>
> In the days
> when no one is
> willing to hire me
>
> In the days
> when the system
> wears me down

Remind me God
you love me
and need me.

PROPER 21

Ordinary Time 26

Sunday between September 25 and October 1 inclusive

| Exodus 17:1–7 | Philippians 2:1–13 |
| Psalm 78:1–4, 12–16 | Matthew 21:23–32 |

The characteristics of humanity

Instead of looking at Jesus for all the marks of what we commonly mean by divinity—such as omnipotence, omniscience and general works of astounding power, we are instructed to look at Jesus for what are properly the characteristics of humanity. So we look at Jesus and see someone vulnerable, someone who suffers and dies, someone who knows himself to be subject to his maker, called to do God's will, even when he does not entirely understand it, someone who has to struggle to understand his own vocation.

These things are part of the human condition as we know it, yet most of us are constantly fighting against them, and trying to make ourselves invulnerable, and to claim total control over our own lives. We are trying, in other words, to be like our image of God. Jesus, on the contrary, is being what we are created to be. And because Jesus accepts his fate and is totally obedient to God, he is actually mirroring God, as we should.

Jane Williams, *Perfect Freedom: Becoming the Person We Were Meant
to Be* (Norwich: Canterbury Press, 2001), pp. 22–23.

The good boy

Show me the book of rules
the good boy said
I'll be obedient.

The rules of God
are in this Holy Book
the parson said.

But how can I
be sure that
you are right?

> *You can't be sure.*

> *I have created you*
> *in my own image.*
> *Do you think that I*

> *Crave for security?*
> *Go out upon*
> *a limb, the way I do:*

> *Create a world,*
> *be crucified,*
> *and be obedient*

> *Only to what you are.*

Get thee behind me
Satan, the good boy said
I only want

To see the book of rules
to be obedient.

Sydney Carter, *The Two-Way Clock: Poems* (London: Stainer & Bell, 2000), pp. 21–22. © 1974 Stainer & Bell Ltd. Used by permission.

From Psalm 78

We will tell each generation
all that you, our God, have done;
how you called and led our nation,
chose us out to be your own:

Tell the times of our rebelling—
how we wandered from your way,
how your law our love compelling
taught us humbly to obey:

Tell how once, when spite and terror
threatened to engulf our land,
you defended us with vigour,
saved us by a mighty hand.

Tell the grace that falls from heaven,
angels' food as faith's reward;
tell how sins may be forgiven
through the mercy of the Lord.

Michael Perry, from *Psalms for Today* and *Songs from the Psalms:
Combined Words Edition,* ed. Michael Perry, with David Iliff and
David Peacock (London: Hodder & Stoughton, 1990), no. 78. © 1989
by Jubilate Hymns, Ltd. © 1996 Mrs. B. Perry. (Admin. Hope
Publishing Company, Carol Stream, IL 60188.) All rights reserved.
Used by permission.

Fanaticism

Faith and prejudice have a common need to rely on authority and in this they can sometimes be confused by one who does not understand their true nature. But faith rests on the authority of love while prejudice rests on the pseudo-authority of hatred.

Everyone who has read the gospel realizes that in order to be a Christian one must give up being a fanatic, because Christianity is love. Love and fanaticism are incompatible.

Fanaticism thrives on aggression. It is destructive, revengeful and sterile. Fanaticism is all the more virulent in proportion as it springs from inability to love, from incapacity to reciprocate human understanding. Fanaticism refuses to look at another man as a person. It regards him only as a thing.

He is either a 'member' or he is not a member. He is either part of one's own mob, or he is outside the mob.

From its very birth, Christianity has been categorically opposed to everything that savours of the mass movement. A mass movement always places the 'cause' above the interests of the individual person, and sacrifices the person to the interests of the movement.

Thomas Merton, *The Power and Meaning of Love* (London: Sheldon,
1976), chap. 6.

Under thirty feet of water

It was announced at Tel Aviv that God was going to send a tidal wave, thirty feet high, over the city because of its sins.

Muslims went to their mosques to pray for a speedy translation to the paradise of the prophet.

Christians went to their churches to pray for the intercession of the saints.

The Jews went to the synagogues and prayed, 'Lord God, it's going to be difficult living under thirty feet of water!'

Lionel Blue, *To Heaven with the Scribes and Pharisees*
(London: Darton, Longman & Todd, 1984), p. 73.

Layers of meaning

Many readers of the Gospels forget John [the Baptist] after the opening scenes, but neither Jesus nor the evangelists made that mistake. Jesus' right to challenge the whole Temple system, and for that matter the current royal and priestly claims, stemmed directly from John's baptism, a counter-Temple movement with a counter-Herodian edge. John had dug the field, Jesus had sown the seed, and now it was harvest time. It was at John's baptism of Jesus that the voice from heaven had named Jesus as messiah, God's beloved son.

The parable of the two sons has at least two layers of meaning. Of course, it is better to do what the father wants than to say you will and then change your mind; but, as usual, the shallow moralistic surface meaning invites us to go beneath for the real thrust. Those who seemed to be flouting God's will ended up being baptized by John; those who seemed to be following God's instructions to the letter refused to do so. This suggests a further reason for Jesus' Temple action: he was following through John's warnings, verbal and symbolic. His authority came from the God in whose name and power John had prophesied. But the parable has a further twist as well. Now that the chief priests were in a rebellious state, they too, like the ne'er-do-wells, could have changed their minds and obeyed after all. Even at this stage the challenge contains a coded final appeal.

N. T. Wright, *Twelve Months of Sundays: Reflections on Bible Readings*
Year A (London: SPCK, 2001), pp. 108–9.

From the apple in the garden

From the apple in the garden
To the manger and the star,

from the rainbow and the promise
to the moment where we are,
you are our hope, loving God.

From the manna in the desert
to the breaking of the bread,
from the hunger of the ages
to our hunger to be fed,
you are our hope, loving God.

From the prisons of the prophets
to the growing light of day,
from the death within the darkness
to the stone that rolls away,
you are our hope, loving God.

From the curse of Eve and Adam
to the blessing of the Christ,
from the spirits of division
to the Spirit in our midst,
still be our hope, loving God!

Two tales

So passionate was Mulla Nasruddin's love for truth that he travelled to distant places in search of Koranic scholars and he felt no inhibitions about drawing infidels at the bazaar into discussions about the truths of his faith.

One day his wife told him how unfairly he was treating her—and discovered that her husband had no interest whatsoever in that kind of Truth*!

*'Truth, when spelt with a capital T, means the truth about you, [so] make sure that each time you read a story you singlemindedly search for a deeper understanding of yourself. The way one would read a Medical Book—wondering if one has any of the symptoms; and not a Psychology Book—thinking what typical specimens one's friends are.' [*Author's advice preceding this tale.*]

A priest's daughter asked him where he got the ideas for his sermons. "From God," he replied.

"Then why do I see you scratching things out?" asked the girl.

Anthony de Mello, *The Prayer of the Frog: A Book of Story Meditations*, vol. 2 (Anand, India: Gujarat Sahitya Prakash, 1989), pp. xxii, 39.

PROPER 22

Ordinary Time 27
Sunday between October 2 and 8 inclusive

Exodus 20:1–4, 7–9, 12–20   Philippians 3:4b–14
Psalm 19   Matthew 21:33–46

The desire to live freely, to live meaningfully, robs death of its power. For some in El Salvador, a chosen death is preferable to mute submission to the murderous machinery of terror. It is a choice that promises liberation not only for oneself, but also for others.

Mary Jo Leddy

Deep in the core of earth
Deep in the core of earth,
primeval sources flow,
their cycles ever pressing on
unseen, alive, below.

Here on the planet's face
is birth and life and death,
the seasons ever rolling on
with every fleeting breath.

Far in the skies beyond
the stars and planets turn,
their every movement set in space,
each with its time to burn.

God of the worlds you made,
we offer praise and prayer,
with human need for faith and trust,
and confidence to share,

that all the work we do
will harvest in your name—
while life develops, changes, turns,
your love remains the same.

Heather Phillips, in *Worship Now* no. 26 (Summer 2003), p. 21.
© Heather Phillips. Used by permission.

If you notice something evil in yourself, correct it; if something good, take care of it; if something beautiful, cherish it; if something sound, preserve it; if something unhealthy, heal it. Do not weary of reading the commandments of the Lord, and you will be adequately instructed by them so as to know what to avoid and what to go after.

Bernard of Clairvaux (1091–1153)

Just round the corner

The story could be apocryphal except that to the best of my knowledge it is true. . . .

It is Yom Kippur, the Day of Atonement, the holiest day of the year. The synagogue is packed with people present for their annual visit. Sometime during the morning the police send a message that they wish to talk urgently with the rabbi. Obviously he is disturbed to be called out on such an occasion, but the service is in the safe hands of the *chazan*, the Cantor. What do they want? Could the rabbi please explain something puzzling to them. In front of the synagogue is a carpark which is totally empty. Yet the entire High Street is filled with the cars that belong to his congregation, so much so that they are blocking the traffic.

Of course the rabbi can explain, though he may hardly have wished to. We are encountering here a curious phenomenon that I remember from my childhood and which I regarded then with considerable scorn. Jews are forbidden to drive on the *Shabbat* or the main festivals—they are technically 'days of rest', and driving, with its use of energy, constitutes work. When Jews lived in small towns or villages, within easy walking distance of the synagogue, walking there on the special day posed no problem. But living in London, few people live that close unless they consciously choose to do so. . . . So a lot of people, unless *frum* (pious), drive there by car, but so as not to be seen as desecrating the *Shabbat*, park 'around the corner'. Or if, as in this case, there was clearly no corner to park around, block up the High Street.

Jonathan Magonet, *The Explorer's Guide to Judaism* (London: Hodder & Stoughton, 1998), pp. 211–12.

The heavens declare

'Heaven,' says George Bernard Shaw, 'as conventionally conceived, is a place so inane, so dull, so useless, so miserable, that nobody has ever ventured to describe a whole day in heaven, though plenty of people have described a day at the seaside.'

The trouble with perfection is that it is indescribable, so seldom do we come across it. Shaw's somewhat acerbic comment is too near the mark to make us feel anything other than uncomfortable. The reason for this lies not in 'heaven' itself but in what the great critic and playwright calls its conventional conception. 'Misconception' would be a far more accurate way of describing the heaven characterised by popular imagination: its inanity caused by the endless plucking of myriad harps; its dullness a result of the sheer monotony of the same boring routine; its uselessness due to the absence of anything to do but rest eternally; its misery a direct consequence of the removal of all challenge from the lives of its inhabitants.

Yet this is emphatically not the heaven of Scripture, where activity is one of its keynotes, and the worship of God the most significant component of that activity. Somewhere along the line, the Christian understanding of heaven has been derailed or shunted into a particularly curious siding. That state of perfection, which we often describe as 'heavenly', is in fact a mode of existence of which we already experience tantalising glimpses. Some of these liftings of the curtain are revealed in the beauty of nature and in those awe-inspiring natural phenomena which, though we can now explain them scientifically, still have the power to strike awe into our hearts. The sight of a volcano in full eruption or the sound of a violent thunderstorm immediately overhead can leave few of us totally unmoved, whatever our understanding of their genesis. That, certainly, was the effect on one person of his contemplation of the sky: 'the heavens declare the glory of God and the firmament sheweth his handywork', as Coverdale translates the first verse of Psalm 19.

David Shearlock, *When Words Fail: God and the World of Beauty* (Norwich: The Canterbury Press, 1996), p. 150.

Prayer for all of life

God of our life, through all the circling years,
We trust in Thee;
In all the past, through all our hopes and fears,
Thy hand we see.
With each new day, when morning lifts the veil,
We own Thy mercies, Lord, which never fail.

God of the past, our times are in Thy hand;
With us abide.
Lead us by faith towards hope's promised land;
Be Thou our guide.
With Thee to bless, the darkness shines as light,
And faith's fair vision changes into sight.

God of the coming years, through paths unknown
We follow Thee;
When we are strong, Lord, leave us not alone;
Our refuge be.
Be Thou for us in life our daily bread,
Our heart's true home when all our years have sped.

Hugh Thompson Kerr, reproduced from *The Presbyterian Hymnal.*
© 1990 Westminster John Knox Press. Used by permission of
Westminster John Knox Press.

PROPER 23

Ordinary Time 28
Sunday between October 9 and 15 inclusive

Exodus 32:1–14
Psalm 106:1–6, 19–23

Philippians 4:1–9
Matthew 22:1–14

Contemporary idolatries

The worship of idols takes many forms, some direct and unmistakable, some far more deceptive and subtle. In our own times, we witness people, relationships, institutions, ideologies, movements, and nations caught in the grip of contemporary idolatries. The contemporary idolatries that have captured our worship and servitude are familiar realities: money, possessions, power, race, class, sex, nation, status, success, work, violence, religion, ideology, causes, and so on. The militant power of the contemporary idolatries has captured the corporations and institutions of commerce, the state and the branches of government, the private and public bureaucracies, the various professions, the schools and universities, media and entertainments, and the churches. The presence of these idols or gods is felt in our economic and political systems, our social and cultural patterns, crucially affecting the way we relate to one another. Idols perpetuate themselves by erecting self-justifying ideologies and informational systems with the ability to turn falsehood into seeming truth by the distortion of language itself.

Biblically understood, idolatry originates in the human decision to seek life and salvation apart from the source of life in God. Idols are 'imposters of God', as William Stringfellow has described them. They may be things, ideas, persons, or institutions exalted and worshipped as gods. Rather than these finite realities serving people, people come to serve and worship them as objects of ultimate concern that are allowed to substitute for God. Idolatry denies the place of God as the giver of life and the author of salvation, dehumanizes people by making them pay homage to objects not deserving of worship, and denigrates the proper vocation of things meant to be servants of human life, not rulers over it.

Jim Wallis, *Agenda for Biblical People* (London: Triangle, 1986), pp. 38–39.

Addition to Exodus

You know, in those days too they made
a golden calf and worshipped it.

Trust, sincerity of love,
such basic necessities of existence,
thrown aside like old sticks or worn-out boots,
they became beasts,
fighting one another, simply wearing human masks.

The world, with Aaron's hordes in charge,
became a place of submissiveness.

But even then there were people
trusting, waiting for Moses to come down from Sinai,
simply, in solitude.

Ah, Canaan,
flowing with milk and honey!
Ah, how far off and how hard to reach.

Ku Sang, from *Wastelands of Fire*, trans. Anthony Teague
(London and Boston: Forest Books, 1990), p. 32.
© 1990 Ku Sang and Anthony Teague.
Used by permission.

I wasn't God's first choice for what I've done in China.

Gladys Aylward

Path of discipleship

The way [of discipleship] is unutterably hard, and at every moment we are in danger of straying from it. If we regard this way as one we follow in obedience to an external command, if we are afraid of ourselves all the time, it is indeed an impossible way. But if we behold Jesus Christ going on before step by step, if we only look to Him and follow Him, step by step, we shall not go astray. But if we worry about the dangers that beset us, if we gaze at the road instead of at Him who goes before, we are already straying from the path. For He is Himself the way, the narrow way and the strait gate. He, and He alone, is our journey's end. When we know that, we are able to proceed along the narrow way through the strait gate of the cross, and on to eternal life, and the very narrowness of the road will increase our certainty.

Dietrich Bonhoeffer, *The Cost of Discipleship,* trans. R. H. Fuller
(London: SCM Press, 1956), p. 162.

Round-table church*

The church is like a table,
a table that is round.
It has no sides or corners,
no first or last, no honours;
here people are in one-ness
and love together bound.

The church is like a table
set in an open house;
no protocol for seating,
a symbol of inviting,
of sharing, drinking, eating;
an end to 'them' and 'us'.

The church is like a table,
a table for a feast
to celebrate the healing
of all excluded-feeling,
(while Christ is serving, kneeling,
a towel around his waist).

The church is like a table
where every head is crowned.
As guests of God created,
all are to each related;

*Suggested tune: HOLLY LANE.

the whole world is awaited
to make the circle round.

The redefinition of identity

At the heart of a theology of reconciled place must be the belief that human identities and places are determined by God rather than by social or economic net-
works or obligations. In the redefinition of personal and collective human
identities brought about in baptism, Christian disciples are bound into solidarity
with those they have not chosen or whose presence they have not negotiated and
indeed would not choose of their own free will. Consequently, the new community, the new world, spoken of in eucharistic place is deeply disturbing of any
humanly constructed social order.

The Eucharist does not simply bind individuals to God in a vertical relationship
or bind people to each other in another kind of purely social construct. We are
bound to one another *en Christo*. And Christ, who is the head of the body, is to be
found persistently on the margins in those who are the least in the Kingdom of the
world. The margins include those who are other, foreign, strange, dangerous, sub-
versive—even socially, morally or religiously distasteful in our eyes. Yet the
Eucharist insists that humans find solidarity where they least expect it and, indeed,
least want to find it. We may recall the story of Francis of Assisi's encounter with
the leper by means of which he passed from a romantic sense of God's revelation
in the natural world to embrace the incarnate God in the excluded 'other'.

Philip Sheldrake, *Spaces for the Sacred: Place, Memory and Identity*
(London: SCM Press, 2001), p. 81.

Establishment, ministry, ecclesial structures, theological methods are all tempo-
rary instruments that inevitably reach their use-by date. If we cling to them
beyond that they become idols.

Richard Holloway

PROPER 24

Ordinary Time 29
Sunday between October 16 and 22 inclusive

| Exodus 33:12–23 | 1 Thessalonians 1:1–10 |
| Psalm 99 | Matthew 22:15–22 |

A good neighbor

An ordinary woman [once] lived in a small town near Modesto, California. She was not famous, powerful, or influential. . . . I was told this true story about her. She was the kind of person we'd call a good neighbor. She was friendly, liked by her neighbors, and was good to her family. When the United States entered the Second World War, she supported our government—until California Supreme Court Justice Earl Warren signed an order requiring all U.S. citizens of Japanese ancestry to be interned in relocation camps.

Many of this woman's neighbors were Japanese Americans. She knew them and loved them as her friends. She went to Sacramento and lobbied the legislators. She wrote to the president to try to stop the camps and the government confiscation of Japanese property. She could not move the powerful and famous. She was a lone nobody. . . . The Disciples of Christ was the only official church body to protest the order to intern Japanese American citizens. So this lone woman . . . bought all the Japanese farms and homes in her town for a dollar each and watched her friends be taken away. When the camps were closed, when the Japanese who survived had no homes left, when their lands were stolen by our government, this woman's neighbors were lucky. She gave her friends and neighbors back their homes and land so that they might live.

> Rita Nakashima Brock, "The Courage to Choose/The Commitment to Being Chosen," in *And Blessed Is She: Sermons by Women*, ed. David Albert Farmer and Edwina Hunter (Valley Forge, Pa.: Judson Press, 1994), p. 109.

Grace is love that cares and stoops and rescues.

> John Stott

Drawing the right lines

God of authority,
you have called us to a life of obedience
which follows your commandment of love
and gives our contemporary Caesars their dues.

God of rebellion,
you have created in us a conscience
which questions unjust impositions
and smarts when convictions are compromised.

How should we draw the line
between the right to strike
and the responsibility of vocation?
Can we staunch the lifeblood of the old and weak
by the struggle for acceptable practice and pay?

How should we draw the line
between paying a tax
and defying the law?
Can we tighten the strings of the communal purse
by holding on to our belief that a charge is unfair?

How should we draw the line
between acceptable suffering
and merciful release?
Can we stifle a positive will to live
with the right to sanction dignified death?

God, we do not ask you to make up our minds for us,
Guide us when moral distinctions are blurred.
Steer us away from the line of least resistance.
Strengthen us in our struggle with difficult decisions.
Help us, as free people, to do what we believe to be right.

Janet Orchard, in *Exceeding Our Limits: Prayer Handbook 1991*,
ed. Graham Cook and Jean Mortimer (London: United Reformed
Church, 1991), September 1. © Janet Orchard 1991.
Used by permission.

Communities of loving defiance

Christ's calling is to a radical alternative society which will, by its existence and values, profoundly challenge the existing society of today. 'The church should consist of communities of loving defiance. Instead it consists largely of comfortable clubs of conformity' [Ronald J. Sider]. No one will bother to persecute dull conformity. But as soon as we adopt a lifestyle of 'loving defiance' which challenges the status quo concerning covetousness, oppression or self-centredness, there is likely to be some strong and bitter opposition. Fellowship for those first Christians 'meant unconditional availability to and unlimited liability for the other brothers and sisters—emotionally, financially and spiritually'. This striking statement exposes the superficiality of many church fellowships today. It is interesting that the word for fellowship (*koinonia*) in the New Testament occurs more frequently in the context of sharing money or possessions than in any other. If the church is to become a community of God's people in the way that Christ demonstrated with his own disciples, it means much more than singing the same hymns, praying the same prayers, taking the same sacraments, and joining in the same services. It will involve the full commitment of our lives, and of all that we have, to one another. Yet it is only when we lose our lives that we will find them, so bringing the life of Jesus to others. In fact, this practical expression of love will speak more powerfully of the living God than anything else.

David Watson, *Discipleship* (London: Hodder & Stoughton, 1983),
pp. 42–43.

The foundation of mission

We long to have contact with more people, but all our wishes and longings must come under one desire: that at any hour, in any place, not our will but God's will be done. We must willingly submit to this. The last few years have shown us—or should have shown us—our incapability, our sinfulness, and our powerlessness. Mission depends on whether our faith is a living faith.

J. Heinrich Arnold, *Discipleship* (Farmington, Pa.: The Plough
Publishing House, 1994), pp. 226–27

Religion

[*written while a resident of Cromwell House, a Methodist Home for the Aged*]

That this is a religious House is true;
but not in the monastic sense. We own
allegiance to a Church that does not frown
on any enterprise that keeps in view
the love of Christ for all humanity.
Was not our founder, Wesley, catholic
in his contentious age, himself so quick
to see a need and find a remedy?

Religion here is neither hot nor cold,
which, despite Laodicea, I confess
suits my desire, in dotage, for toleration.
What is the use, I ask, of growing old
if we've not learned that truth is manifold,
and caring a chief part of our vocation?

PROPER 25

Ordinary Time 30
Sunday between October 23 and 29 inclusive

Deuteronomy 34:1–12   1 Thessalonians 2:1–8
Psalm 90:1–6, 13–17   Matthew 22:34–46

A solidarity of care and concern

Intercession, on one level, draws near to contemplation. It is a way of seeing people and placing them at the source of Love. This source, or wellspring, is something, over time, you have got to know, and which you trust and wish to share with another. We are not praying for someone who is outside God's care and love, nor are we praying outside God's care and love ourselves; we are entering into a relationship with both God and the other person in a solidarity of care and concern. We do not pray for someone imagining that we are the strong one and they the weak, with God hovering somewhere in between. We are all beggars before God, and God also has shown himself vulnerable and human in Jesus Christ. We do not pray from a position of super health for the sick, or from super strength for the weak; we enter into a relationship with them, with God, and rest in that. In that relationship many questions remain unanswered. There is sometimes a limit in our desire to say 'why?' We just want to rest in the fact that something is, and trust that God who made us is also at the point where something just is. The relentless 'why?' gives way to simple trust.

David Scott, *Moments of Prayer* (London: SPCK, 1997), p. 12.

You can never love your neighbour without loving God.

Jacques Bénigne Bossuet (1627–1704)

Mutuality

It astonished me how often [my mother] folded her hands during a nearly four-weeks-long death struggle. As if crying out loud were not enough.

. . . While singing to her, I had a feeling of being connected to her, as if she had found contentment through it. It did not seem as if I were doing something 'for her,' but as if we were together walking toward something greater than we are. An old theological conviction of mine was strengthened during those nights at her deathbed, namely, that without mutuality, without giving and taking on both sides, there can be no love. God cannot 'give' us anything if we do not become the bearers and givers of God's power.

Dorothee Soelle, *Against the Wind: Memoir of a Radical Christian,*
trans. Barbara and Martin Rumscheidt (Minneapolis: Fortress Press,
1999), p. 156.

A wedding or relationship blessing

In the starshine and sunshine of God
may you be warmed and welcomed.

In the stories and laughter of Jesus
may you be called and challenged.

In the fire and breath of the Holy Spirit
may you be awakened and kept from harm.

May your home be a place of hospitality and kindness,
a beckoning lamp in the darkness,
a shelter for questions and dreaming,
a safe space for joy and tears.

Live well————and————
May you celebrate life together
May you grow in love for each other
May you dance with the little ones,
the saints and the angels,
May you be cherished
May you be blessed.

Ruth Burgess, from *A Book of Blessings—and How to Write Your Own,*
comp. Ruth Burgess (Glasgow: Wild Goose Publications, 2001), p. 54.
© Ruth Burgess 2001. Used by permission of Wild Goose
Publications, Glasgow G2 3DH Scotland.

The church and the kingdom of God

The criterion for what the church is remains the kingdom of God; the church arises out of its proclamation, and organizes itself in its direction. . . .

. . . 'Already there' and 'not yet' represent a complex structure, a 'both–and' which cannot be grasped within positivistic logic. They represent a dialectic, an indissoluble and necessary contradiction in which the church on the way to the kingdom of God shares.

We can see how both the 'already there' and the 'not yet' belong together if we think of relationships between human beings, which must necessarily be different from relationships between people and things. Things can be got by having, acquiring, owning. Actions like acquiring, buying, taking over, lead to a having—in the present. But relationships between human beings are more complicated, and in them the present 'having' destroys the future being. For example, if I think I know someone completely, if I think that by loving him or her I utterly possess him or her in the present, expect no more of him or her, if his or her reactions are predictable, then present security has completely swallowed up future expectation. The eschatology of love destroys itself in a pure present without expectation.

When transferred to the church, that amounts to a self-destruction which begins when the church feels sure of the present Christ and thinks that it 'has' him in word and sacrament. The present possession of the Spirit has then swallowed up the incalculable future of God. If Christ has become completely the possession of such a community, if there is no longer anything unknown, dark, mysterious, about him, then the Christness is stamped with a false triumphalistic certainty, the boundaries are drawn clearly between within and without, church and world, us and them, and God becomes a household object to make use of.

The kind of enduring and all-embracing loving relationship in which we need both the 'now already' and the 'not yet' must be paralleled by the relationship between the church and the kingdom of God.

Dorothee Soelle, *Thinking about God: An Introduction to Theology*
(London: SCM Press; Philadelphia, Pa.: Trinity Press International,
1990), pp. 137, 139–40.

The school of love

My Love, my God,
the only way to make progress here
is to follow you totally

and love you alone unceasingly.
Let me not be left behind in the school of your love . . .
but in you and through you and with you,
let me progress day by day from strength to strength
and so bear fruit for you, my Love,
in the new vineyard of your love.

> Gertrude the Great, in *The Heart of Love: Prayers of German Women
> Mystics,* trans. Brian Pickett (Slough: St. Paul Publications, 1991),
> p. 85. © Brian Pickett. Used by permission.

There is no more sensitive conscience than that of a person who loves God. It registers every shadow that passes over the heart of God.

> Helmut Thielicke

PROPER 26

Ordinary Time 31

Sunday between October 30 and November 5 inclusive

Joshua 3:7–17
Psalm 107:1–7, 33–37

1 Thessalonians 2:9–13
Matthew 23:1–12

Everyday God

She was suddenly aware of how blessed she was in the symbols of family and friendship that surrounded her. She was warmed by the fire, supported by the cushions of her chair, and delighted by the view from her window. Gratitude and joy for the richness of the life she had led were the emotions in her heart. Just as she had been instructed, she made no special effort to pray, but inevitably, she thanked God for all that this room and its contents represented to her. Gradually, she realised that it was as if she was listening to God speaking words of love to her—and every aspect of her life was one of those words, mediated to her by the physical contents of the room in which she was sitting.

Mark Barrett, O.S.B., *Crossing: Reclaiming the Landscape of Our Lives*
(London: Darton, Longman & Todd, 2001), p. 75.

Praise

I've been looking for a suitable word
to praise you, Lord. Something enthusiastic
but not too formal, the sort of happy shout
a child gives to its mother.
I've tried Hallelujahs, Glorias and Hosannas,
but really, what I'd like is a word
from my own language, a word that is me.
If I were a bellbird, I'd fill my throat
with ecstatic song. Or, as a lamb,
I could fling myself into spring dance.
As a mountain stream I would spill out

inarticulate babblings of joy.
And if I were the sea, my waves would explode
in a thunder of love for you.
Lord, you overwhelm me with your great goodness.
Praise should not be difficult and yet
I can't find the exact word. Perhaps
it doesn't exist, though if it does,
I'm sure that it sounds like 'Yippee!'

> Joy Cowley, in *Aotearoa Psalms: Prayers of a New People* (Wellington:
> Catholic Supplies [N.Z.] Ltd., 1989), no. 19. Used by permission.

Practical wisdom

Nowhere does St Benedict suggest that he is interested in encouraging unusual people to perform spectacular feats. His monks are ordinary people and he will lead them in ways that are accessible to ordinary people. In fact the importance of the weak and the ordinary is one of the great guiding principles of the Rule, one which 'makes it possible for ordinary folk to live lives of quite extraordinary value,' as Cardinal Basil Hume puts it. Time and again the Rule makes allowances for human weakness. 'In drawing up its regulations we hope to set down nothing harsh, nothing burdensome' (Prologue 46).

> Esther de Waal, *Seeking God: The Way of St. Benedict*
> (London: Fount, 1984), p. 30.

The more we depend on God, the more dependable we find he is.

> Cliff Richard

A silly disposition

A vain man is a nauseous creature: he is so full of himself, that he has no room for anything else, be it ever so good or deserving. It is I, at every turn, that does this, or can do that. And as he abounds in his comparisons, so he is sure to give himself the better of everybody else; according to the proverb, 'All his geese are swans.' They are certainly to be pitied that can be so much mistaken at home. And yet I have sometimes thought that such people are, in a sort, happy, that nothing can put out of countenance with themselves, though they neither have, nor merit, other people's. But at the same time, one would wonder they should not feel the blows they give themselves, or get from others, from this intolerable and ridiculous temper; nor show any concern at that which makes others blush for, as well as at, them viz. their unreasonable assurance. To be a man's own fool is bad enough; but the vain man is everybody's. This silly disposition comes of a mixture of ignorance, confidence and pride: and as there is more or less of the last, so it is more or less offensive, or entertaining. And yet, perhaps, the worst part of this vanity is its unteachableness. Tell it anything, and it has known it long ago; and outruns information and instruction, or else proudly puffs at it. Whereas the greatest understandings doubt most, are readiest to learn and least pleased with themselves; this, with nobody else. For though they stand on higher ground, and so see further than their neighbours, they are yet humbled by their prospect, since it shows them something so much higher above their reach.

And truly then it is that sense shines with the greatest beauty when it is fed in humility.

William Penn, *Fruits of Solitude* (A. W. Bennett, 1863), p. 91.

The meaning of Christ

Christ is a name which for me expresses solidarity, hence suffering with, struggling with. Christ is the mysterious power which was in Jesus and which continues on and sometimes makes us into 'fools in Christ', who, without hope of success and without an objective, share life with others. Share bread, shelter, anxiety, and joy. Jesus' attitude toward life was that it cannot be possessed, hoarded, safeguarded. What we can do with life is to share it, pass it along, get it as a gift and give it on.

Dorothee Soelle, *Theology for Sceptics,* trans. Joyce L. Irwin (London: Mowbray; Minneapolis: Fortress Press, 1995), p. 93.

He lays upon us no other burden than that of putting our whole trust in him— no difficult self-immolation, no exaggerated austerities, no excesses of ascetic practice. He wants us to be kind and just and true in all the little dealings of our daily life, but even that he does not expect of us in our own strength.

John Baillie

PROPER 27

Ordinary Time 32

Sunday between November 6 and 12 inclusive

Joshua 24:1–3a, 14–25	1 Thessalonians 4:13–18
Psalm 78:1–7	Matthew 25:1–13

Into your hands

The final recorded words of Jesus are the Psalmist's words, 'Father, into your hands I entrust my spirit.' They are the simplest, most childlike form of faith. Jesus had often spoken of such trust in God's overarching power and goodness as the only way in which to live. And to die. When I come to die it will be the ultimate test of that trust in God that I have been trying to learn all my life. It will be the acid test of whether I am willing to let go of all that would bind me to earth, not just because I am old and tired and ready to depart, but because of my desire for God. Yet I hold back, for I cannot bear the thought of parting from those I love most in the world, nor of their grief; nor the thought of leaving the sights and sounds and scents that make this world so beautiful. One of the wistful delights of growing old is a new need to 'seize the day'. Each morning I say the prayer that begins: 'The night has passed and the day lies open before us' [from *Celebrating Common Prayer* (London: Mowbray, 1992)], and most days I notice some simple wonder I thought I had outgrown. To believe that beyond death lies resurrection might be thought to make departing (and the grieving process) less painful. It doesn't. What it does is to change the whole context in which you see your life.

Michael Mayne, *Learning to Dance* (London: Darton, Longman & Todd, 2001), pp. 235–36.

Let us now praise noble women

Let us now praise noble women
   and our mothers who lived before us,
through whom God's glory has been shown,
   in each successive generation.

Some ruled nations with authority
   and were renowned as queens;
others gave counsel by their wisdom
   and spoke with prophetic power;
a few were leaders of the people
    because of their deep understanding;
    their custody of tradition.
Some composed musical tunes
   and set forth verses in writing;
others were rich and respected
    peacefully keeping their homes.
All these were honoured in their lifetime
   and were a glory of their day.
Such women have left a name which is remembered
   so that their praises are still sung.
But others have left no memory,
   have vanished as though they had never lived.
These are the nameless women of the ages;
   the work of their hands is not remembered.
These women planted, picked,
   preserved, baked, boiled and brewed;
they washed, cooked, cleaned,
   fed, clothed and nursed the world.
A few were barren but most bore
   children, children and more children
to carry on the father's name
   so his posterity continues forever.
All these were different in their lives,
   different and yet the same;
and they died in different ways,
   in childbirth, sickness,
fever, madness, ripe old age;
   all died.
They are now as though they had never been
   and so too are their daughters who followed them.
There are numerous men whose good works have not been forgotten

whose descendants remember their names
and recall their forefathers with pride,
rejoicing in their heritage.
Their bodies were buried with honour
and their names live on
so that their glory lasts for ever.
Few of our foremothers are so remembered;
most lie forgotten in their graves
until their daughters shall claim their inheritance,
recollecting them with joy and pride.
Now their glory is not blotted out
as we declare their wisdom and proclaim their praise;
Noble women and nameless ones,
our mothers who lived before us.

Janet Crawford, in *Celebrating Women: The New Edition*, ed. Hannah
Ward, Jennifer Wild, and Janet Morley (London: SPCK, 1995),
pp. 64–66. © Janet Crawford. Used by permission.

In the depth of the anxiety of having to die is the anxiety of being eternally
forgotten.

Paul Tillich

A grave warning

If I read this parable aright as it addresses us in *our* century (as in past centuries),
there is grave warning here. Having in other parables been reminded by Jesus that
others' exclusion is a matter for sorrow, not joy, we are now warned that never-
theless some people *will exclude themselves,* and those people *may be us.* For if we
have taken no steps to ensure we are ready and prepared for our encounter with
God, whenever that might come, to do our task of living for him ('carrying our
lamps') and to be known of him, then we are 'outside' the ambience of joy and celebration which others, who have cared more, share with him. We are unfitted by
our whole way of being to be there with them. . . .

It is a frightening parable, none the less so for being so familiar that it has
almost been tamed. Almost. The concepts of *separation* from those with whom we
had apparently shared a calling, and *exclusion* from the ultimate life together, as a

result of our own heedlessness, uncaring and laziness, is not one that lodges easily in our current culture. Yet the parable probes us. In the end, it says, is not this the truth of how things ultimately work? Then why should it not be so in our encounter with God?

Ruth Etchells, *A Reading of the Parables of Jesus* (London: Darton, Longman & Todd, 1998), pp. 116–17.

Sleeping in trust

It's said that every time we sleep
we rehearse our deaths.
However wise that sounds
I doubt many of us think that.
We are like children as we sleep,
needing to refresh, recover, recharge ourselves with energy,
preparing ourselves for the next day's (or night's) activity.
Unable to defend our selves from any assault
we lie helpless,
trusting that protected and secure
we shall be defended from all
perils and dangers and rise again
recreated, renewed, released.
So I prefer to think of sleep
not as a rehearsal of death,
but as an act of faith, that whenever I rise,
and wherever I go
I shall find myself
within the boundaries of the Kingdom.

May God be with us
this day, and every day,
this night and every night
always.

John Young, in *Kneelers: Prayers from Three Nations,* ed. Norman Hart (London: United Reformed Church, 2001), p. 129. © 2001 United Reformed Church. Used by permission.

As wisdom dawns with age, we begin to measure our experiences not by what life gives to us, not by the things withheld from us, but by their power to help us to grow in spiritual wisdom.

Evelyn Sturge

Proper 28

Ordinary Time 33
Sunday between November 13 and 19 inclusive

Judges 4:1–7   1 Thessalonians 5:1–11
Psalm 123   Matthew 25:14–30

A palm tree rather than a briefcase

A younger-than-middle-aged woman stands in her perfect silk suit with every hair in place. Her makeup and a little airbrushing eliminate any flaws. In one hand is a gleaming leather briefcase and curled in the other arm is the most adorable toddler you have ever seen in designer overalls and Weeboks.

This is the picture of superwoman brought to you by Madison Avenue. Inside the magazine there is an article about how this wonder-woman organized her day in order to have fresh crabmeat crepes on the table by six and a not-very-hostile takeover merger signed by noon the next day.

I never met one of those women who could work full-time in a demanding job, mother young children, and get through a whole week without take-out Chinese food *and* pizza.

Deborah had a palm tree rather than a briefcase. And though we are not told explicitly, a woman who had attained the designation of prophet was probably past her time of childbearing. It is curious that in her song, the only role Deborah refers to is that of mother: "you arose, Deborah, arose as a mother in Israel" (Judges 5:7a). She is the best candidate for superwoman in the Old Testament, carrying the multiple roles of mother, judge, and prophet.

. . . The tone of the story conveys Deborah's confidence in herself. That confidence has a social and political base since judges were elected by the people of Israel, and she is the only female judge recorded. Her spiritual wisdom as a prophet enhanced her role as judge. When the people determined to seek justice for their oppression, they went to Deborah and she did not fail them.

Mary Zimmer, from "Deborah: Choosing Battles," in *Sister Images: Guided Meditations from the Stories of Biblical Women* (Nashville: Abingdon Press, 1992), pp. 32–33. Used by permission.

In weariness

O Lord Jesus Christ
who art as the shadow of a great rock in a weary land,
who beholdest thy weak creatures
weary of labour, weary of pleasure,
weary of hope deferred, weary of self,
in thine abundant compassion,
and fellow feeling with us,
and unutterable tenderness,
bring us we pray thee,
unto thy rest.

Christina Rossetti

God is a free giver

What happens to the parable [of the talents] if we reverse the figure of the boss (as we would with the crooked judge) and say, 'Look, our God is not a ruthless, exploitive God'? If we reverse the boss's moral status, then we end up out of the parable, trying to figure out how to conduct our lives in response to a free-grace God. We don't play it safe, because God is patient and ever merciful. But we don't *have* to invest, produce, and hand over a profit either to get along with God. No, if God is a free giver, we can step out of the parable and be free givers as well.

Has our espousal of capitalism prevented us from hearing the parable? Perhaps. Or maybe clergy using the parable in connection with church fund-raising have blinded our sight. Without really hearing the parable, we tend to assign hero status to the investors. Of course, Matthew has done the same thing—morally investing yourself will earn approval when God hands out rewards and punishments in judgment.

How do we preach the parable? Initially, I think, let's admit that the parable has nothing to do with innate abilities, with what we sometimes call 'talents.' The word 'talent' comes from the parable but should not be used to interpret the story. The parable may have been spoken to Sadducees and Pharisees. The Sadducees lived within the law, playing it safe, guarding their religious purity. The Pharisees, on the other hand, were pietists; they intended to extend God's law into all areas of their lives, investing their energies in virtue so as to glean a reward in the resurrection of the just. Although Jesus guards God's law—'not one iota,

not one stroke of a letter, will pass from the law until all is accomplished'
(Matthew 5:18)—and indeed urges radical virtues, obviously his love commandment poses a broader way.

David Buttrick, *Speaking Parables: A Homiletic Guide* (Louisville, Ky.:
Westminster John Knox Press, 2000), pp. 173–74.

Stewardship

The pew preached to the pulpit,
    all the while clutching its checkbook.
The pulpit hung its head,
    and tried to quiet its conscience
with these considerations:
    If the greatest givers are offended,
        mission will go unfunded.
    If the boat is rocked,
        it is the poor who will be drowned.
The conscience spoke back:
    Answer me this one:
        Do we owe our soul to the Company Church?

Ann Weems, from *Kneeling in Jerusalem* (Louisville, Ky.: Westminster
John Knox Press, 2000), p. 41. © 1992 Ann Barr Weems. Used by
permission of Westminster John Knox Press. Not to be duplicated
without written permission from Westminster John Knox Press, 100
Witherspoon Street, Louisville, KY 40202.

The heart of our spiritual nature

Conscience is that depth of human nature at which it comes in touch with God,
where it receives God's message and hears his voice. . . . Conscience is the remembrance, in our sinful life, of God and of life divine. . . . Conscience is the organ of
reception of religious revelation of truth, of good, of integral truth. It is not a separate side of human nature or a special function, it is the wholeness of our spiritual nature, its very heart. . . . Conscience is also the source of original primary
judgments about the world, and about life. More than this, conscience judges
God, or about God, because it is an organ of the perception of God. God acts on
our conscience, awakens our conscience, awakens our memories of a higher

world. Conscience is the remembrance of what we are, to what world we belong to by the idea of our creation, by whom we were created, how and why we were created.

Nicolas Berdyaev, *Christian Existentialism,* selected and trans. Donald A. Lowrie (London: George Allen & Unwin, 1965), p. 88.

Look, I am going to play the part of God and seat myself on the throne of judgment. What do you want me to do for you, then? If you say, 'Have mercy on me', God says to you, 'If you want me to have mercy on you, do you also have mercy on your brother; if you want me to forgive you, do you also forgive your neighbour?' Can there be injustice in God? Certainly not, but it depends on us whether we wish to be saved.

Anonymous saying of a desert mother or father

A matter of imagination

The key feature of this parable is that it is the imagination of the servants as to what their master is like which is the determining factor of their conscience and thus the wellspring of their activity. The first two servants . . . trusted that their master was the sort of daring fellow who would do rash and crazy things for which there was no script, would dare, would experiment, would risk losing things and so would end up multiplying things greatly. In other words, they perceived their master's regard for them as one of liking them enough to be daring them and encouraging them to be adventurous, and so, imagining and trusting that abundance would multiply, they indeed multiplied abundance.

James Alison, *On Being Liked* (London: Darton, Longman & Todd, 2003), p. 109.

Entirely too much has been said in most churches about the stewardship of money and too little about the stewardship of power. The modern equivalent of repentance is the responsible use of power.

Harvey Cox

PROPER 29

(Christ the King or Reign of Christ)
Ordinary Time 34
Sunday between November 20 and 26 inclusive

Ezekiel 34:11–16, 20–24   Ephesians 1:15–23
            Psalm 100   Matthew 25:31–46

Visiting the sick

Another matter on which I feel much more reluctant to write, is the effect my illness had on my family. . . .

The way husband and wife experience and respond to the vow to love and cherish each other 'in sickness and in health' is private to themselves, though observed by others. I am beginning now to understand the strain there was on Alison, and I shall always be grateful that a number of people understood this and quietly supported her. . . .

Alison, like me, learned more about the difficult art of visiting the sick: the importance of giving of yourself, of being interested, *really* interested, when you ask how someone is; not coming when you are tired; not staying too long; not sharing your own experience of illness; sharing an item of common interest. . . .

One of the minor problems about looking after someone you love at home is to know whether to go out, sit with them, or simply try to carry on life as before: it is a constant juggling act. . . .

Looking back now, Alison cannot remember what she read, what kind of winter it was, what happened at Christmas. There is a kind of amnesia, a blotting out of those difficult months which for me remain so vivid.

Michael Mayne, *A Year Lost and Found* (London: Darton, Longman &
Todd, 1987), pp. 40, 42.

No place

No place had you to lay your head
O Christ whom we call King of Kings;
you came to share the painful lot
of all the homeless, life's foundlings.
    You had no home to call your own
    though earth's your footstool, heaven your throne.

At last, through wood and nails, you found
a home, spread-eagled on the cross,
where all could see the face of God
made one with human pain and loss:
    and hear God's call, and find God grants
    to each a niche of relevance.

Lord, make us restless till we rest
in your good will for humankind
that, while the birds have each a nest
and foxes holes, we learn your mind
    that all your cherished human race
    may claim a sheltered dwelling place.

When we are at peace, when we have assumed our deep wounds and weakness,
when we are in touch with our own heart and capacity for tenderness, then actions
flow from our true selves.

Jean Vanier

Converted betrayers?

The gospels are written from the perspective of converted betrayers, disciples who
knew that they had been unable to hear the radical character of his message of
abnegation of power in his own lifetime, and only in the light of the resurrection

were able to re-evaluate this mistake. Yet we have to ask whether that mistake has not, in fact, been perpetuated by the successors of the apostles in the church. Even as the church picks up the cross as a symbol of triumph over death and as rebuke to the Jews, they continue the betrayal of Jesus, which is to use his name as a means of power and domination over other people. The Jesus who made himself one of the poor, one of the outcasts, and, finally, one of the dead, in order to witness to the true conditions for entering God's reign, witnesses against this betrayal of his name. He flees from those who use his memory as a means of power and domination. To adapt the Jewish legend, he is perhaps to be found among the beggars at the gates of Rome.

> Rosemary Radford Ruether, *To Change the World: Christological and Cultural Criticism* (New York: Crossroad, 1988), p. 18.

Caring presence

It is through caring that the power of illness and death is broken. Curing, thankfully, sometimes may take place, but caring is central. The ministry of presence breaks alienation. It is presence that relieves the sting of death.

The church has some experience in knowing the central mission of the hospital: it is *hospitality*. . . . Indeed, by the fourth century it was common for congregations to have "houses of lodging for strangers." These were the first rudimentary hospitals in the West. Caring for the stranger's ailments was part of their task, but central was their ministry of presence and hospitality. If too often the modern hospital is a place of isolation—isolating the sick from the rest of us—we can try to recover the central meaning of the original hospital movement.

> James B. Nelson, *Body Theology* (Louisville, Ky.: Westminster/John Knox Press, 1992), p. 136.

From the heart of the world

From amidst diversified and often warring creeds: over a vast span of history: in the language of many a tribe and many a nation: out of the mouths of the learned and simple, the lowly and great: despite oceans of bloodshed, and torturing inhumanities, and persecutions unspeakable—the single voice of a greater Humanity rises confidently to heaven, saying "We adore Thee, who are

One and who art Love: and it is in unity and love that we would live together, doing Thy will".

Victor Gollancz, from the Preface to *God of a Hundred Names: Prayers of Many Peoples and Creeds,* sel. and arr. Barbara Greene and Victor Gollancz (London: Victor Gollancz Ltd., 1962), p. 9.

The soul of one who loves God always swims in joy, always keeps holiday, and is always in a mood for singing.

John of the Cross

ALL SAINTS

November 1 or the first Sunday in November

Revelation 7:9–17   1 John 3:1–3

Psalm 34:1–10, 22   Matthew 5:1–12

Recovering a vision of heaven cannot be achieved simply by biblical exegesis, intellectual rigour, artistic passion or cultural nostalgia. It has to emerge as human beings in their diversity encounter the friendship of Jesus within the brokenness and confusion of human life.

Michael Vasey

Saintly choir

Sometimes when I bow before the glory of God, singing the doxology at the end of a psalm, I see from the corner of my eye, as mirrors reflect into other mirrors, an infinite line of shimmering figures bowing with me. Sometimes I see them en masse, as crowds are painted in early Byzantine art. Or sometimes I see a lone shepherd or hermit, voice roughened by years of singing against wind and sun, wandering in solitude.

There is a reality of the communion of saints that becomes transparently apparent through psalmody, a reality that has force and power, a there-ness that seems more fully manifest in this way than any other. The music of the long-vanished psalm-singers lingers in the silence. You can feel it in churches; you can feel it in ruins; you can feel it wandering through mountains where holy ones have lived.

Maggie Ross, *The Fire of Your Life: A Solitude Shared* (London: Darton, Longman & Todd; New York: HarperCollins, 1992), p. 75.

Meeting the others

We would like to see the World Council of Churches facilitating the meeting of people with others whom they would normally never have the chance to know. Instead of so many centralized consultations we would recommend that there be greater numbers of teams travelling to share in the everyday life of the faithful men and women who make up the local communities that week by week share in the communion of the body of Christ. In encounters of that kind people can be encouraged to go beyond the limits of their own experience and enter into the lives and concerns of their sisters and brothers in other parts of the world.

Bertrice gave us a moving illustration of such an experience happening to her on a visit to Romania. She had grown up in a tradition of worship which prides itself on its simplicity. So she had reacted strongly against any kind of iconography. But on a festival day she was invited to attend the liturgy. There came a point in the service when the people moved forward to kiss the icons. "That," she thought stubbornly, "I am not going to do." But a nun nearby beckoned to her and took her hand. What should she do? Risk offending the nun, or offend her own conscience by kissing the icon? She decided the relationship with her new friend was more important than her old scruples. So she went forward to kiss the icon, and burst into tears as a whole new experience of reverence overwhelmed her. In that moment, she realized that through the nun the Spirit had helped her to go a step beyond in her own spiritual journey.

Pauline Webb, *She Flies Beyond: Memories and Hopes of Women in the Ecumenical Movement* (Geneva: WCC Publications, 1993), pp. 65–66.

Everything is related

I attended a course led by a young woman theologian from the United States. It was the 4th of July. When she came in, someone called out, "Happy Independence Day!" She stood at the lectern for some time without speaking.

It was the time when N[ew] Z[ealand] had told the U[nited] S[tates], "We would rather not have your nuclear warships tied up to our country." The U.S. responded, "We will not tell you our military secrets, and we may not buy your beef for our hamburgers."

Finally she spoke.

"I look forward to the day when my country will remember we were once a tiny nation standing against a powerful one." She went on, "And I look forward to the day when we will celebrate not Independence Day, but Interdependence Day, for we each need one-another."

John Hunt, *We Spirited People: A Personal, Enriching and Uniquely New Zealand Guide in Celtic Spirituality* (Christchurch, New Zealand: The Caxton Press, 1998), p. 72.

Praying in the face of death

On a recent visit to Christians in rural western Kenya, I was greatly impressed by the practical and prayer support to bereaved families. In this community of small family farms, the whole neighbourhood turns up to sit with the mourners for several days. Their closest friends and members of the extended 'clan' sleep outside the house in the fields. The day is spent in talking, dancing and prayer, with the deceased loved one being interred eventually on the family's own land, often very close to the small, mud-built house in which his or her relatives still live.

Strangers as well as friends are welcomed. I know, as I received a very warm welcome indeed. Among the guests were children who didn't seem to belong to anyone. I was told that they were the equivalent of what in a city would be street children. In a country devastated by HIV/AIDS, many were orphans. They came to funerals because they knew they would find food, and they were not disappointed. They were not turned away, but received as part of the gathering.

As evening fell on the first day of one such funeral, a group of women arrived, singing and dancing. They were all neighbours and friends, and many were members of the clan. They came bringing water and maize, basic provisions for the bereaved family during their time of loss.

This was an intensely moving moment. As the sun dropped towards the horizon, the songs of the women and their practical care brought a sense of comfort and hope in a time of sorrow.

Janet Wootton, in *Worship Live* no. 25 (London: Stainer & Bell,
Spring 2003), p. 13.

The Passing of the Foremothers

All my dear old friends,
The Grandmas of the church,
Limp gamely home.
We waved off Marjorie
On Easter Saturday,
Her little coffin underneath
The banner HE IS RISEN,
And so is she.
And Peggy, Sylvia, Gladys
And the rest,

Foremothers of the faith
Who wiped my nose
When first I came to Jesus;
Steely-haired and golden-hearted
Women twice my age,
Yet sisters, pushing forward
Fearlessly to meet their God
Seen dimly through the dust
At the end of a long road.

> Rowena Edlin-White, in *Dancing on Mountains: An Anthology of
> Women's Spiritual Writings,* comp. Kathy Keay and Rowena Edlin-
> White (London: HarperCollins, 1996), p. 137. © Rowena Edlin-
> White. Used by permission.

From darkness to light

Grant us your light, O Lord, that the darkness in our hearts being wholly passed away we may come at last to the light which is Christ. For Christ is the morning star, who when the night of this world has passed, brings to his saints the promised light of life, and opens to them eternal day. Amen.

> The Venerable Bede, in *Christ the Golden-Blossom: A Treasury of
> Anglo-Saxon Prayer,* ed. and trans. Douglas Dales (Norwich:
> The Canterbury Press, 2001), p. 17.

In heaven, the mystery of God, precisely as mystery, will be our eternal blessed-ness.

> A Carthusian

INDEX OF LECTIONARY READINGS

Index of Themes

INDEX OF AUTHORS